'While it is deeply rooted in Continental thought, this important work takes this enterprise in many new and sometimes illuminatingly surprising directions. We live in a curious time in which we imagine that we are at home everywhere in an increasingly homogenous world, but we cannot see that this is precisely the mark of our alienation: although we are all over the place (and place is increasingly the same place everywhere), we have no real sense of place. Kuperus's wake-up call allows us to see Nietzsche's refusal of the homogenous herd and his call to be true to the earth as having made the "turn to place". The book also builds powerful new bridges into classical Zen thought (especially Dōgen Zenji) and indigenous Tlingit thought.'

Jason Wirth, Seattle University, USA

'Place remains one of the most central and compelling themes in environmental philosophy, and Gerard Kuperus's *Ecopolitical Homelessness* makes one of the most noteworthy contributions to this central concern in recent years. Kuperus insightfully diagnoses the unique form of homelessness that afflicts much of the industrialized global north and, increasingly, the world – a form of homelessness obscured precisely by the degree to which globalization and homogenization give us the superficial sense of being at home everywhere, while simultaneously alienating us from the particular local realities that make up genuine places. Calling for a radical transition in our thinking and acting, Kuperus outlines a persuasive new ecopolitics of belonging, which incorporates both implacement and nomadism. In so doing, he points toward the way in which we can be responsible inhabitants of a planet faced with diverse environmental, social, and political challenges.'

Brian Treanor, Loyola Marymount University, USA

'Kuperus provides a fresh approach to what at times is in danger of becoming a worn topic. We all can benefit from the exceptionally clear expositions of Nietzsche, Heidegger, Deleuze and Guattari that convincingly connect their ideas to environmental problems. More than that, the sure use of Latour to reassess the relationships between nature and politics is extended beyond Euro-centric positions by the interesting attention to Dōgen and Tlingit peoples.'

Robert Mugerauer, University of Washington, USA

Ecopolitical Homelessness

While our world is characterized by mobility, global interactions, and increasing knowledge, we are facing serious challenges regarding the knowledge of the places around us. We understand and navigate our surroundings by relying on advanced technologies. Yet, a truly knowledgeable relationship to the places where we live and visit is lacking.

This book proposes that we are utterly lost and that the loss of a sense of place has contributed to different crises, such as the environmental crisis, the immigration crisis, and poverty. With a rising number of environmental, political, and economic displacements, the topic of place becomes more and more relevant and philosophy has to take up this topic in more serious ways than it has done so far. To counteract this problem, the book provides suggestions for how to think differently, about ourselves, our relationship to other people, and to the places around us. It ends with a suggestion of how to understand ourselves in an ecopolitical community, one of humans and other living beings as well as inanimate objects.

This book will be of great interest to researchers and students of environmental ethics and philosophy, as well as those interested in the environmental humanities more generally.

Gerard Kuperus is Assistant Professor at the University of San Francisco, USA, specializing in philosophy of nature and environmental philosophy.

Routledge Environmental Humanities

Series editors: Iain McCalman and Libby Robin

The *Routledge Environmental Humanities* series is an original and inspiring venture recognising that today's world agricultural and water crises, ocean pollution and resource depletion, global warming from greenhouse gases, urban sprawl, overpopulation, food insecurity and environmental justice are all *crises of culture*.

The reality of understanding and finding adaptive solutions to our present and future environmental challenges has shifted the epicenter of environmental studies away from an exclusively scientific and technological framework to one that depends on the human-focused disciplines and ideas of the humanities and allied social sciences.

We thus welcome book proposals from all humanities and social sciences disciplines for an inclusive and interdisciplinary series. We favour manuscripts aimed at an international readership and written in a lively and accessible style. The readership comprises scholars and students from the humanities and social sciences and thoughtful readers concerned about the human dimensions of environmental change.

Endangerment, Biodiversity and Culture
Edited by Fernando Vidal and Nélia Dias

A Cultural History of Climate Change
Edited by Tom Bristow and Thomas H. Ford

Ecopolitical Homelessness
Defining place in an unsettled world
Gerard Kuperus

Ecopolitical Homelessness

Defining place in an unsettled world

Gerard Kuperus

 Routledge
Taylor & Francis Group
LONDON AND NEW YORK

 earthscan
from Routledge

First published 2016
by Routledge

2 Park Square, Milton Park, Abingdon, Oxfordshire OX14 4RN
711 Third Avenue, New York, NY 10017

Routledge is an imprint of the Taylor & Francis Group, an informa business

First issued in paperback 2017

British Library Cataloguing in Publication Data
A catalogue record for this book is available from the British Library

Library of Congress Cataloging-in-Publication Data
Names: Kuperus, Gerard, author.
Title: Ecopolitical homelessness : defining place in an unsettled world / Gerard Kuperus.
Description: New York, NY : Routledge, 2016. | Includes bibliographical references and index.
Identifiers: LCCN 2015045351| ISBN 9781138649859 (hardback) | ISBN 9781315625676 (ebook)
Subjects: LCSH: Place (Philosophy) | Human ecology—Philosophy. | Environmental ethics.
Classification: LCC B105.P53 K86 2016 | DDC 304.2/3—dc23
LC record available at http://lccn.loc.gov/2015045351

ISBN: 978-1-138-64985-9 (hbk)
ISBN: 978-0-8153-5580-9 (pbk)

Typeset in Bembo
by Keystroke, Station Road, Codsall, Wolverhampton

Contents

Acknowledgments

As Plato, quoting Homer, recalls in the *Phaedo*, "when two go together, one observes before the other [Iliad, x. 224]; for somehow it makes all of us human beings more resourceful in every deed or word or thought" (*Protagoras*, 348d). A philosopher is not merely a friend or lover of wisdom, but the pursuit of wisdom itself requires friendships. This project has been greatly influenced by many friends and others who observed before me, or who in some other way made me more resourceful.

Many parts of the book were at some point presented as papers. Questions and comments provided at those occasions, as well as more informal discussions afterwards, have shaped the papers and encouraged me to keep working on the ideas and to develop the book. Of the many places where initial versions of the chapters were presented, I will mention the annual meetings of the Pacific Association for the Continental Tradition (PACT), the International Association for Environmental Philosophy (IAEP), and the Comparative and Continental Philosophy Circle (CCPC). An early version of parts of the first chapter was presented at the 2014 DePaul Humanities Center's series of lectures and events on "The Humanimal" organized by Peter Steeves. Some of the parts of the final chapter were presented to the Philosophy Department at the California State University, Stanislaus. Parts of chapters 4 and 5 were presented to the philosophy department at the University of Wageningen. I want to thank everyone who engaged in a dialogue about the presented papers. Comments and questions have greatly contributed to the book.

Writing itself is often a solitary activity, but I have been in the fortunate position to be able to regularly write with others at writing retreats and with the on-campus "writing teams." Of the many writing partners I would like to thank in particular Stephanie Vandrick, one of the few colleagues who will show up on a Friday at 3 p.m. for a few hours of writing. I could fill a page mentioning all other writing partners, but you know who you are: thank you for your company, suggestions, and friendship!

Many of the initial papers that became chapters were written during writing retreats offered by the University of San Francisco. I would like to thank the Dean's Office for funding these retreats, which have been incredibly

helpful. I am also extremely grateful to have been selected as the Davies
Professor during the semester I was finishing the book, which provided the
opportunity to teach the Davies Forum on "Displacements: Retrieving a
Sense of Place." Working on the book while teaching the course to highly
talented students and with numerous guest speakers who work on place was
a highly motivating circumstance. In addition, I want to thank the University
of San Francisco's Faculty Development Fund (and our union that secures
the fund) for always funding my conference travels and research assistants.

Although he might not always agree with my stance on ecology, my
discussions (and a debate) with my colleague John Callaway have been
incredibly helpful in thinking through the parts on ecology, included in the
last chapter of the book. In Sitka, Alaska, I want to thank ecologist Scott
Harris for the insights he provided during our walk through Staragaven,
marine biologists Lon Garrison and Jim Seeland for explaining hands-on the
functioning of a salmon hatchery, and anthropologist Richard Nelson for
sharing his insights into the knowledge of the land. On the Big Island, I want
to thank Tim Freeman and Chris Lauer for their hospitality and providing
insights in the local discussions regarding invasive species. I have discussed
parts of the work over lunch, dinner, coffee, or something stronger with
local friends Sam Mickey, Marjolein Oele, Amanda Paris, and Ron Sundstrom.
I am grateful to all of you!

In terms of finishing and polishing the book, I would like to thank Bob
Mugerauer, Brian Treanor, Jason Wirth, and the two anonymous reviewers
for Routledge for reading (parts of) the manuscript and for the insightful
comments that helped me improve the final manuscript. Research assistants
who helped me along the way were Brian Burke, Alex Binsfield-Debus,
Shara Love, Kristin Aakvik, and Allison Rodriguez. The latter was of invaluable assistance in editing the chapters and preparing the final manuscript.
In addition, it has been a real pleasure to work with Helen Bell, Rebecca
Brennan and Claire Garner at Routledge.

Finally, I would like to thank Marjolein, Lars, and Imma, who define "my
place" in an unsettled world.

Of course, as always, all mistakes are mine.

A note on the front cover images

All the images on the front cover are taken by NASA's Earth Observatory. On the surface the images might seem depictions of nature without humans, but all, in fact, show the relationship and close connections between humans and the earth. Clockwise, starting on the right top the images show 1) the calving of ice at Yakutat Glacier in Southeast Alaska, one of the effects of global warming; 2) Algae blooms in Lake Erie, caused by agricultural runoff and warm temperatures, and 3) the Sundarban forest in Bangladesh and Southeastern India. The first two images show the destructive effects of the lack of human responsibility while the latter shows an ecosystem in which humans who live in it can sustainably use and protect it (ecopolitics at work). The images are, as such, a reflection of the book's main argument to move from ecological destruction to responsibility, and it encourages us to truly live in the places that determine us.

Introduction

When Odysseus returns to his home in Ithaca, he does so as a stranger. Twenty years away from his place – traveling, fighting a grueling war, and living through all kinds of adventures – has turned him into a stranger, someone who is homeless, without a place. Odysseus emphasizes his homelessness by dressing up as a beggar, presumably in order to spy on the household. He is out of place in his own place. This situation is reversed by an act of violence: once he announces his homecoming he slays all the suitors of his wife as well as 12 of the maids. Welcome home!

Homer's *Odyssey* contains one of the ailments of our society: our tendency to explore, to travel everywhere, and to violently make every place our own. While Odysseus returns home to a particular place, our current culture is less and less tied to particular places. This means that anywhere in the USA and increasingly abroad we can feel "at home" since we find the same corporations not only invading, but in many cases constituting the public sphere. While I know many people to whom this familiarity creates an uncanny feeling, to many others these universal spaces create a home. Places are no longer constituted by a history, by a specific culture, and certainly not by its geography, its rivers, its mountains. We humans move around, often uprooting our own family history, as well as the cultures that used to live on the land that we now call our home. When we think today of home or dwelling, we are, in a sense, nomads; we are at home everywhere, including those places that are explicitly not our home. We are drawn to cultures that are not our own, to different climates, to the exotic, and so forth. Yet, we will always find the certainty of belonging. Tourism provides us with foreign places that offer people who speak our language beds with mattresses similar to our own, technology that creates a bearable climate (at least indoors) and companies that will bring us to the sites we have read about in our guides. In short, today we are at home everywhere. Yet, what it means to be "at home" is grounded in a shallow sense of home or place.

The shallow understanding of home or place indicates a situation in which the topic of place has become pressing. To start, we are facing a population crisis. In the last couple of centuries the world population has exploded. With this the question arises whether this place, the earth, is large enough to provide a home for nine billion people. As Hardin has discussed, over-population is a topic most people try to avoid, but is something that we cannot keep denying (Hardin 2002). This population crisis is closely tied to the environmental crisis: do we have enough natural resources for this huge world population, of which some are consuming an incredible and unsustainable amount? Both population and consumption are closely tied to issues of immigration and displacement. The current immigration crisis is only in its first steps toward a full-blown crisis, as natural resources continue to deplete, oceans start to rise, and many find themselves in politically unstable situations. As the wealthier countries in the world vehemently protect their borders, the question that needs to be asked is to whom do particular places belong? Can we claim the places that we inhabit and own by paying our mortgage or paying the tax dollars that support our towns, states, and nation? On legal terms the answer is straightforward – ethically, historically, and philosophically, less so. Internally we have divided our land, resources, and pollution in problematic ways, burdening those who somehow do not count as much, and benefitting those who count more. Also externally, i.e., outside of our borders, we exploit, using resources that we either buy from corrupt regimes, or that are acquired under the false pretense of bringing new wealth. Many natural places are treated as private property. Common property is an idea that has been successfully suppressed. Privatization is seen as the solution. We build fences and walls, and heavily patrol the borders around the land that we claim as ours. Even while the land that we live on once was inhabited by the ancestors of those we keep out, these displaced strangers are not welcome because of a different skin color, because of a different language, or simply because they were not born in the right place. Thus, despite or because of our nomadic existence in which we feel at home anywhere, we have constructed strong ideas about what and whom belongs and what and whom does not belong.

Finally, besides the environmental and population crises, we face an identity crisis, both personally and culturally. The fact that we move around and can settle anywhere means that we lack knowledge of the places in which we live. It also means that our cultural and personal identities are diminished or impoverished. Who we are – as a culture and as individuals – is determined by a few superficial aspects (such as music and food), lacking deeper systems of knowledge rooted in place. Places have become moldable "plastic" places, mostly defined through commerce and street names such as "Market Street," "Main Street," First Street," and so forth. The names of places, even if they refer to a past, have little to no cultural significance. Being at home in every place is partly explained by different places appearing increasingly homogeneous. The "McDonaldization" and "Hiltonization" of the world provide us with a familiar setting even in the strangest of places. We find people everywhere, or almost everywhere, who mostly look and behave like us. We avoid unsafe areas; we can explore the world on cruises that bring us to exotic places, neatly framed within the familiarity of other English-speaking tourists who could live down the street. Meanwhile, we move around. While in the past people looked for jobs where they lived, today we live where we find a job. Lack of job security, the temporary status of jobs, and the constant need for upward mobility contribute to the mobility of our lives. Since national and multinational companies have taken over, many people work for these companies that require traveling and/or relocation. Both the job and the place we live in are less permanent than ever. Thus, we are nomadic, traveling around the world without settling permanently. Our nomadic existence has, likewise, resulted in a lack of knowledge of the places around us. We do not recognize changes, or falsely think something has radically changed. Besides a few one-liners, we do not know the stories that used to tie people to their places.

These crises, and in particular the crisis concerning our identity, play a significant role in the central part of this book, in which I tie the analysis of homelessness to our contemporary nomadism and the constant changes we make to the places in which we live.

Being at home, as suggested by Homer, involves violence. There are many ways in which we create "home" through ideas of belonging and inclusion. Belonging or inclusion always involve exclusion. For example, on our vacations, and at home, we avoid places or people that might disturb us. We have built high borders around our country. The nice middle-class neighborhood has many strategies at its disposal that will keep those out who might bring the value of houses down. Gender neatly divides the human population into two groups, excluding those who do not quite fit in either category. The human species as a boundary excludes all other species. Boundaries determine who we are as a community, as a society, a nation, a species, and as individuals. Boundaries determine what is right and wrong, what should be and what should not be. These certainties create a home, which occurs through the categories that we as a species invent. For example, the idea of species only exists for the human being.

When we think about home, our place, we can first consider the dwelling we live in, or the place where we grew up. Place in that regard can be a country, city, village, province, county, district, or region. We can also call the world or the earth our home. As world travelers and conquerors, we are at home everywhere. We have guidebooks, maps, and technologies that can point out our exact location on our cellphone or other device. If we know where we are, the thought seems to be, we are at home, however unfamiliar our surroundings. We create a sense of home by mapping and making the place.

Perhaps it is because of this strange and violent relationship to place since Homer that the Western tradition of thinking has, particularly in the last centuries, largely ignored place. Philosophers write and speak about space, the more abstract concept in which we find more particular and specific places.[1] Nevertheless, in the last couple of decades discussions of place in the field of philosophy have occurred with some frequency. Without questioning the significance of the few works on place, the fact remains that they are few. A so-called "spatial turn" that occurred in many of the humanities did not occur in philosophy.

Besides the few recent discussions of place, philosophy has not always ignored place. *Topos* (as well as *atopos*, "being out of place," or "strange") plays a significant role in Plato's dialogues. "Where" is one of Aristotle's categories. Neo-Platonism and scholastic thinking certainly did not ignore place. Yet, what happened to place in the modern era? Ed Casey provides a compelling insight in this regard. It is worthwhile to quote him here at length:

> In the past two centuries in the West – the period of "modernity" – place has come to be not only neglected but actively suppressed. Owing to the triumph of the natural and social sciences in the same period, any serious talk of place has been regarded as regressive or trivial. A discourse has emerged whose exclusive cosmological foci are Time and Space. When the two were combined by twentieth-century physicists into the amalgam "space-time," the overlooking of place was only continued by other means. For an entire epoch, place has been regarded as an impoverished second cousin of Time and Space, those two colossal cosmic partners that tower over modernity.
>
> (Casey 2009, xiv)

Thus, Casey argues that philosophy has simply accepted the theories of the natural sciences and assumed that thinking about place is unimportant and not scientific – not "worthy" of the queen of the sciences. Yet, place is such an important topic since it intersects with all aspects of our world, those aspects that we pay attention to and those that we ignore or forget. Senses of place determine borders and play a significant role in creating and maintaining racial identities. Our (gendered) human body is also a place, creating a boundary as well as a connection between self and other. The human as a place provides identity to who we are by separating us from animals, and nature in general. Place and senses of home determine whom we are in terms of, among other things, nation (or tribe), race, gender, and species.

As a phenomenologist, Casey attempts to emphasize place over space: we do not experience space, but places (Casey 2009, 319).[2] In emphasizing place over space, the starting point, for Casey, is not a blank canvas of space in which particular places occur. Rather, we start with the experience of places. Space is only a secondary concept derived from these experiences. Casey argues that both space and time are, "first and last, dimensions of place, and they are experienced and expressed in place" (Casey 2009, 340). Space (and time) is, thus, not a foundation but rather a derivative of place, since the first could never be experienced without the latter.

In this book I analyze our experience of place, with little discussion of space. I use place as location, site, home, body or any unified entity that we experience spatially. As such, it can be a cultural (how places, and which places, define a culture), social (how do places unify or separate people), economic (who owns, makes profits and how is property and commerce driving the identity of places), scientific (how is place and its significance defined), ecological (how does a place function as a natural system), historical (what happened here), or a political entity (how is a place run, what hierarchies are in place, who is excluded, etc.). Whether we speak of a body, a province or state, a city or village, a house or neighborhood, or a bioregion, I argue that the way we understand these places is through the conglomeration of these discourses. Place is conceived as something that determines who we are through our collective experiences.

As we will see in Chapter 4, other philosophical traditions have done much more to emphasize place as a significant component of who we are. Zen Buddhism and Native American thinking tie human existence and identity immediately to place. These traditions place the human in its environment, not as some external entity in which we find ourselves, but rather we find ourselves as an internal part of these places. We should first seek to understand the places that we inhabit before we can start to understand ourselves.

While these traditions provide a valuable alternative approach, the main framework of the book is Western, criticizing and rethinking the system from within, even while it attempts to radically break out of it. Through thinkers such as Nietzsche and what we could call "other Nietzscheans," I rethink place from within our Western understanding. The book, thus, calls for a transitional thinking, or a re-placing of ourselves. As already mentioned, the last couple of decades brought to life an interest in the topic of place. Ed Casey, cited above, has done extensive and important work on place through a phenomenological framework. Casey's former student, David Abram, wrote the well-known work *The Spell of the Sensuous*, in which place plays a prominent role. Jeff Malpas's book on the experience of place used Heidegger's ideas on place, as have numerous phenomenologists in works concerning, among other things, architecture and urban planning. Heidegger remains an important thinker for many who work on place. The second chapter of this book is dedicated to Heidegger's thinking. Besides the relevant insights he provides, it is important to keep in mind that Heidegger's main interest is not place, but being, and that he understands being in terms of time. What Heidegger provides is an analysis of our being.

Although there is in Heidegger's work some tension between place and time, for him our contemporary being is determined through a loss of place: homelessness. This sense of being lost, of not being tied to a place, is both a positive and a negative component of who we are: we can identify two forms of homelessness. One provides the possibility to philosophize while the other form is the condition in which we try to escape from any philosophizing or confrontation with ourselves. Thus, from the outset Heidegger's thoughts on homelessness are complex, and we always have to keep both directions in mind. We should not settle in the everyday gossip and concerns, but we cannot remain homeless either. Heidegger's analysis of our "being there," *Dasein*, makes significant appeals to ideas about location and dwelling.

Being-in-the-world (written with dashes since "being" and "world" are intrinsically tied together) suggests that we cannot think about being without the place in which we exist.

Heidegger's thinking is deeply rooted in Nietzsche. In relationship to the topic of place and homelessness, Nietzsche places all our values and ideas in question and as such he makes us wander, without a secure dwelling in language or thinking. Deleuze calls Nietzsche's philosophy "nomad thought" (Deleuze 1985). It is, in fact, Nietzsche's thinking that forms the guiding thread of this book. For that reason the book starts with a chapter on Nietzsche and his wandering philosophy, or a thinking-in-transition. That said, it is not a book about Nietzsche, however Nietzschean in spirit.

As suggested above, we re-create the same places and appropriate all places through a sense of what and who belongs and what and who does not belong. These appropriations and exclusions create, for us, a being at home. By ordering the world, in a sense we own it, even while we lack autonomy, since we simply follow the political, social, economic, philosophical, religious, and scientific values in which we live. We are what Nietzsche calls "herd animals," not applying the ability to think for ourselves and predominantly concerned with what others might think of us.[3] For him, our herd mentality creates a false home that makes us think we are wise and know who we are, while we are in fact utterly lost. This form of being lost is a negative form of homelessness, which can be opposed with a more positive one of philosophical wandering, or existential homelessness. The latter form of homelessness can be interpreted as a crisis, since all values are gone and, as a result, we have nothing to hold on to. Yet, for Nietzsche, this homelessness is ultimately positive since we are given the opportunity to create our own values and with that we can become who we are, i.e., overcome ourselves. The herd mentality is similar to what Heidegger describes as the anonymous structure of "the they" – the no one that is also everyone. We care about celebrities, what kind of car our neighbors drive, what they might think of ours, and so on. Any philosophical thoughts are left far away. A reflection on who we are in relation to the places in which we live is entirely excluded from our lives. As such, we feel entirely at home in the world while we are utterly lost.

The idea I want to stress in this project is that this superficial form of being at home is a false sense of home, or homelessness: the universal market places, national banks, strip malls, chain restaurants, chain coffee shops, and the alienating experiences of (sub)urban dwelling machines, decorated according to the latest fads, indicate an alienation from the world around us. Technology *is* the connection to the world, in effect limiting the world to all that is expressed through technology. The car is in many ways a displacing and alienating technology. Modern technology, literally, has brought the structure of Heidegger's "they" into our home. Talk-show hosts, news anchors, and sports commentators cozily join us at the breakfast table to discuss the latest news and gossip, always making a joke when appropriate. They have become part of the family. We then hop into our car, drive to work while listening to more chatter, and feel at home in the landscape as we experience it from the car. It is familiar as we pass through it every day. We focus on the bottle-necks, changing lanes, traffic lights, and speed limits. This is how we feel at home in our world. Meanwhile, we are constantly connected: we check our messages through whatever technology every one else is using and are tied to whatever keeps us busy and creates a feeling at home. Whenever work is not entirely occupying us, we call and text with our friends and loved ones in order to hear the latest gossip from and about our colleagues, friends, and family.

Through our attachments to technology our experience of the world is filtered and, arguably, impoverished. All places, in a way, turn into the same. The places that we mostly experience, such as freeways, offices, coffee shops, restaurants, malls, hotels and, to a certain degree, our homes are universal places. The homogeneity of places creates a sense of feeling at home wherever we are. This universality of places has significant consequences. By constantly moving we lose a sense of history and memory of a place. By feeling at home, even while we are not, we are lulled into a false comfort that keeps us from thinking philosophically and from paying attention to the actual world behind the façade of commercialized planning and architecture. We fail to notice possibly important changes around us. Changes in climate, water and air quality, and the way our bodies respond to our environment are lost upon us, simply because we have not been around long enough.

The 2011 tsunami in Japan is a very tragic example of how we are not attached or in sync with the places we live in. Old traditions to avoid building anything below a certain level were forgotten, even while stone markers (some of them more than six centuries old) are still present. The stones had mostly become artifacts without a meaning, even while the message carved in the stones was clear: "Do not build your homes below this point" (Fackler 2011).[4] The tsunami was violent, but not without precedent. It took so many human lives because inhabitants forgot the past of the place. Thus, they built villages (and nuclear power plants) in an area that was known to be dangerous.

In the USA we are likewise on unknown grounds. Columbus only arrived six centuries ago and all the existing knowledge of the place we now call our home has been wiped out with those who carried the knowledge. To provide an example, in the San Francisco Bay Area, where I work and live, the seasonal climate is very predictable. San Franciscans think they know this climate so well that they always seem to notice something extraordinary. Rain in the summer is rare, but a little shower occurs almost every year. Interestingly, hardly anyone seems to remember this rare but reoccurring phenomenon, and everyone will talk about it when it happens. It might even make the front page of the newspaper. Likewise, only native inhabitants seem to remember that the spring and fall are typically the warmest in San Francisco, with little fog. Everyone else is surprised by the number of beautiful days during these times of the year. Most people, it seems, have not been here long enough to remember the subtleties of the weather cycles. Would we, then, be able to recognize significant changes in the climate – changes that might indicate an upcoming catastrophe? The irony is that we think that we know so much more than ever before. We are recording the weather with reliable instruments. Yet, our experiences have become dramatically less reliable, and we might not even know what to look for.

We experience fewer natural places directly (because we are glued to our gadgets and because we have fewer natural places to begin with). We also lack the experience of places that are other than our own. As a white person one has no business in a black or Hispanic neighborhood. In fact, visiting such places is not without risk. Likewise racial minorities face risks in visiting white places. Many cities have successfully moved poverty to their fringes, and, thus, the mainstream does not experience such places. In our explorations abroad, tour guides will make sure we are kept away from other dangerous places, and so we end up only visiting beautiful, historical sites, rather than the places that actually constitute the country, and where people live. Of course, no one would want to visit a ghetto on vacation, but our experience of a foreign place is a lopsided one that consists of great weather, incredibly friendly people, and astonishing beauty.

Because of this shallow experience of places and the earlier discussed population and environmental crises I argue that we not only should take up the issue of place in a serious manner, but also argue for making a radical transition in our thinking as well as in our actions. I call this new way of existing an eco-politics since it positions the human in the greater realm of ecology: all that lives and makes life possible. It is, to some degree, a Nietzschean affirmation of life. This is not merely an eco-politics in the sense that we should take care of the earth. It is also an eco-politics that emphasizes that we should take care of one another. It actually works under the assumption that the way we treat nature directly correlates with the way we treat one another. A society that oppresses animals and its environment also oppresses human beings. This idea is certainly not new. Civil rights and environmental activist Van Jones uses it in the *Green Collar Economy*, and the Marxist philosopher Marcuse argues that capitalism dominates man through the domination of nature. According to the latter, the "non-social" man (the product of capitalism) lacks the kinds of senses the social man possesses (Marcuse 1972). He calls for an emancipation of the senses, in which we experience the world in a richer way, as opposed to the impoverished world we experience today and that leads to environmental destruction and the destruction of human lives.

We can then speak of a lack of experience of places, such as the places that frighten us, the places that are racially different, and we can speak of a poor or impoverished experience of places. In fact, these two shortcomings both contribute to an oppression of other places and those who inhabit them. As indicated, place also has significant implications for our identity. In this book I discuss this through ideas of homelessness and nomadism, in both a positive and negative way. On the one hand, we need to become homeless in order to experience these other places and to reinvigorate our senses. We need to step outside the boundaries we have created, and this implies a loss of home as well as a loss of our very identity. In truly encountering what we are not, the other, we ourselves are changed. Thus, the book, in particular the first chapters, largely focuses on homelessness in order to make such a transition. On the other hand, we need to overcome the negative homelessness of our contemporary being that is lost without the actual recognition that we are lost. The idea that we think we are at home while we lack any real grounding in the places where we live is ultimately unsustainable and dangerous. We can and have to attempt to change who we are, by first of all relating differently to the places that we encounter, not in a false nomadic sense, but in a philosophical sense of being homeless.

This book marks the need to move ourselves both physically and intellectually. To move our thinking and being by retrieving a sense of place implies that we are becoming a different person, redefining ourselves. This move involves homelessness for us, yet moves towards a more inclusive unity. I have called this unity "ecopolitics," which emphasizes the environmental aspects of the relationships within the proposed unity. As I will argue, the step to a new politics can only be made in a radical rethinking of who and what is included in a political unity. The most radical way to do this will involve the inclusion of nature. I am using in this regard Latour's idea of a democratizing of nature in which all beings, human, living, and inanimate have a voice in how to live together. This might sound like a "tree-hugger" hippie dream, yet I will draw our attention to some aboriginal cultures that fairly recently were living (and some still do live) in such a politics of nature. I do not in this regard propose to return to this previous state, but rather advance to another state in which we use technology and industry along with and in harmony with nature. The book, thus, proposes an ecopolitical homelessness that merges aboriginal and technological cultures in such a way that technology is not going to dominate and dictate how we think and act.

This is, obviously, an ambitious agenda, and the proposed ecopolitics – discussed in the concluding chapter – will not move beyond a few tentative ideas. Most of the book is dedicated to shaking the foundations of who we are, by an investigation of home, senses of place, and homelessness. The following provides a brief summary of each chapter.

In the first chapter – "Nietzsche, the wandering philosopher" – I introduce the necessity as well as complexities of the idea of wandering, of becoming nomadic in a philosophical sense, through Nietzsche. It will become clear that we are, in fact, dealing with two forms of homelessness: the common way of being lost in the herd is a form of homelessness that is (ironically) rooted in a strong attachment. This homelessness is one that we fail to recognize. The second form of homelessness is an existential one that we explicitly experience as a loss. I use Nietzsche's declaration of the death of God as the starting point of wandering since it marks the loss of all values.

While some have used Nietzsche combined with postmodern relativism to argue that anything goes in this vacuum of values, I question such a direction. In particular, I think through Nietzsche's idea that we are a part of nature, thus placing us in an environment, in a place. Nietzsche's *Zarathustra* thus exclaims that we must remain true to the earth. While our thinking tends to artificially distance ourselves from animals, and nature in general (a common theme throughout the book), this tendency is also, in a way, natural. Nietzsche, thus, places us in nature, in which we are naturally related against nature. How we should remain true to nature given this antagonism is one of the driving questions in this book. Nietzsche's *Übermensch*, I argue, is a being tied to the earth, but also to particular places from which it derives its values. To "become yourself" means to relate to the place in which and through which one is becoming.

Chapter 2, "Lost at home: Heidegger and the phenomenologists on being-in-the-world," continues the theme of wandering, specifically through notions of homelessness. For both Heidegger and Nietzsche language is an important element that forms our world, something on which we rest, or under which we take cover. As such, language provides a home in the world. Heidegger analyzes and deconstructs this home of language in order to create a new way of thinking. This deconstruction often creates a sense of homelessness. Through this homelessness I discuss in particular our place in the world, and what it means to have, or to not have, a place in the world. While we have clear notions of what belongs and does not belong in particular parts of the world (among others through language), we ourselves (as Western white people) seem to be at home everywhere. Yet, for Heidegger, this being at home is grounded in a being lost: we are at home while removed from ourselves, or lost. Here we again encounter the two forms of homelessness. First of all, a homelessness that is rooted in an inauthentic feeling of being at home. We are at home in the world, through or in, among other things, language, technology, and science. It is through these media that we experience our world. Second, we can experience homelessness in a philosophical, existential way, through which we recognize the inauthenticity of our existence. It is a moment of being ourselves, of being authentic, a homelessness that brings us home, so to speak.

Chapter 3, "Plastic places; settled nomads: an analysis of our sense of place through Foucault and Deleuze," is the central chapter of the book. It moves from notions of philosophical homelessness and nomadism to historical and current relationship to place, partly defined as nomadic, yet simultaneously settled, in the sense that all places have become the same. Through Foucault's ideas of genealogy and abnormalcy, I think through how we have arrived at and are comfortable with our unprecedented nomadism and a rapid change of the places that we occupy. The last part of the chapter ties these thoughts back to Nietzsche through Deleuze's essay "Nomad thought," in which he compels us to think nomadically. Here we return to the fine line that exists between inauthentic and authentic nomadism.

While the first three chapters are mostly critical of our homeless or nomadic being, the last two chapters are thinking forward, and find a more positive way of being and thinking nomadically. Chapter 4, "Walking and thinking mountains: Dōgen, Leopold, and the Tlingit," discusses a few non-Western approaches to place. The chapter is framed by Western thinkers: Aldo Leopold and Bruno Latour, who provide both an entry and exit point to, among others, Dōgen and some indigenous cultures. The thinkers and traditions discussed in this chapter provide an intricate relationship between being and place. What it means to be and that we are at all is, for these traditions, deeply tied to place. While many of the thinkers discussed in this book attempt to rethink the relationship between subject and object, between the human active perceiver and the perceived natural world, the traditions discussed in this chapter already find themselves in such a relationship. In other words, they do not need to rethink a tradition they have never been a part of. The aim of this chapter is to propose a non-anthropocentric approach in which we are closer to nature, as a member of a community, as opposed to an oppressor or a controller. Latour provides such an idea in terms of his actor–network theory, in which human and non-human actors or actants are placed in a political unity.

In order to think through the implications of a non-anthropocentric approach, the last chapter, "Conclusion: toward an ecopolitical homelessness," discusses a new political unity, partly based on Latour's actor–network theory and Esposito's work on "immunity." The latter is, in short, a new approach to biopolitics by thinking about our society as seeking too much security, a process in which it incorporates the other in order to destroy it as invasive or as an intruder. The chapter brings together these ideas in relationship to home and homelessness by thinking through, among other things, restoration ecology. While this field is anthropocentric, among others by using notions of place and by determining what belongs in certain places, it also provides an opportunity to engage and share places with beings that are non-human. Moreover, since restoration ecology thinks about ecosystems in a very rigid sense, in terms of what belongs and what does not belong, it provides a helpful contrast with our own lack of a relationship to place. The chapter tries to bring these opposites together, in which we learn from other species how to become more attached to places and how to identify ourselves with the places in which and through which we live. We can become more tied to places, somewhat more like a species in an ecosystem. Likewise, ecology can become more flexible in its assessment of belonging and non-belonging. Plants and animals, as species, can become more nomadic. I will situate this argument in the context of a changing climate in which we might need not only *Übermenschen* ("overhumans"), but also *Überbaume* ("overtrees") and *Übertiere* ("overanimals") – species that overcome themselves through their environment. Through this re-assessment of both the ecosystem as conceived by ecology and our place as human beings, we will find ourselves in a new homelessness or nomadism.

Notes

1 I have no intention to provide here a complete summary of the concept of space, but merely want to point out that we find throughout the history of philosophy an extensive discussion of space. One notable example is Kant, who conceives of space as one of the two forms with which we order our perceptions. Two important aspects of space should be noted from Kant: (1) it is subjective, in the sense that it does not exist outside of human experience; (2) the other form is time, tying spatial experiences immediately to time (Kant 1965).
2 As he points out, this is not a new, but rather a forgotten idea. Archytas and Aristotle have already put place before space.
3 Nietzsche uses terms such as "herd animal" and "herd mentality" throughout his works (most prominently in Nietzsche 1998).
4 Fackler's article describes one tiny village that survived the tsunamis for the simple reason that they followed the message their ancestors had carved in the stones. The waves stopped 300 feet from the stones.

References

Casey, Edward S. 2009. *Getting Back into Place: Toward a Renewed Understanding of the Place-World*. Bloomington: Indiana University Press.

Deleuze, Gilles. 1985. "Nomad thought." In David B. Allison (ed.) *The New Nietzsche: Contemporary Styles of Interpretation*. Cambridge, MA: MIT Press.

Fackler, Martin. 2011. "Tsunami warnings, written in stone." *The New York Times*, April 21.

Hardin, Garrett. 2002. "Poverty as an environmental problem: living on a lifeboat." In: David Schmidtz and Elizabeth Willott (eds.), *Environmental Ethics: What Really Matters, What Really Works*. New York: Oxford University Press.

Kant, Immanuel, 1965. *Critique of Pure Reason*. Translated by Norman Kemp Smith. New York: St. Martin's Press.

Marcuse, Herbert. 1972. *Counterrevolution and Revolt*. Boston: Beacon Press.

Nietzsche, Friedrich Wilhelm. 1998. *Beyond Good and Evil: Prelude to a Philosophy of the Future*. New York: Oxford University Press.

1 Nietzsche, the wandering philosopher

Introduction

In what I take as a simultaneously comic and tragic passage in *The Gay Science*, Nietzsche writes

> Have you not heard of that madman who lit a lantern in the bright morning hours, ran to the marketplace and cried incessantly: "I seek God! I seek God!" – As many of those who did not believe in God were standing around just then, he provoked much laughter. Has he got lost? asked one. Did he lose his way like a child? asked another. Or is he hiding? Is he afraid of us? Has he gone on a voyage? Emigrated? – Thus they yelled and laughed.
>
> (Nietzsche 1974, 125)

Perhaps Nietzsche was longing for living in this environment where not he – the atheist – but the Christian was the madman. However, Nietzsche does not merely mock the Christian for believing, nor does he ever claim to be closer to the truth than a Christian. Truth is always historical and continuously changing. This idea comes to the fore in the same section when Nietzsche continues: "The madman sprang into their midst and transfixed them with his gaze. 'Where has God gone?' he cried; 'I'll tell you where! *We have killed him* – you and I! We are all his murderers'" (Nietzsche 1995, 125). Nietzsche suggests that God did exist, at least in our minds. The image of killing God reflects the idea that we have killed one truth, and consequently we are in need of another truth. In fact, the murder of God does not resolve our problems. On the contrary, it creates a whole range of new problems. I quote Nietzsche again: "Where are we moving? Away from all suns? Aren't we falling constantly? Backwards, sideways, forwards, in every direction? Is there still an above and below?" (Nietzsche 1995, 125). Without the belief in God, we have lost our whole orientation. The lantern, lit in the bright morning, indicates the impossible nature of the madman's search (similar to the impossible nature of Diogenes's search for an honest man). Dark and light, up and down: all direction is gone.

Here we are immediately thrown into existential homelessness. Without a god who created the world with a goal, all direction is lost: values, boundaries, borders, and categories dissolve. We encounter an absolute freedom. Yet the gift of freedom poses a serious problem. To be absolutely free is to lose all order. In this position we can start to philosophize. It is the first, positive form of homelessness, which I will call an existential homelessness, since one is confronted with oneself, with one's very existence. To be without direction and certainty means that the only remaining certainty is our being, the fact that we are. Yet, this existential homelessness, to be without any direction, is impossible for us. Nietzsche's death of God is an attempt to make everything fluid, but we cannot really accept a world of fluidity, in which we find nothing to hold on to. Opposed to this first form of homelessness we will find homelessness in a lack of reflection, in constantly being immersed in what Nietzsche calls "the herd." Ironically, in finding our place or home in the herd, we are in fact far removed from ourselves. Thus we are lost, homeless in a false sense of home.

Returning to existential homelessness, its lack of direction and values could be represented as empty space, the void. This idea, indeed, proved pivotal in Nietzsche's early thinking, when he encountered the atomism of Democritus, which arguably provided an inspiration for the rest of his life. The void represents life as devoid of meaning. Everything in nature is fluid, and without necessity. Thus, we arrive at Nietzsche's assessment of nature, which is, first of all, valueless and without order. In all its aspects, nature is chaos. In this chapter I think through Nietzsche's idea of nature without value, in conjunction with our tendency to produce and create value. Throughout the book, I discuss notions of boundaries and borders that identify what should and should not be. Who or what should be where and who or what is deemed to be the other that needs to be excluded, either through subtle mechanisms or through violence. Ordering the world into places of identity creates a home as well as exclusion from that home. It is an appropriation that can only be realized through alienation. In this chapter I focus on the ways in which this appropriation or creation of a home at the cost of exclusion is created through order, purpose, and norms in a world that is, according to Nietzsche, without order, purpose, and norms.

In particular I evaluate our own position and who we are. In a world without absolute values, a sense of homelessness and fluidity arises. In the last section, I will use H.G. Wells's novel *The Island of Dr. Moreau* and the film *The Island of Lost Souls*, based on Wells's novel. The book and film introduce hybrid beings that provide an interesting take on Darwin's theory of evolution, which also greatly influenced Nietzsche. I argue that we can understand ourselves as fluid and changing beings in relationship to our environment – the place in which we live, grow, and develop.

The void

When we give up all values and move toward an understanding of nature without any order, how exactly do we understand place, provided that we can still have any understanding at all? A picture of "nature as chaos" emerges, in which all places and placement is arbitrary, and we return to a sense of space in which such random placements occur. Can we, however, really imagine such chaos? To think chaos – if at all possible – is not an easy task. Defining chaos is difficult at best. In fact, Nietzsche claims that our inability to think chaos is a result of more than two millennia of order, teleology, and value. We define chaos negatively, as the opposite of order. Inspired by Friedrich Lange, Nietzsche argues that a conception of nature without a purpose, value, and order has been long lost with the loss (and destruction) of the ideas and works of Democritus.

While Democritus and this concern appear in Nietzsche's very early writings, the project to retrieve a conception of nature that is without order is, arguably, a driving force throughout his career. As Deleuze, Nehamas, and Safranski (to name just a few) have pointed out, one of Nietzsche's tasks is to define the natural world of forces without falling into the determinism and teleological ideas of Western thinking. It is well-known how, for Nietzsche, all life is determined as a will to power, which can be a force that acts or re-acts against other forces (Deleuze 1983) and even a force that acts against its own nature (Nehamas 1985). One way to think of this world of forces without a source or goal is through the atomism of Democritus.

The fragment attributed to Democritus that inspired Nietzsche, among others, reads as follows: "Nothing exists but atoms and empty space; every-thing else is opinion" (Lange 1925, 18). Nietzsche translates this fragment into the following:

> Whatever has *value* in our world now does not have value in itself, according to its nature – nature is always value-less, but has been *given* value at some time, as a present – and it was we who gave and bestowed it. Only we have created the world *that concerns man!*
>
> (Nietzsche 1974, 301)

Perhaps Democritus can be understood as Nietzsche's Greek predecessor. For both thinkers, Gods, form-giving principles, as well as good and evil, are classified as mere opinions, or in Nietzsche's words, "perspectives."[1] The philosopher who celebrated the death of God was certainly enthused to find an account of the world in which only atoms and empty space exist. It gave Nietzsche hope that an understanding of the world "beyond good and evil," a philosophy without anthropomorphism and supernatural ideas, existed in the very beginning of Western thought.

Democritus's account of atomism places the human being in a decentralized position, questioning all values and ideas of determination. This atomism provides us with absolute freedom without any kind of determinism (besides the fact that atoms and empty space existed). For the Western world, how-ever, such a freedom is a prison: without truth, boundaries, values, norms, or any determination, one is nothing but homeless. Nietzsche is seeking such homelessness, moving against the grain of the tradition of Western thinking that, for him, is seeking truth rather than homelessness or chaos. Within that context, Nietzsche raises some serious suspicions about the history of philosophy in relation to Democritus's reclaimed works. These are suspicions that, arguably, became the foundation of Nietzsche's relation to the history of philosophy, to him a history of sick thinkers who needed philosophy and its "truths" as a crutch (Nietzsche 1974, i). The suspicion starts with a question about what happened to Democritus and his non-teleological account of nature. Have Plato, Aristotle, the neo-Platonists and, finally, the Christian thinkers burned Democritus's atomism – either literally or figuratively – simply because it did not match their view of the order of nature? Influenced by Friedrich Lange's *History of Materialism*, Nietzsche discovers, through the oppression of Democritus's philosophy of nature, the dynamics of the history of philosophy.

Reconstructing Democritus is not an easy task since so little is left of his writing and what is left comes from a variety of different sources.[2] Democritus is known for his atomism, the theory that everything in nature is made out of invisible and indivisible parts. Hermias writes that the theory is a full explanation of all that is: "Being is the full and non-being the void. And the full produces all things by its impulsion and proportion in the void" (Nahm 1964, 160).[3]

The second-century physician and philosopher Galenus writes that atoms do not have qualities:

> Since all the atoms are minute bodies, they have no qualities and the void is a kind of place in which all these bodies, as they move up and down through all time, either [sic] become somehow entangled with each other by reason of such contacts, and in this way produce all other combinations including our own bodies with their affections and sensations.
>
> (Nahm 1964, 160)

We encounter here, thus, a complete randomness in the way atoms entangle. Whether we talk about mountains, rivers, plants or human bodies (with their affections and sensations) we find a random entanglement of atoms that have collided. In this entanglement, bodies come into being.

Besides the causes of movement and entanglement, commentators such as Galenus, Simplicius, and Dionysius, over the course of almost 500 years, are quite consistent in their respective accounts of atomism.[4] All take a materialistic approach in which we indeed have only atoms and empty space. How movement comes about and how atoms entangle are not agreed upon, but all think of perceivable objects as merely the temporary states of the entangled atoms.

While most sources do seem to take the role of "objective" reporters or historians, some other sources include objections to Democritus.[5] Aristotle (and Plutarch) questions the growth and decay of the body within the theory of atomism. In *On Parts of Animals* he writes: "[Democritus] says it is clear to everyone what sort of shape man is, since he is known by his shape and color. And yet a corpse has the same shape, but it is not therefore a man" (Aristotle 1937, 1640b29). Indeed, if Democritus's world only consists of atoms and the void, his theory seems to run into some obvious problems. Aristotle asks what the difference between a living and a dead body is. In addition, we can ask questions about the randomness of the collision of atoms. Even while we lose millions of body cells every single day, and while apparently over time most of our cells are replaced, on a day-to-day basis our bodies are quite consistent in appearance. Moreover, we resemble our biological parents as well as other members of our species. Understood this way, it seems that our bodies are considerably organized forms, rather than random conglomerations. This implies that a human being is more than simply an aggregate of her material parts. What constitutes a self, how a self remains to some degree consistent, and how we appear similar over time, even while material parts continuously change, are questions that certainly lie beyond the scope of my discussion here. Yet this version of atomism fails to address these issues if it simply regards the human body as a collision and entanglement of atoms.

We do find answers to these objections in some other accounts of Democritus's atomism. Besides the previously discussed materialistic approaches, in which atoms are regarded as physical entities that are indivisible, we also find supernatural explanations. Sextus Empiricus, for example, seems to interpret atoms as platonic forms.[6] Some others also mention that atoms are forms, and many suggest that atoms are eternal. In addition, Aristotle makes a somewhat puzzling comment that could be interpreted in line with this "form-giving atomism." In the *Metaphysics*, while discussing generation, he writes: "Democritus's doctrine would be better expressed as 'all things were together potentially, but not actually'" (Aristotle 1997, 1069b22). Aristotle appears to want to correct the theory of atomism by suggesting that atoms should be seen as pure potentiality. When things come into being, they are no longer simply elements; they become actual things. Atoms should, then, not be seen as the actual beings that make up the universe, but the potentiality for those things.

This can perhaps be better understood through the vortex that Aristotle discusses in *The Physics*. He mentions that for "some . . . the vortex and shifting that disentangled the chaos and established the cosmic order came by chance" (Aristotle 1934, 196a24). A few lines later he adds, "This is surely most amazing – for these people actually to say that" since plants and animals "are all caused by nature or mind" (Aristotle 1934, 196b32). Although Aristotle does not mention Democritus by name, commentators such as Simplicius interpret "some" as referring to Democritus.[7]

The Greek word for vortex is *dine*: a rotating heaven, whirlpool, or eddy. Simplicius explains the vortex as separated from the universe: "'[a] vortex of all sorts of forms was separated from the universe.'" This vortex "seems to produce the world by chance and luck" (Simplicius 1992, 327). In a sense, Simplicius merges the material and form-giving approaches. The vortex or swirling movement is invisible and is separated from our world, but the vortex produces the material world "by chance and luck."[8]

Diogenes Laertius also mentions the vortex: "[atoms] are borne along in the whole universe in a vortex, and thereby generate all composite things." It is interesting that a few lines later he adds, "In nature there is nothing but atoms and void space" (Diogenes Laertius 1972, 34). It seems that the vortex is a birthplace for atoms in which some kind of transference from form or pure potentiality to matter or actuality takes place. Nature is matter or actuality, while the vortex is separated from nature, and some kind of transformation between the divine or intelligible world and nature.

In Democritus we, thus, find an account of nature that lacks organization beyond atoms and space. We do not find any necessity in bodies, events, or places. All the meaning attributed to reality is merely an interpretation. We also note that thinkers such as Aristotle were highly critical of this account, and Nietzsche, as we see in the following, focuses on the ways Democritus's thinking was not merely criticized, but purposefully destroyed.

Burning atomism

That meaning is interpretation, and that beyond interpretation only chaos exists, is certainly important for Nietzsche. He provides an additional interesting twist to the history of Democritus. He accepts the account of atomism that includes the vortex. Even with a vortex that implies a source outside of nature, atoms can still be constantly moving without an aim, or without a plan. Nietzsche does seem to think that some commentators were confused, however; he suggests that Anaxagoras and Democritus are "blurred together" (Nietzsche 2005, 21).[9] Indeed, Anaxagoras's (as well as Empedocles's) theory does include a vortex.

Instead of focusing on the sources, Nietzsche focuses on the fact that Democritus's theory did not survive. It is, indeed, striking that according to Diogenes Laertius, the books of Democritus were widely distributed during Plato's time, he lived to 109 years old, and traveled all over the ancient world (including Egypt, Persia, the Red Sea, India and Ethiopia). If these facts about Democritus are true, one would expect that he was well known by Plato and his student Aristotle. Nietzsche was intrigued by the fact that Plato never discusses Democritus, as well as by the rumor that Plato wanted to burn all Democritus's books (Laertius 1972, 449). Plato's theory of the forms and Aristotle's teleological system provided order not merely to human existence, but to all that is. In their theories, everything in nature acts according to certain principles that determine its place in the universe and how it relates to other beings. In Democritus's theory the only principle is chaos. Bodies are random entanglement and a telos does not exist. Considering this opposition and the power that both Plato and Aristotle enjoyed, is it possible that Democritus and his theory became the victims of a conspiracy that "assassinated" anti-teleological systems?

Although Nietzsche's accusations against Plato's assumed censure of atomism might sound like a paranoid reaction, it is remarkable that Democritus's theory has been almost completely neglected in the Greek world. Friedrich Lange's *The History of Materialism* inspired Nietzsche's accusation of a conspiracy against atomism. Both Nietzsche and Lange argue, in the words of Paul Swift, that "the dominant history of Western Platonism has been written according to an implicit value structure that sanctions and favors the very tendencies towards supernaturalism and teleology which Democritus rejects" (Swift 2005, 21). Lange and Nietzsche certainly do portray Plato as a tyrant philosopher. Corrupted by Socrates, who forced him to burn his own tragedies, Plato himself wants to burn those books that reject his own philosophical beliefs. Whether the rumors about book burnings are true or not is, for Nietzsche, beside the point. More interesting (and plausible) is that Plato "burned" the atomistic tradition by ignoring it.

Yet, how was Plato put on the map while Democritus was overlooked? According to Nietzsche, "Bad things have happened to the writings of Democritus" (Nietzsche 2005, 30). In particular, "Christian scholars and monastic transcribers forced their hands from Democritus, to remove him as if he were possessed, a plan which Plato had kindled, to throw the collected writings of Democritus into the fire" (Nietzsche 2005, 30). The devil that needed to be burned was, according to Nietzsche, the anti-teleological view of nature, the view he advocated for himself. It is the view against a world that is organized along borders and boundaries of what belongs and what does not belong, a world of values and categories. None of that could exist in the atomism of Democritus, and so we find in that thinking an absolute homelessness, a void, a world without proper or improper places.

Nietzsche's Democritus

This reading of the history of Democritus shows that although the Greeks inspire Nietzsche, he is quite often cynical in his assessment. Nietzsche's relationship to the Greeks is complicated, to say the least. The figure of Socrates, famously, plays a double role in his writings, in which Nietzsche often ridicules the philosopher who is in many ways close (perhaps too close) to him. Socrates is, after all, a wanderer, literally since he is not tied to a school and likes to wander in the streets of Athens. He is also figuratively a wanderer: he is a homeless thinker, whose only knowledge is that he does not know. Yet, Socrates is also a thinker tied to places: he does not want to leave Athens in order to save his own life (the ultimate denial of life); his dialogues always occur at significant places, such as in front of the courthouse or his prison cell; he might also be rooted in a theory of forms, which seems to suggest in the *Phaedo* that we should not wander away from the care of our soul; and finally, he views the body, which makes it possible to wander, with suspicion (Plato 1998, 118).[10]

Thus, for Nietzsche, who wants us to return to our bodies, Socrates is to be read with suspicion and he is often the target of ridicule. The pre-Socratic thinkers are not exempt from his ridicule either. Thales, for example, "started with an absurd notion, with the proposition that *water* is the primal origin and womb of all things" (Nietzsche 1962, 38). Despite this absurdity, Nietzsche does show appreciation for the creative imagination behind the theory.

Within Nietzsche's cynical assessment of the Greeks, Democritus is somewhat of an exception. Many have emphasized the influence of Democritus on Nietzsche. For example, in his biography of Nietzsche, Safranski spends several pages explaining the significance of Democritus for the development of Nietzsche's ideas on nature. He defines Nietzsche's Democritus as follows: "[a]lthough it is true that the way atoms fall, collide, and become linked happens with causality, these are only effects and not causes, occurring as a 'blind' necessity devoid of teleology and 'meaning'" (Safranski 2002, 150–1). Even while we find certain patterns, there is no meaning or driving force behind these patterns and, thus, "nothing exists besides atoms and empty space" (Safranski 2002, 151). Safranski therefore takes the materialistic Democritus as an inspiration for Nietzsche. Indeed, Nietzsche does often describe nature in a similar fashion. In *The Gay Science* he writes:

> Let us now be on our guard against believing that the universe is a machine; it is assuredly not constructed with a view to one end; we invest it with far too high an honor with the word "machine" [. . .] The general character of the world, on the other hand, is to all eternity chaos; not by the absence of necessity, but in the sense of the absence of order, structure, form, beauty, wisdom, and whatever else our aesthetic humanities are called.
>
> (Nietzsche 2005, 109)

This is Nietzsche's atomism in which he emphasizes the lack of order, and argues that all orders we do find are merely opinions or "aesthetic humanities." What he finds in Democritus is a philosophy that is not simply the negation of order, but a thinking before any order. Democritus (and Nietzsche) does not deny necessity, but denies that necessity is driven by an order or toward a goal beyond these effects. With this theory we could say, for example, that it is necessary that the human species came into existence considering all the circumstances. However, our existence is not part of a plan; it is rather the mere result of the chaos of nature, i.e., the random collision of atoms. The fact that we as individuals exist is the result of a random event, or rather, of multiple random or coincidental events. Likewise, the fact that the human species came into existence is not the result of any necessity. If circumstances had been slightly different, the chimpanzee might have developed its strength rather than its intelligence.

We do constantly order and give value to nature, but this is a value created by man. For Democritus only atoms and the void exist. We have seen that, similarly for Nietzsche, "[w]hatever has *value* in our world now does not have value in itself" (Nietzsche 1974, 301). Both positions contrast the Platonic tradition in which all unknown aspects of the cosmos are attributed to a lack of knowledge on our side. If we see chance and random chaos it means we have not discovered the structure yet. The history of Western thinking can be characterized by the search for such truths, which most of the pre-Socratic thinkers were already seeking. Democritus argues exactly the opposite by stating that everything we discover beyond atoms and the void is merely human opinion.

Following Nietzsche (and Lange), we can suggest that atomism has been deified in the history of ancient philosophy and its reception by Christian thinkers. It is incredibly difficult today to de-deify nature, i.e., to conceive of nature without a telos. Even in our secularized understanding of nature we still hold on to the model of a rational system that moves toward a goal (in which we, for example, regard our own species as the ultimate goal of evolution). Thus Nietzsche asks us, "When shall we have nature entirely de-deified? When shall we be permitted to naturalize ourselves by means of the pure, newly discovered, newly redeemed nature?" (Nietzsche 2005, 109). Interestingly, Nietzsche ties the word "de-deification" to the (Christian) concept of redemption. The discovery of nature is the discovery of a beyond, i.e., to think of nature beyond the terms of life and death and to stop anthropomorphizing the world as a living thing. Instead, we could say, atoms and empty space are all that exists.

Fires, both literally and metaphorically, have destroyed important ideas and important ways of thinking. Some required thousands of years to be rediscovered; others are perhaps today unthinkable, and thus lost forever. Nietzsche himself was a thinker who attempted to recover those unthinkable thoughts and was often disappointed by his own efforts that ended in dull words (Nietzsche 1998, 296). Ironically, those dull thoughts were almost burned as well, albeit for different reasons. In the third and fourth chapters we will encounter more recently lost and destroyed ideas and knowledge in the form of aboriginal knowledge. Although these form different losses, we find in both a destruction of knowledge, and a loss of ways of thinking that are replaced with a way of thinking that assumes it either knows or will know everything.

Creating home

The main message we can take away from Nietzsche's interest in Democritus is that nature is represented as non-ordered. If everything, including ourselves, is not ordered, or chaotic, how do we find ourselves in this lack of order? Are we simply homeless, without a proper place? Being entirely without a home is not easy to accept, if it can be accepted at all. Even Nietzsche seems to struggle with such an idea. He wants to pull us away from the herd, from thinking that attempts to solidify things, find truth, and create a home in establishing boundaries, laws, categories and so forth. For Nietzsche such a home is false, and should be overcome.

Sometimes Nietzsche seems to suggest that we are separated from everything, and that we do not even have a home in nature. For example, in *Beyond Good and Evil* he writes (mockingly) about a return to our unity with nature:

> According to nature you want to live? Oh you noble Stoics, what deceptive words these are! Imagine a being like nature, wasteful beyond measure, indifferent beyond measure, without purposes and considerations, without mercy and justice, fertile and desolate and uncertain at the same time; imagine indifference itself as a power – how could you live according to this indifference?
>
> (Nietzsche 1998, 9)

Nietzsche ridicules the (Stoic) idea of a predetermined unity in the organization of the cosmos and our behavior. The comment also displays his understanding of nature as a chaotic and indifferent being that we never should or could take as our example. However, Nietzsche does not simply separate us from nature. He adds, "Supposing your imperative 'live according to nature' meant at bottom as much as 'live according to life' – how could you *not* do that? Why make a principle of what you yourselves are and must be?" (Nietzsche 1998, 9). Thus, while Nietzsche initially suggests that we are separate from nature, he then draws us into the realm of chaos, wastefulness, and purposelessness. We are nature, driven by the same force that drives all of nature: the will to power. Everything we do is in this sense natural since we are driven by this natural principle. Yet, the passage indicates a tension with our own nature: we should not want to become nature, and yet we are nature. This means that we often act against nature. This is the anti-natural attitude, which Nietzsche describes as asceticism. Asceticism is an attempt to accept our suffering, the result of an original sin. Since this sin itself is our nature, we hate our own nature and everything that hints at it. And so we try to deny that we are nature and we try to find a position of superiority in the destruction of everything that is natural. It would be a mistake to understand asceticism as a position that Nietzsche wants to overcome in order to become natural. As Nehamas has argued, asceticism itself is a natural attitude, even while it acts against nature. It is natural to not want to be natural. It is part of the human condition to reject its own nature. Every attempt to become who we are naturally involves this rejection of our own nature (Nehamas 1985, 106–37). This is part of Nietzsche's will to power, a will to overcome our own natural weakness. This will to power can, ironically, involve life-denying tendencies, like those we find in asceticism.

In the *Genealogy of Morals*, Nietzsche famously declares that the roots of our thinking regarding ethics indicate a slave morality in which we find virtue in weakness, oppression, and suffering. Strength, power, and enjoyment of life, on the other hand, are qualities always observed with suspicion.[11] For Nietzsche, our herd or slave morality is derived from an anti-natural idea in which we move against ourselves. This is a movement that is both positive and negative: positive in the sense that it can initiate the process to overcome ourselves, negative in the sense that it can lead to a denial of life. This negative asceticism is tied to original sin, a basic denial of life. To deny oneself life is to deny nature. Since such a denial involves suffering and recognizing oneself as insignificant, one is tempted to fight this suffering and insignificance. One way of doing that is to master nature itself. The mastery (and destruction) of nature can then be seen as an expression of the will to power, an attempt perhaps to be at home in the world.

Applied to our creation of order, and with that a place or home, we can understand that creation as an expression of our will to power, a natural force. It is our particular nature to create and assign values. It is what creates a place, a sense of home for us, because an ordered world is a place that is ours. It is again a false sense of home, which is a negative homelessness, or a home based on ignorance. Nietzsche pushes us away from this home into an existential homelessness, one that creates the preconditions for becoming who we are. Yet, this move at first results in a crisis – what are we left with when, as Nietzsche suggests, we do not create values any longer and we smash the old ones to pieces? The lack of any value is perhaps the hardest thing to accomplish, as we always replace the old values with new ones. Without a value system, we return to the image encountered in the introduction of this chapter: the madman looking for any sense of direction, with a lantern in the bright light, indicating the impossibility of the search. However, the joke of the madman (as well as the joke of Diogenes) is on us: Can we live in sanity without direction?

Nietzsche does not simply leave us without any values. The *Übermensch* is a new value, one that perhaps is more than a perspective, but rather a multiplicity of perspectives. Instead of narrowing perspectives in the name of (a singular) truth, which has been the trend in the history of philosophy, we move here toward multiplicity. For Nietzsche truth in an absolute sense does not exist; yet without any "truth," i.e., the appearance of a perspective as truth, we would probably go mad. As Nietzsche writes in the preface to *Beyond Good and Evil*, a perspective is the "basic condition of all life" (Nietzsche 1968, 193). This seems to suggest that we cannot give up perspectives, but rather than cling to one perspective as the Truth, we should seek as many truths as possible. This can be explained, then, in terms of the "reevaluation of all values" as well as his idea of the *Übermensch* – the overcoming of the human – a move beyond our current values and toward a self-creating of values. For Nietzsche, a multiplicity of perspectives and the re-evaluation of all values means that we stop thinking in terms of dichotomies that state that something is either true or false, right or wrong, good or evil, straight or crooked, etc.

Seeing ourselves as separate from or as a part of nature are perspectives or values that we create. Following the idea that we need a multiplicity of values or perspectives and to move away from dualistic thinking, we can perhaps argue that we need to keep both ideas alive: that we are and that we are not nature. Nature, and the dichotomy between nature and the human being are then to be recognized as human creations. How we think as well as feel about nature are always determined by the values *we* attribute to it. This means that for us the meaning nature does not have an origin outside of the human realm. Nietzsche's perspective, as such, problematizes a return to nature in which we live closer to nature. By living "in harmony with nature" (eating locally according to the seasons, for example), we still use values that we created. A so-called return to nature is in fact a turn toward some other perspective on nature, toward some other value that we have ascribed to it.

We arrive at a position that can be characterized as fundamentally homeless: since all values are human constructions we have, in the end, nothing on which to hold. For someone like Schopenhauer – Nietzsche's great inspiration – this creates the existential situation of nihilism as suffering, since we constantly look for meaning in a world that is without meaning. Nietzsche famously emphasizes the positive side of nihilism: since there are no absolute values, we can create our own. Such a possibility can only arise by first completely ridding ourselves of all the values that our culture, religion, and society have indoctrinated us with, i.e., we need to become homeless in order to build a new home. Instead of homelessness, we find rather a transitional state in which we move beyond the feeling of a lack of home. In fact, we start to find home in the transition itself, in nomadism. Deleuze, discussed in Chapter 3, uses the term "nomad thought" to describe Nietzsche's philosophy. Nomadic thinking is thinking in a transitional state, always challenging the borders, boundaries, concepts, categories, and ideas that we encounter, including the idea of nomadism itself.

Humanimal transformations

In order to think through this idea of nomadism, to understand ourselves as fluid, transforming or nomadic beings, I will use the science fiction classic *The Island of Dr. Moreau* by H.G. Wells, as well as one of the films based upon the book, *The Island of Lost Souls*.[12] The novel and film feature Dr. Moreau, a talented but somewhat crazy scientist. He works far away from human civilization on an unmapped and unnamed island, indicating the homelessness of his creations, the strange hybrid of man and animal. Moreau has grafted humans from animal forms, named "the beast folk" by Wells, and in the later film version referred to as "the humanimal."[13] Homelessness (as well as homesickness) is also found in the main character, Edward Parker, a young man shipwrecked and thrown off the boat that initially rescued him.[14] After the captain abandons him on a strange island he finds himself in the world of Dr. Moreau and his assistant, who fled to the island in order to avoid imprisonment. Moreau himself is a homeless scientist whose work is brilliant, but too controversial to perform in the academy. His creations are "lost" homeless beings, hovering between human and animal. This humanimal certainly does not constitute the transitional nomadic existence that Nietzsche envisions, but the film, rooted in Darwin's work, does provide an existential homelessness as a basis for some interesting Nietzschean reflections.

The novel and films contain many narratives, those of colonialism, of ethics, of human–animal relationships, to name a few. The narrative I focus on here is that of speciation, of how we have instituted boundaries and how such boundaries create norms about what should and what should not be. The very idea of the humanimal, the hybrid between animal and human, is horrific, an idea we seek to avoid, and thus makes good material for a horror movie. The idea of the humanimal questions what a species is, a question we mostly avoid asking.

Darwin (to whom both Wells and Nietzsche are indebted, albeit in different ways) mostly avoids the question regarding species, as well.[15] *On the Origin of Species* focuses predominantly on explaining origins, but never attempts to explain what a species is in the first place. In other words, what is the origin of the notion or concept of species? In *The Descent of Man*, Darwin is somewhat less certain about what a species is. He at least once engages in a discussion about the differences between races and species, and discusses at length hybrid species. However, in the end he still seems comfortable maintaining a concept of species that revolves entirely around the possibility to interbreed. If two beings can successfully interbreed – i.e., produce fertile offspring – they belong to the same species. Darwin's theory seems to run into a contradiction here. If all species descended from common ancestors, the criterion of interbreeding seems problematic. *The Descent of Man* makes explicit what was already implied in the *Origin of Species*: We descended from the chimp, and other animals. In the end, all life is one big family. In other words, our ancestors at some point were not only able, but actually did interbreed with a chimp.[16]

Darwin was certainly under political pressure in dealing with the challenging notion that all life, and in particular human beings, evolved out of other life forms, instead of as the result of intelligent design. He nevertheless states the inevitable conclusion of his theory. Once he takes that step he seems to come close to the idea that species do not exist. If species evolve do we have a clear ground for distinguishing between a chimp and a human being? The idea of a species, as others have argued, is then perhaps a social construct.[17]

If the idea of a species is, indeed, a social construct, what does this construct tell us about who we are, about what we want to be and what we do not want to be? Darwin (and the rest of us) holds on to the notion of species. Why can we not accept a fluidity of beings, but need boundaries and identity? The answer I would like to advance is that the idea of species creates values, and that the underlying motive for instituting these boundaries is an attempt to institute and maintain (ethical) ideas about what should and what should not be through a value system. In order to develop this point, I will discuss, first of all, what Darwin himself writes about ethics.

Darwin, in *The Descent of Man*, argues that the emergence of ethics is an important evolutionary step. In order for some species (including *Homo sapiens*) to survive, cooperation and selfless services to the community are necessary. While Darwin starts his analysis of sympathy from what he calls the lower animals and eventually reaches the human being, he applies the concept of morality only to human beings.[18] Following J.S. Mill, he writes, "A moral being is one who is capable of comparing his past and future actions or motives, and of approving or disapproving of them" (Darwin 1981, 111).[19] Since, for Darwin, animals lack such a reflective ability, the moral aspect of our character distinguishes us from other animals.

Interestingly, it is this separation between the moral human being and other animals that produces an ethics: the human judges who possesses morality and who does not. In making that judgment we re-inscribe a morality that institutes a limit. Maintaining the boundaries between human and other species creates a home for us. It tells us where we belong. It shelters us as it provides security about our identity and tells us what should and what should not be.

This shelter is under attack in Wells's *The Island of Dr. Moreau*. The novel and the film based upon the novel introduce hybrid creatures, humanimals or "beast people," who challenge the boundaries of human and animal. The suggestion that the boundary between human and beast is fluid challenges one of our homes, namely the very idea that we are separate from animals. We can feel at home in the idea that we are better, smarter, and more sophisticated than any animal. Every other aspect in the world, including the world itself, is in flux, but the idea that we belong to this species, the only moral species, creates stability; stability creates a home. The film and the novel create a feeling of homelessness, or homesickness, by creating a hybrid between human and animal. The transformation of the other into the familiar challenges the familiar.

The novel and *The Island of Lost Souls* also confirm the familiar through racist and colonial comments. The narrative reminds us of the nasty history of colonization and the establishment of the New World, with some moved here involuntarily, and others displaced or killed in the process of invading. The novel and film reflect these histories by calling the hybrid beings "natives" or "strange natives." Their darkness is often mentioned. Darwin's narrative is partly a narrative about strangers, "savages" who have not acquired the moral sense, and only have feelings for members of the same tribe, not for the species. Darwin argues these strangers lack habit, instruction, and religion (Darwin 1981, 119). Dr. Moreau claims to "humanize" the animal, the savage. In the novel and in the film he calls them "strange natives." He teaches them exactly what Darwin believes the savage is missing: habit, instruction, and religion. The Law is ceremoniously repeated after the sayer of the law. It instructs them to not walk on all fours, to not eat meat, and to not shed blood. When they break The Law, they will be punished in the house of pain. Interestingly, but not surprisingly, it is Dr. Moreau himself who breaks The Law, telling a common colonial story – of trying to educate the cruel savage, while being oneself a cruel savage.

Even while he thinks he is, Dr. Moreau is then not "humanizing" the animal or savage. He, first of all, invades the natives' home by treating them as "strange natives" and instead of creating humans he creates true strangers. They have become, in their own words, "things" that are neither human nor animal. By radically altering their bodies and behavior they have become estranged from themselves, even feeling out of place in their bodies. This is homelessness in a very negative sense. Even the body does not provide a place for oneself. In that regard, the humanimal can also be understood as (an unintentional?) criticism of Western philosophy since Plato views the body mostly as an impediment or prison. For Moreau, both the body and the mind are moldable entities. The humanimals recognize the essential nature of their bodies. In their new bodies they have become "things." They are in that regard Nietzschean, since it is Nietzsche who brings back the body in the philosophical discourse, bringing us back to our very nature.

What do the above-mentioned analogies between natives and animals tell us? We have a few obvious points: natives are treated as animals; animals are treated with cruelty. The natives are re-educated, but somehow their underlying animal nature persists. The experiments always fail in the end, as the humanimals return to their original form. The biggest victory that Moreau can claim is that Lota, the panther woman, can fall in love with a human being, Parker. She eventually cries about the fact that she is not fully human. The development of these emotions, love and sadness, both related to a human being, draw her closely into the human realm.

Darwin's discourse, and in less subtle terms the *Island of Dr. Moreau*, powerfully reinforce some of the existing prejudices against natives, whose homes have been invaded, and who have become a marginalized subtext within the grand narrative of the West. It tells us again that it is fine to conquer and colonize, to normalize and to turn the other into the same.

The evidence that Darwin relies on for this argument is highly problematic, but interesting for the purposes of this chapter:

> Most savages are utterly indifferent to the sufferings of strangers, or even delight in witnessing them. It is well known that the women and children of the North-American Indians aided in torturing their enemies. Some savages take a horrid pleasure in cruelty to animals, and humanity is an unknown virtue.
>
> (Darwin 1981, 117–18)

While I do not seek to excuse his comment – though he, among other things, strongly opposed slavery – he certainly lived and worked in a time when negative conceptions of "savages," a problematic word to begin with, were prevalent. Darwin's analysis of the savage classifies the savage as being more animal and less human, closer to its instincts, removed from its more reflective activities, which it can cultivate but has not been able to take up. It is then a stranger who is closer to the animal, the being s/he, supposedly, treats with cruelty.

In fact, as we know today, the white Westerners were the savages treating colonized others as animals, i.e., with cruelty, indifferent to their suffering, even delighting in seeing them suffer.[20] Likewise, as Westerners we treat animals and the land, especially when it is not our own land, with cruelty. Darwin's claims regarding ethics then establish an interesting and familiar story about our values: Western, white, male, *Homo sapiens* are seen as the superior race. This idea in itself provides a home, since it places all human beings in a hierarchy, clearly marking who belongs where. Even while Darwin explicitly draws the conclusion that we descended from the ape and that we are tied to other human races, he can comfort his audience with the idea that we are not savage, that we have evolved to some extent of distinction.

The film and novel can then, as can Darwin's scientific work, be read as a very familiar story of colonization, in which we both move and institute boundaries. Our home can be at any place, while others, animals and natives alike, are excluded. Both *The Island of Lost Souls* and *The Descent of Man* tell us stories. We might accept Darwin's story as the more compelling one since he is a scientist, but let us not forget that Darwin, as any scientist, fabricates stories. When we talk about species, we create a story about inclusion and exclusion: who is in, who is not? Whether we are talking about different plants or different races of human beings, how we group them together, or separate them, is, ultimately, a choice, and often a political one. Science does not escape the political.[21]

The problem of this politics of exclusion is not limited to science; we dwell in categories and distinctions created by a number of narratives. Derrida speaks about the politics of exclusion in *Of Hospitality* when he writes that the foreigner (*xenos*) does not exist before or outside the pact (*xenia*). Only by the institutions of political pacts or social contracts do we start to exclude. By naming those who belong we also, implicitly or explicitly, name those who do not belong. The term "species" institutes similar boundaries, as it is a pact between humans, and excludes the non-human. The species thus provides a shelter for us. *The Island of Dr. Moreau* questions this home. The very idea that animals could become humans, that humans can become animals, or that the animal is somewhere in us, thus that boundaries stop making sense, is a terrifying thing to think. It puts us in the situation of existential homelessness that we also find in Nietzsche's re-evaluation of all values. Dr. Moreau is Nietzschean in so far (and only in this regard) that he crosses a boundary that should not be crossed. By mixing the human and the animal, by going through the steps of evolution in the individual, who we are, our identity as a species, is questioned. We feel lost. This is the – perhaps unintended – twist of the novel: it is, in fact, our and not the animals' souls that are lost.

Nietzsche makes us feel comfortable with the idea of being lost. He is a wanderer in many ways. Nietzsche, both the person and the philosopher (for they are ultimately the same), is not tied to a particular place. He wanders in his language and thought, and finds promise in wandering, in burning our bridges and destroying the land behind us (Nietzsche 2005, 180). Being lost, even at home, or perhaps *especially* at home, seems a necessary element to Nietzsche's philosophy. When we seriously question all our values, boundaries, distinctions, language, thinking, consciousness and so forth, then we cannot remain at home in the world. If all ideas of belonging are put into question, where do we still belong; how do we retain or retrieve a sense of community or self?

For Darwin, ethics determines who we are. For Nietzsche, the opposite is true: ethics determines who we are not. Ethics is a reflection of the herd mentality, the need for security, for order, to be at home, and so forth. Nietzsche's rethinking of values can be found in the different movements of Zarathustra, who repeatedly leaves and returns home to his cave. Perhaps he follows Plato's idea to not only leave the cave, but to return to it as well. In comparison to Plato's cave, Zarathustra's cave is quiet. It is his home and yet he always has to leave again, "to go down and under," i.e., leave the mountain and his solitude. One cannot overcome oneself by simply ascending and separating oneself from humanity. Even the very last action undertaken by Zarathustra is to leave his cave: "Thus spoke Zarathustra, and he left his cave, glowing and strong as a morning sun that comes out of dark mountains" (Nietzsche 1976, 439). He is not, as Plato instructs us, seeking the sun, the good. Zarathustra himself becomes the sun who comes out of the cave, his home. While he is attached to his cave, it is not the only place he calls home. His world is everywhere and nowhere. He is constantly expanding his horizons and is lost everywhere, including in his cave. He has to go down and under.

The issue of species for Nietzsche, the wandering thinker, is an important one, as it is a home we also should leave behind. The idea of the *Übermensch* is the next step in evolution, or a revolution in the individual. The task of Zarathustra, as stated in the "prologue," is to teach the *Übermensch*. With that attempt, Nietzsche is questioning the rigidity of species. As difficult as it might be, the very possibility to overcome ourselves, to move beyond the human, emphasizes the fluidity of who we are.

When we speak about species we seem to rely on some kind of image of an original form, platonic or otherwise. We tend to forget that language created this form, which, as we saw earlier, always equates what is unequal.[22] The term species thus becomes its own reality and creates its own values.[23]

For this reason, one of the biggest struggles for Nietzsche is language, the words and sentences that make his great thoughts so dull (Nietzsche 1998, 296). Zarathustra is the prophet who announces the death of God, and with that he announces that it is time to overcome ourselves through teaching and learning, as well as forgetting and leaving behind. The biggest obstacle is language and the home it institutes, for us and for our values.

Dr. Moreau also teaches, but it is exactly the kind of teaching that Nietzsche so despises. It is a dogmatic indoctrination of The Law, telling the humanimals to not walk on all fours, to not eat meat, and to not shed blood. They are also told to worship their creator, Dr. Moreau.[24] For Moreau, the animal (or the native) is a lower being that can be improved, both physically and morally. In wiping out hundreds of thousands of years of evolution he sees himself as playing God, which in fact seems to be his main motive: "Do you know what it means to feel like God?" (*The Island of Lost Souls* 1932). Moreau embodies the estranged scientist who cannot reflect on the true meaning of his work. In fact, he has created beings, things, that like himself lack the ability to reflect. The humanimal is the ultimate embodiment of becoming who you are not. Dr. Moreau, the mad scientist, creates sickness, inventing a being that thinks without originality. Although he claims to "study the plasticity of living forms" (Wells 2008, 131), the animal bodies are painfully grafted into a pre-determined form, following the mantra of intelligent design: essence precedes existence. The humanimals are thinking machines that merely follow laws and bodily shapes. They are without autonomy, without any sense of self, until they escape from The Law and kill the creator of The Law and their bodies.

While Nietzsche's death of God is an uncertain search for values, in which we have nothing to hold on to, the death of Moreau is a wild celebration of regained freedom by the humanimals, who are now again animals and abandon their "humanity." Within the genre of the horror film this event has to be a moment of catharsis, involving fire and the escape of the few surviving human beings. "Don't look back" are the last words spoken in the film.[25]

In other words, forget about our past, forget about these beings that we are so closely connected to, biologically and otherwise. We suppress the animal in us: the animal that lusts and desires, the animal that is embodied. Thus we say, "don't look back"; it is not I. I am not an animal; these creatures are not I.

For Nietzsche, not looking back is the hardest thing to do. It is *the* problem in overcoming ourselves. Homelessness is difficult, and so we long to return to our home, forgetting again that the human being is a mistake that we have to leave behind. Thus we are still tied to our values, our past, our reason, our thinking, language, and consciousness. How can we leave all that behind?

This is, certainly, Nietzsche's struggle: how to leave everything behind, move out of the shadow, and laugh about the search for God. As evident in Zarathustra, it is not as simple as climbing or descending a mountain and leaving it all. Plato (and Socrates) shows us that it is necessary to return to the cave full of people who are unknowingly prisoners to their false beliefs.[26] Likewise, Nietzsche argues that we cannot remain hermits in an empty cave. Again we find the image of the wandering, homeless, or nomadic philosopher.[27]

Darwin understood ethics as a necessary condition for making an advanced social species such as the human race successful. While he finds evidence of certain social behaviors in other species, only in human beings are such behaviors developed into morality, which involves a reflection on our actions and motives. Through his genealogical method, Nietzsche identifies the grounds of our ethical system not in a necessary component for survival as a species (as Mill and Darwin argue), but as a weakness, a slave morality, in which we sympathize with the position of the conquered and declare any power as evil. With that, we ourselves have become slaves to a morality that we blindly accept.

God has disappeared from this ethics, and yet his shadow looms larger than ever. Nietzsche writes:

> [a]fter Buddha was dead, his shadow was still displayed in a cave for centuries – a colossal, horrible shadow. God is dead. But as is the way of human beings, there may still be caves for millennia in which his shadow is displayed. And we – we must still defeat his shadow!
>
> (Nietzsche 1974, 108)

In yet another re-reading of Plato's cave we are still dealing with the shadows of a past we cannot forget. In order to leave the cave, one must first defeat the shadow, i.e., the past. To become who you are means to deal with the past, the shadows that haunt us, and thus we must look back and return to the cave.

In a secular world, we follow a Christian morality that lacks both a ground and a telos. Thus Nietzsche writes at the beginning pages of *Thus Spoke Zarathustra*,

> Once the sin against God was the greatest sin; but God died, and these sinners died with him. To sin against the earth is now the most dreadful thing and to esteem the entrails of the unknowable higher than the meaning of the earth.

And thus, Zarathustra exclaims, "remain faithful to the earth" (Nietzsche 1995, 13).

The call of Nietzsche's Zarathustra to remain true to the earth can and has been interpreted in many ways. I have previously discussed Nietzsche's complex relationship to nature. Nature is something that we cannot live according to (since it is without measure, wasteful, and indifferent) *and* that we have to live according to (since we are nature). To remain true to the earth can be interpreted along the lines of being faithful to nature as a force that is wasteful and indifferent, and without measure. This also implies that we are being true to ourselves in terms of life affirmation: we recognize that we are life. Since Nietzsche brings up the idea of being true to the earth within the context of sinning, he seems to urge us to think beyond Christianity and its notion of sinning, and instead stop sinning against the earth, or nature. This is a move toward an ethics of the earth, which is also an ethics of our animal being, our body, our desires and lusts, all that we have suppressed. It is an ethics of the humanimal that resides somewhere in us. In other words, we do not need a crazy scientist to create the humanimal. It is already in us. We want to keep it away, out of sight, hidden, but it is there and will continue to emerge. To turn to an ethics of the earth is, however, not merely a turn to the animal in us, as if we are returning to some prehistoric state of being. In doing so, we create something new. After all, we seek to overcome ourselves, and a return to some animal state that is still lingering in us would not constitute an overcoming, but rather a regression.

To remain faithful to the earth is, thus, an earth ethics in which we are true to ourselves, or our future selves. To be true to the earth means to be true to our past and our future, not a future in the form of some afterlife, but a future existence. In terms of the past, we, first of all, attempt to find the stranger, the other, within ourselves. In doing so, we recognize our evolution, our own history, the past that first has to be recognized and dealt with. Such recognition, then, evolves into a more fluid understanding of ourselves as individuals and as a species. It is a new nomadism of ourselves, but also of the world in which we live.

While an ethics of the earth recognizes the earth itself as our home, it is not a solidifying thinking that grounds and leaves no room for homelessness. Hybridization and nomadism, not only of us, but also of all beings are part of being true to the earth. We and other species become homeless and hybrid, i.e., we attempt to rethink and let go of the categories and boundaries that constitute who we are and what is "other"; what belongs and does not; what is native and non-native. Thus we become open to the other, or otherness, that we ourselves already are, to the other or otherness we will become, and to the otherness that escapes our labeling.[28] We thus find the other, the humanimal, in ourselves, and we find ourselves in the world that we inhabit. Derrida, in this regard, speaks of an absolute hospitality, in which we open our place, our home, to the other, without any conditions (Derrida 2000). I suggest that we can only move toward such hospitality if we first embrace the *xenos*, the other in ourselves. This is a proposal for a nomadic thinking in which we are first and foremost transient, changing, always questioning whatever truth we have found. For, let us not forget, to speak in the words of Zarathustra, "What is great in man is that he is a bridge and not an end: what can be loved in man is that he is an *overture* and a *going under*" (Nietzsche 1995, 15).

Back to nature

For Nietzsche the natural world does not have any values. Consequently, we consider ourselves, as opposed to nature, a-natural. We are not naturally connected to nature because we think, a value-giving activity. Moreover, nature itself is to be seen as chaotic and lacking harmony. Nature, or "what is natural," is a human value. In fact, every understanding, every rationalization of nature is necessarily missing the essence of nature. What's more, to attribute an essence to nature is an interpretation or perspective.[29]

Are we then simply left with the conclusion that nature is chaos (whatever that exactly means), and that all the ideas we have about nature are mere perspectives? It seems contentious to claim that nature is pure chaos, especially considering that the natural sciences continue to expose all kinds of patterns in nature – albeit through ever-changing paradigms or perspectives. Nietzsche does not question the fact that we are able to find certain patterns in nature. For example, we do not have to question whether all objects move toward the earth. However, the law of nature with which we explain such phenomena, in this case gravity, is an anthropomorphic rationalization of the tendency of objects to move toward the earth. Laws of nature are not actual phenomena. We cannot experience these laws directly. We only use the theory of the law to explain the phenomena that we observe. Thus, the idea of the natural law structures our experience, while another idea or law would have structured it differently. As hard as this might be to imagine, someday (if the human race does not extinguish itself before that time) gravity, and even the very idea of natural laws all together, will be replaced by a different paradigm that will restructure our experience. For Nietzsche these are perspectives, mere interpretations of nature. As he writes in *On Truth and Lie in an Extramoral Sense*:

> After all, what is a law of nature as such for us? We are not acquainted with it in itself, but only with its effects, which means in its relation to other laws of nature – which, in turn, are known to us only as sums of relations. [. . .] All that we actually know about these laws of nature is what we ourselves bring to them – time and space, and therefore relationships of succession and number. [. . .W]e produce these representations in and from ourselves with the same necessity with which the spider spins.
>
> (Nietzsche 1976, 46)

In this passage, Nietzsche seems quite moderate in still holding onto the idea that a natural law exists outside of human perspective or rationalization. A decade later, in *The Gay Science*, Nietzsche appears much more radical:

> Whatever has *value* in our world now does not have value in itself, according to its nature – nature is always value-less, but has been *given* value at some time, as a present – and it was *we* who gave and bestowed it. Only we have created the world *that concerns man*!
>
> (Nietzsche 1974, 242)[30]

Thus, we ascribe values – such as natural laws – to a realm that is without values and without laws. Our urge to anthropomorphize the other than ourselves can be regarded as an attempt to find order in chaos, to find control in the uncontrollable.

Nietzsche harshly criticizes the significance we attribute to thinking, the instrument with which we order. Thinking is also used, in fact (and this is the problem) uses itself, to mark the boundary between the world around us and ourselves. Throughout the history of philosophy, reason is linked to language, and these features are used to distinguish us from all other animals. We have seen that Darwin uses, among other things, the criterion of ethical decisions guided by rational reflection as a benchmark to distinguish the animal from the human. Much earlier, Plato called the body a distraction or impediment to thinking, while Descartes went as far as to call us a thinking thing, separate from the body or the bodily. What exactly is so great about thinking, Nietzsche asks. Why should we want to separate ourselves from the body (representing the animal) and aspire to a life of the mind? These questions that confront us with our animal bodies as our home place us in the face of an existential homelessness in which our assumed home, reason, is questioned in the most radical way.

While in later works Nietzsche goes on to call thinking a mistake in evolution, in earlier works he focuses more on what thinking exactly does when it works with concepts. In *On Truth and Lie in an Extramoral Sense*, Nietzsche writes: "We believe that we know something about the things themselves when we speak of trees, colors, snow, and flowers; and yet we possess nothing but metaphors for things – metaphors which correspond in no way to the original entities" (Nietzsche 1976, 46). He adds:

> Every concept originates through our equating what is unequal. No leaf ever wholly equals another, and the concept "leaf" is formed through an arbitrary abstraction from these individual differences, through forgetting the distinctions; and now it gives rise to the idea that in nature there might be something besides the leaves which would be "leaf" – some kind of original form after which all leaves have been woven, marked, copied, colored, curled, and painted, but by unskilled hands, so that no copy turned out to be a correct, reliable, and faithful image of the original form.
>
> (Nietzsche 1976, 46)

When we speak, for example, about species we seem to rely on some kind of image of an original form, platonic or otherwise. We tend to forget that this form is created by language, which, according to Nietzsche, always equates what is unequal. Any classification creates a unity and in doing so it uses an element of violence, on the one hand by excluding everything else that does not fit within this classification, on the other hand by creating equality, negating the differences and forgetting distinctions.

Contrary to this urge to order (or the urge for a home), we have seen the image of nature as a mystery that we cannot structure; we can only grasp in nature what is similar to ourselves. Only what is of my own kind speaks to me (Nietzsche 1974, 166). The idea that nature does not have any value could mean that I either do not care at all, or that I could change my perspective on nature and let it speak to me in a different way. Since Nietzsche emphasizes how we should grasp our own view of the world as one perspective among many others, we must recognize the perspective of the tree hugger, the perspective of the person who thinks nature lies at our command, and possibly the perspective of the tree. Likewise, we should include the perspective of nature as a violent force, as well as nature as peaceful tranquility. Most of all, we have to recognize that these perspectives *are* perspectives; through recognizing the multiplicity of perspectives we can move on to a view that is perhaps less anthropocentric and anthropomorphic – toward a view that lies beyond our value systems and that regards nature as valueless (cf. Nietzsche 1974, 294, 301). Nature, then, is not judged in our terms but is regarded instead as an entity that constantly becomes in unpredictable and spontaneous acts.

This brings us to a picture of nature that is perhaps less anthropocentric and anthropomorphic. However, if nature is an entity that constantly becomes through unpredictable and spontaneous acts, then how can we be true to the earth? It seems to imply that we ourselves must become in unpredictable and spontaneous acts. When we, indeed, turn to nature it is not a turn to some origin, or to a lost connection. It is rather a turn to something that we have never been.

I take this to be part of Nietzsche's notion of the will to power, a will to overcome our own natural weakness. This will to power can involve life-denying tendencies, like those we find in asceticism. Yet, we want to survive and find a way to live with as little suffering as possible. The will to power can certainly be a motive for acting against nature; when we destroy nature we conquer it, we overcome this force that makes us suffer. Nevertheless, such a conquering does have negative consequences for us as a species. We cannot destroy nature without destroying ourselves. The way we have been dealing with this is through faith in our technological possibilities and a resulting sense of control over nature.

We have seen now that since, for Nietzsche, God has not created the world, the only meaning it has is a perspective (or range of perspectives) given by us. There is no purpose to the world: only we attributed a certain meaning and order to it. Nature itself is chaotic, a struggle of different wills to power. The only order that has been created is the human order. We as creators have not created the world in a physical sense (although we do alter the physical aspects of the world). What we have created is the meaning and value of the world, a world that follows laws, as if it is a machine that revolves toward a goal. In understanding the world we attribute those values to whatever we see. How we think about nature as well as how we experience nature are always determined through the values we ascribe to it.[31] Recognizing that all values are ours and that they can be otherwise is the first step toward nomadic thinking. The next step is to actually change values and to give up existing boundaries.

Conclusion: nomadic thinking

Since Nietzsche describes nature as chaos, our attempts to rationalize the way nature acts are, for him, necessarily a failure. Thus the question arises whether a language beyond good and evil can be helpful at all. For if nature acts without any ethical standards, then our actions toward nature, or rather toward natural things, cannot be judged in terms of our ethical standards. In other words, it becomes impossible to argue that my violence toward someone else, society, an animal, or a natural object is ethically despicable, or that there is any value in the world. In this final section, I want to use one of the most famous aspects of Nietzsche's thought, the *Übermensch* (a beyond ourselves), to argue that Nietzsche, in fact, does make a few demands.

Within our sober and oppressed life, we generally deny ourselves. The ascetic ideal in philosophy seems, for Nietzsche, to be a necessary poison: unhealthy to the core, but needed in order to overcome our sickness. It is an anti-natural attitude in which we deny ourselves, but this self-denial is ultimately a self-affirmation. Nietzsche expresses this in the metaphor of the butterfly that needs to release itself, but is still in the form of a caterpillar: "Has that many-colored and dangerous winged creature, the 'spirit' which this caterpillar concealed, really been unfettered at last and released into the light, thanks to a sunnier, warmer, brighter world?" (Nietzsche 1968, 552). Here, again, Nietzsche describes us in terms of nature. We slowly free our spirit as a butterfly that struggles to get out of its cocoon. Without this struggle we cannot become a free spirit: to overcome and to strengthen ourselves we need to struggle. We need to be homeless and wander in order to find ourselves, a new self still to come.

For Nietzsche this self-contradictory struggle, in which we first deny ourselves, is part of who we are: it is our nature. Ironically, this denial of life that we find in the anti-natural attitude of asceticism arises out of a tendency to become master over life itself. It does this by reducing everything to error, since "it will look for error precisely where the instinct of life most unconditionally posits truth" (Nietzsche 1968, 554).[32] The tendency to become master over life itself Nietzsche famously calls *ressentiment*, "an insatiable instinct and power-will that wants to become master not over something in life but over life itself, over its most profound, powerful, and basic conditions" (Nietzsche 1968, 553–4). The anti-natural attitude that leads us to this notion of *ressentiment* is contradictory, and Nietzsche emphasizes this once more in describing this *ressentiment* as "a discord that wants to be discordant" (Nietzsche 1968, 554).

We derived our herd and slave morality from an anti-natural idea in which we move against ourselves as well as against life. To deny oneself life is to deny nature. We find a home by creating one, denying ourselves the possibility to search and wander, to experience an existential homelessness. Since such a homelessness involves suffering and recognizing oneself as insignificant, one is tempted to fight it. One way of doing that is to master nature itself. The mastery (and destruction) of nature can then be seen as an expression of the will to power.

With that we are natural: nature is a multitude of striving forces and we are one of those forces. Our will is expressed in an attempt to control the struggle itself, for example, by introducing and extinguishing invasive species. We affirm ourselves in both acts as masters of nature. By asserting that control, we are also denying life; we decide which species can live and which ones should die. In many cases the most powerful species, i.e. the "invasive" species that are thriving, are the ones that should not live.

Contrary to this urge to order, we have seen the image of nature as something that we cannot order (cf. Nietzsche 1974, 166). The idea that nature does not have any value could mean that I either do not care at all, or that I could change my perspective on nature and let it speak to me in a different way. Nietzsche emphasizes how we should grasp our own view of the world as one perspective among many others. Most of all, we have to recognize that through recognizing the multiplicity of perspectives we can move to a view that is perhaps less anthropocentric and anthropomorphic, a view that lies beyond our value systems and that regards nature as valueless (cf. Nietzsche 1974, 294, 301). Nature is, then, not judged in our terms but is regarded instead as an entity that constantly becomes in unpredictable and spontaneous acts. As opposed to the mastery of nature as an expression of the will to power, Nietzsche thus proposes an idea of nature without an inherent order, or the possibility of different, conflicting orders.

In a passage in *Thus Spoke Zarathustra*, Nietzsche describes the tree that has grown so tall that if it wanted to speak no one could hear it. Zarathustra comments, "It is the same with humanity as with the tree. The more he seeks to rise into the height and light, the more vigorously do his roots struggle earthward, downward, into the dark and deep – into the evil" (Nietzsche 1995, 42). To grow, to overcome ourselves, also means to find ourselves in the herd, in the slave morality that tries to stay away from the earth, from "evil."

It is also through Zarathustra that Nietzsche describes the human being as a bridge between the ape and the overman (and it might be that this is the same bridge that he sometimes wants to burn, e.g., in *The Gay Science*). The overman is the meaning (*Sinn*) of the earth and thus we (who are being taught the overman by Zarathustra) should remain true to the earth (Nietzsche 1974, 97). Since Nietzsche contrasts the earth with "super-earthly hopes" he seems to emphasize the importance of enjoying life, as opposed to life-denying values. "To remain true to the earth" then perhaps most of all means to live and to recognize ourselves as natural beings, i.e., beings who are alive, who can change, who are homeless, and are thus not tied in any absolute sense to values, labels, and ideas.

"To become who we are" is, then, not a return to nature, but rather a development of a new nature in which we first of all accept that we are nature. The human species is after all just a step along the way to the overman, an animal evolving to a new way of being. Our new way of being is not some state, but a nomadic being, a way of thinking in transition. Nothing is fixed, but everything is continually supplemented, negated, denied, and affirmed. Our new home is to be nomadic, to be in transition.

Notes

1 The word "perspective" appears at many places in Nietzsche's work. The word indicates, on the one hand, the lack of an absolute truth, yet also indicates that we cannot live without some sense of "truth." This is what Nietzsche calls a perspective (Nietzsche 1998, 46).

2 Since the respective sources are inconsistent, we do encounter at least two different Democriti: the first theory is the purely materialist one, while the other includes supernatural aspects. I do not discuss such inconsistencies in the main text, since they are not taken up by Nietzsche and not entirely relevant to the main argument.

3 Hermias Philosophus is known for reading few primary sources and reading biographies instead.

4 Simplicius (about 400 years after Galenus) in "Simplici in Aristotelis de Caelo Commentaria" does attribute qualities to Democritus's atoms which are "so small that we cannot perceive them, yet they have all sorts of forms and shapes, and differences in size" (Nahm 1964, 154). According to Simplicius's account, atoms have qualities such as form and shape and size, and these qualities determine how the atoms entangle.

   Dionysius of Alexandria seems to provide a more random account of the entanglement of atoms when he writes in "On Nature" (cited by Eusebius) about an "irregular momentum," but also includes a "variety of shapes" (Nahm 1964, 158–9). Further, in his work, too, dissimilarity or variety of atomic shapes cause entanglement. Still the explanation of why things move in the first place is not due to a dissimilarity of shape, but rather an "irregular momentum."

5 For example, in "Adversus Colotem" Plutarch writes, "There is no generation from non-being nor can there be any generation from things which exist because the atoms on account of their solidity neither change nor suffer any impression" (Nahm 1964, 162). While bodies do come into being, atoms do not generate or decay. Democritus, thus, explains the growth and decay of a body merely as a combining and separating of atoms. See also Aristotle (1934, 265b24).

6 In *Adversus Mathematicos*, Sextus Empiricus places Democritus in one category with Plato: "The disciples both of Plato and Democritus held that only intelligible objects are real. Democritus thought so because there is no sensible substratum in nature, for the atoms which gave rise to things by combining have a nature devoid of all sensible quality; Plato held this view because the sensibles are always in a process of becoming, but never really are" (Nahm 1964, 162).

7 Thus it seems that either Aristotle or later commentators introduce a vortex in relation to Democritus's atomism. This vortex is entirely lacking in the earlier sources. Again, I do not analyze the discrepancies in the sources, since it is not important for Nietzsche's argument.

8 It is questionable what chance and luck exactly mean. Is it true chaos – as Nietzsche takes it – or is it rather a cause that is hidden from human intelligence, in the way Plato sometimes explains the forms? I am thinking in particular of the *Phaedo* where the forms are approached, but never known, during the life we live on earth. We can get closer to these divine forms in the afterlife. The *Phaedo* (as well as the *Meno*) suggests that we learn the forms not during this life in our bodies (Plato 1998, 99–102).

9 This passage (and a few of the following) is the translation of Nietzsche's "The Fate of Democritus" from *Frühe Schriften* as it is included in Swift (2005).

10 Certainly, these different ideas seem inconsistent in the sense that Socrates is both a wandering thinker and tied to truths. Some of these inconsistencies might be the result of Plato ridiculing Socrates.

11 A contemporary example can be found in the typical Hollywood villain who is wealthy, powerful, and enjoys life. At the moment we are introduced to this character we already know that he (it is almost always a man) is not up to any good.

12 I would like to thank Amanda Parris for bringing the film to my attention.

13 Recently the term has been used by a number of "posthuman" thinkers such as: Taylor and Signal (2011), Seshadri (2011), and Kapil (2009).

14 In the novel he is called Edward Prendick. I mostly use the film here, since it provides a few interesting additions. The basic concept of the humanimal is Wells's and I focus on Darwin's influence on Wells that led him to this creature.

15 Nietzsche's idea of the *Übermensch* is an evolution in the individual, rather than the species. Wells studied evolutionary biology with T.H. Huxley (with whom he wrote the influential work the *Science of Life*). This background certainly had an important impact on his literary writing.

16 Peter Steeves makes this argument in his essay "Illicit crossings: the familiar other and the feral self," in Steeves (2006).

17 In Chapter 4 I will return to the idea of the social construct at work in scientific discourses.

18 Darwin excluded the non-human animal and the "savage" from the ethical realm. About the latter he writes that for them "these feelings and services are by no means extended to all the individuals of the same species, only to those of the same association" (Darwin 1981, 98).

19 For Darwin, the "ethical feelings" are partly created by habit, but mostly innate or, as Darwin puts it, they are attributed "chiefly to natural selection." In its most basic form, social feelings can manifest as parental affection. More complex forms include "sympathy" and "obedience to the wishes and judgment of the community" (Darwin 1981, 99). Writing, then, specifically about humans, Darwin seems to follow Aristotle's suggestion that we are ethical beings neither by nature nor against nature; we have the capacity to become ethical beings as nature provides the possibility. What this concretely means for Darwin is "a tendency to be faithful to his comrades, and obedient to the leader of his tribe." Other than that, s/he possesses "some capacity for self-command," a willingness to defend "in concert with others, his fellow-men," and a readiness "to aid them in any way" (Darwin 1981, 109).

20 The title of the documentary "Nuclear Savage" reflects this idea in calling the US Army "savages" because of their experimentation with nuclear radiation on "savages." The story repeats itself throughout history. Wells's novel, as bizarre in its setting, reflects our treatment of others. Interestingly, the actual nuclear experiment, like Wells's fictional story, took place on an island (Horowitz and Einhorn 2012).

21 As Ulrich Beck points out, science is constantly involved in political and ethical decisions, for example when it assesses risk. When a scientist tells us that the level of pollution is acceptable and does not pose a risk to humans, she does not simply measure and determine what is still safe. She also already works with a sense of how much pollution is allowed and what is too much pollution, as well as that some pollution is allowed. Scientists here make important ethical decisions regarding how much risk we can take, or how much risk is normal. Such decisions are the result of a political process involving scientists and the industries that pollute (Beck 1992, 24).

22 In *On Truth and Lie in an Extramoral Sense*, discussed in more detail in the following pages, Nietzsche writes: "Every concept originates through our equating what is unequal. No leaf ever wholly equals another, and the concept 'leaf' is formed through an arbitrary abstraction from these individual differences, through forgetting the distinctions; and now it gives rise to the idea that in nature

there might be something besides the leaves which would be 'leaf' – some kind of original form after which all leaves have been woven, marked, copied, colored, curled, and painted, but by unskilled hands, so that no copy turned out to be a correct, reliable, and faithful image of the original form" (Nietzsche 1976, 46).

23 Language also creates home in another way. As Derrida asks, "What in fact does language name, the so-called mother-tongue, the language you carry with you, the one that also carries us from birth to death? Doesn't it figure the home that never leaves us?" Thus, we wander around the globe, at home in our bodies and our language that we carry, as Derrida suggests, "as a sort of second skin you wear on yourself' (Derrida 2000, 89).

24 Wells included an interesting reflection on the birth of morals, as he lets Moreau say: "Very much indeed of what we call moral education is such an artificial modification and perversion of instinct; pugnacity is trained into courageous self-sacrifice, and suppressed sexuality into religious emotion" (Wells 2008, 132).

25 The death of Moreau is also a remembrance of our colonial past. For example, we can think about Captain Cook, who after being welcomed to Hawai'i, and initially considered as a god, was eventually killed. The message of Wells's novel and *The Island of Lost Souls* seems to be that natives are too wild and eventually always fall back in their animal behaviors. Yet, the novel and film also show us that the ultimate animal and savage is, as is the case in most colonial stories, the white male trying to exercise power over and transform the natives, to "humane" standards.

26 Socrates was, like Nietzsche, a wanderer, but he did have a strong sense of Athens as his home. Dialogues mostly take place in the city and when he is offered a chance to escape from Athens to avoid his pending death sentence, he refuses since Athens is his home. Yet, while being born and raised in Athens and having lived there nearly all his life, he is a strange character, often out of place. His strange ideas get him into trouble, his strange ways of speaking as well as his strange stubbornness result in his death.

27 While Darwin was a wandering researcher traveling the globe, his thoughts and ideas are often firm. Should a theory of evolution not bring about fluidity, transformative thinking, and a questioning of boundaries? If species evolve and change, slowly over time, can we then draw sharp boundaries between different species?

28 Michael Naas writes in this regard that autoimmunity (a term used by Derrida in *Voyous, Rogues*) as hospitality is "the welcoming of an event that may thus bring good or ill, that may invite a remedy or a poison, a friend or foe. To be open to the event, to offer hospitality, it is essential *not to know* in advance what is what or who is who [. . .] only someone at war with himself can offer refuge to that which is not the self' (Naas 2008, 33). Naas also discusses hospitality within the context of receiving or accepting the tradition as an heir. To re-affirm the tradition is to choose to keep the tradition alive (Naas 2008, 30–1).

29 In this sense Nietzsche's thinking is very much in contrast to his eighteenth- and nineteenth-century predecessors who often used natural models to describe the self. Hegel, for example, uses the model of the organism when he describes the different stages of consciousness. It is the model of life that he sees as the ultimate model of both reason and reality (Hegel 1977, §§275–7).

30 The choice of words here might lead us to think that Nietzsche merely makes a Kantian move by claiming that we cannot know the thing in itself. Many interpreters argue that Nietzsche separates the physical world from the world of knowing in a way that is very similar to Kant. While I do not dispute this interpretation, focusing merely on this Kantian aspect of Nietzsche's thinking runs the risk of missing a crucial aspect of Nietzsche's point. Whereas for Kant all human beings naturally think in the same way since we all possess the same

structures of knowing, for Nietzsche, instead, our thinking, or the way we think, is determined through all kinds of external factors. We can change the way we think and different people have different ways of thinking. The only reason we have a limited amount of perspectives lies in the herd instinct, the notion that we all think and feel in the same way, since our culture teaches us to think and feel in that way. Although some have, thus, pointed out that Nietzsche argues here that we cannot know the thing-in-itself, others (such as Cox) have pointed out that Nietzsche, moreover, argues that we are the ones who create value for nature (Cox 1999).

31 Heidegger explains this relationship to nature with the notion of "enframing" (*Gestell*) – the idea that we always enframe nature as something useful and exploitable. Whereas Heidegger seems to argue that we have lost nature, for Nietzsche we have never been natural. I am thinking here particularly of Heidegger's contrast between the modern and the old forester. The modern forester works for the paper industry, the old one used to dwell freely in his work environment. For Heidegger, the unity with nature has been lost in our contemporary urban life-style (and on a side-note: with that we have lost being). This will be discussed in more detail in the next chapter (Heidegger 1977).

32 Nietzsche seems to take a Cartesian route here in the sense that he lets all other beliefs fall down by destroying the very foundation of all truth. Yet, with Nietzsche we do not end with a firm foundation for the sciences but, instead, we end with a variety of perspectives, perspectives that are needed for life: "there would be no life at all if not on the basis of perspective estimates and appearances" (Nietzsche 1998, 46).

References

Aristotle. 1934. *The Physics: Books V–VIII*. Cambridge, MA: Harvard University Press.

——. 1937. *Parts of Animals*. Cambridge, MA: Harvard University Press.

——. 1997. *Metaphysics*. Cambridge, MA: Harvard University Press.

Beck, Ulrich. 1992. *Risk Society Towards a New Modernity*. London and Newbury Park: Sage Publications.

Cox, Christoph. 1999. *Nietzsche: Naturalism and Interpretation*. Berkeley: University of California Press.

Darwin, Charles. 1981. *The Descent of Man and Selection in Relation to Sex*. Princeton: Princeton University Press.

Deleuze, Gilles. 1983. *Nietzsche and Philosophy*. New York: Columbia University Press.

Derrida, Jacques. 2000. *Of Hospitality*. Stanford: Stanford University Press.

Diogenes Laertius. 1972. *Lives of Eminent Philosophers*. Cambridge, MA: Harvard University Press.

Hegel, Georg Wilhelm Friedrich. 1977. *Phenomenology of Spirit*. Oxford: Oxford University Press.

Heidegger, Martin. 1977. *The Question Concerning Technology, and Other Essays*. New York: Harper & Row.

Horowitz, Adam and Einhorn, Richard. 2012. *Nuclear Savage: The Island Experiments of Secret Project 4.1*. San Francisco, CA: Primordial Soup Company, and Video Project.

The Island of Lost Souls. 1932. DVD. Directed by Erle C. Kenton. Los Angeles: Paramount Pictures.

Kapil, Bhanu. 2009. *Humanimal: A Project for Future Children*. Berkeley: Kelsey Street Press.

Lange, Friedrich Albert. 1925. *History of Materialism and Criticism of its Present Importance*. New York: Harcourt, Brace & Company.

Naas, Michael. 2008. *Derrida from Now On*. New York: Fordham University Press.

Nahm, Milton C. 1964. *Selections from Early Greek Philosophy*. New York: Appleton-Century-Crofts.

Nehamas, Alexander. 1985. *Nietzsche: Life as Literature*. Cambridge, MA: Harvard University Press.

Nietzsche, Friedrich Wilhelm. 1962. *Philosophy in the Tragic Age of the Greeks*. Chicago: Regnery Publishing.

——. 1968. *Basic Writings of Nietzsche*. New York: Modern Library.

——. 1974. *The Gay Science: With a Prelude in Rhymes and an Appendix of Songs*. New York: Vintage Books.

——. 1976. *The Portable Nietzsche*. New York: Penguin Books.

——. 1995. *Thus Spoke Zarathustra: A Book for All and None*. New York: Modern Library.

——. 1998. *Beyond Good and Evil Prelude to a Philosophy of the Future*. New York: Oxford University Press.

——. 2005. "The Fate of Democritus." From *Frühe Schriften*. In *Becoming Nietzsche: Early Reflections on Democritus, Schopenhauer, and Kant*. Translated by Swift, Paul. Lanham: Lexington Books.

——. 2006. *The Gay Science*. Mineola: Dover Publications.

Plato. 1998. *Phaedo*. Newburyport: Focus Classical Library.

Safranski, R. 2002. *Nietzsche: A Philosophical Biography*. New York: W.W. Norton & Company.

Seshadri, Kalpana. 2011. *HumAnimal Race, Law, Language*. Minneapolis and London: University of Minnesota Press.

Simplicius. 1992. *On Aristotle's Physics 4*. Ithaca: Cornell University Press.

Steeves, H. Peter. 2006. *The Things Themselves: Phenomenology and the Return to the Everyday*. Albany: State University of New York Press.

Swift, Paul A. 2005. *Becoming Nietzsche: Early Reflections on Democritus, Schopenhauer, and Kant*. Lanham, MD: Lexington Books.

Taylor, Nik, and Tania Signal (eds.). 2011. *Theorizing Animals: Re-Thinking Humanimal Relations*. Leiden and Boston: Brill.

Wells, H.G. 2008. *The Island of Dr. Moreau*. Waiheke Island: Floating Press.

2 Lost at home

Heidegger and the phenomenologists on being-in-the-world

In one of Novalis' best-known fragments, referred to by (among others) Lukács and Heidegger, he writes "Philosophy is really homesickness; it is the urge to be at home everywhere" (Novalis 1923, 21). In the previous chapter, I laid out a Nietzschean approach to homelessness, to transitional thinking, or thinking without a home. I focused on the creation of values, the function of language, and how language and values create a "home" that we can hold on to. This home provides boundaries and limitations for us, as well as other species. In this chapter, I elaborate on this notion of home and homelessness, specifically through the thoughts of Heidegger.

Heidegger names the human being *Dasein*, literally meaning "being there." We are beings for whom being is an issue, i.e., we can ask what it means to be, and we can in some ways relate to what it means not to be, or the end of our being, death. "To be," means, first of all, to be in the world. Our being is immediately tied to our world, expressed in the dashes used in "being-in-the-world," the basic state of *Dasein*. The world is not simply the earth or the globe, nor is it the environment, the *Umwelt* that surrounds us. Our world is, instead, the world *Dasein* is in. For the human being, to be is to be *in*. We cannot be without a context, without a place in which we are. Furthermore, the world in which *Dasein* is, is the world of *Dasein*. The world is always mine, Heidegger writes (Heidegger 1962, 26, 163). To be for us, is to be "there" (*Da*). Even while Heidegger has been criticized for emphasizing time over place, we get a sense of how Heidegger is a place-based thinker; we are tied to place and places (consisting of other beings, including human beings) in a fundamental way.[1] Our being is tied to places, even while we easily forget such connections. His notion of being-in-the-world is closely tied to Husserl's lifeworld, the background that is mostly just taken for granted. Events take place, people and things appear within this background, and these events, people, and things make us forget about the background without which nothing could appear or take place. For obvious reasons I cannot constantly acknowledge the fact that because of gravity I am not currently floating through the air, but sitting firmly in my chair. Yet, such facts constitute the lifeworld that we mostly take for granted.

The most important background fact, for Heidegger, is being. We forget the very basic fact that things are, that we are, and what it means for something or ourselves to be. We have become oblivious to the strange but important question of "what is being?" Part of Heidegger's analysis consists of emphasizing how we are immersed in this world, how our being is an issue for us, and how our immersion in the everyday world makes us forget about being; it is usually not an issue for us, at least not thematically.

Heidegger often uses terms of homelessness in his analysis of *Dasein*, the human being. In a very basic form, Heidegger's assessment of the contemporary human being can be summarized as follows: we are lost, even while we feel so much at home. The oblivion of being is the main reason we are not at home in our world, an oblivion caused by, among other things, technology, language, as well as science (or what Heidegger calls "the mathematical"). In this chapter I analyze the different ways in which we are lost, according to Heidegger. It is tempting to think that we can overcome the oblivion of being and become authentic by overcoming our homelessness. As there is a double nature to Nietzsche's idea of absolute freedom, there is a double nature to homelessness in the form of Heidegger's fundamental attunement, which is a gift (in this case to start to philosophize) and a poison: one cannot remain in a state of anxiety or absolute homelessness. Still, a sense of homelessness is necessary to philosophize in the first place, and creating or retrieving a sense of home is part of our inauthentic fleeing. This inauthenticity is similar to Nietzsche's herd mentality. Heidegger provides, I argue, important insights into why we try to create a home, as well as senses of belonging and not belonging, native and foreigner – both in the human as well as the non-human world.[2] In particular, I address how we order the human and natural world in terms of belonging and not belonging. Such ordering and managing of the natural world starkly contrasts our own homelessness.

Lost at home

Heidegger is the philosopher of homelessness and homecoming.[3] Dasein, the human being, is at home in the things and gossip with which it occupies itself. Yet, it is exactly in this sense of being at home that Dasein is homeless and lost; Dasein's dwelling is a fleeing to the stuff in which it immerses itself. Being at home with all that surrounds us is how we flee away from the nothing, from our utmost possibility, the end of any possibility, our own death. Interestingly, and ironically, this being immersed in the things is the homelessness of contemporary Dasein. By tying ourselves to the things around us, we might experience a sense of being-at-home, but it constitutes a repression of who and what we are, thus constituting a being lost. We busy ourselves with everything, know everything and, in doing so, we immerse ourselves in the world, and, still, we know so little about ourselves. We are lost at home.

The idea relates to Nietzsche, who writes: "We remain unknown to ourselves, we seekers of knowledge" (Nietzsche, 1968, 1). We can land a rocket on a comet, fly by Pluto, plan to travel to Mars, but we fail to even begin to grasp ourselves. Both Nietzsche and Heidegger see this lack of self in the midst of so much knowledge as correlated; our urge to know everything is a fleeing away from self-knowledge. For Heidegger, such fleeing is an escape from our own possibilities. Possibilities are tied to our own death – the impossibility of any further possibility. We would rather not connect to the temporality of our being and thus we flee into knowing everything beside ourselves. This is the preamble to Heidegger's investigation into "being."

Being is not some mystical entity that is abstract. It is always my being, which is tied to the world. In order to outline the structure of our being-in-the-world, Heidegger applies the method of phenomenology. As formulated by Husserl, phenomenology is the study of phenomena, of how things appear to us, or in Husserl's words, how the things show themselves. This means that we first of all try to experience things as phenomena without already grasping and placing them in theories. Husserl's original idea of phenomenology stemmed from a criticism of the sciences, which he clamed theorized too much and left little value to experience. Experience is the origin of all knowledge and understanding. It provides a wealth that we often tend to forget. For example, it is impossible to provide an accurate description of walking through the snow to someone who has never experienced walking through the snow. The crispness, the sound, the feeling, sinking a little bit away with each step – there are no words, no numbers, and no visuals that can sufficiently capture the actual experience of feeling snow under one's feet. One has to actually experience it in order to know what it is like. Similarly, hearing a tree in the wind, smelling the ocean, tasting coffee, or driving a car are experiences that one needs to experience in order to understand. Extending the lack of experience to the animal world, we can say that we will always miss out from not being able to fly like a bird, dive and breach like a whale, or ride a storm like a tree. In fact, John Muir tried to experience the latter by climbing a Douglas spruce during a storm. Several paragraphs describe his experience, starting with the following:

> The slender tops fairly flapped and swished in the passionate torrent, bending and swirling backward and forward, round and round, tracing indescribable combinations of vertical and horizontal curves, while I clung with muscles firm braced, like a bobo-link on a reed.
>
> (Muir 1961, 255)

The text is full of metaphors and after reading through it several times I have the strong impression that I still do not have the faintest idea of what Muir experienced while spending hours in the tree, beyond what I already imagined such an experiment would be like. Further, I do not think Muir himself experienced the storm like a tree. This did not seem to be the purpose of either the tree riding, or writing about the experience. It is rather aimed at calling attention to the unknown elements: "Most people like to look at mountain rivers, and bear them in mind; but few care to look at the winds, though far more beautiful and sublime, and though they become at times about as visible as flowing water" (Muir 1961, 255).

In comparison to Muir – who also rode an avalanche, climbed behind the falls at Yosemite, and spent so much time in the wilderness – the rest of us are perhaps living in outer space, looking at "nature" from a distance. Phenomenology, then, approached through Muir, comes with the basic understanding that the earth is full of mysteries that we will never be able to fully grasp.

Thinking outside of values and theories – a turn from "facts" to experience without theory – is extremely difficult if not impossible, since we almost always already have an understanding of what the things are even before we observe them. The phenomenologists argue that we need such a change and a new appreciation of experience. This does not mean that Husserl, or any of the other phenomenologists, argue that we can experience without theories, concepts, or language, nor do they seek to rid us of the sciences: "The scientific rigor of these disciplines, the convincingness of their theoretical accomplishments, and their enduringly compelling successes are unquestionable" (Husserl 1970, 4). The sciences, however, tend to reduce the world to quantifiable facts. Even human existence is reduced to what can be objectively established. It excludes "questions of the meaning or meaninglessness of the whole of this human existence" (Husserl 1970, 6). The crisis of the sciences can be summed up as follows: "Merely fact-minded sciences make merely fact-minded people" (Husserl 1970, 6). We lose something important in reducing the world and human existence to what can be measured. We are not merely facts. Returning to Nietzsche, we can say that "facts" merely present one perspective among many others. As Merleau-Ponty (following Husserl) points out, we are first of all a wealth of experience that is much more than what science grasps.

Merleau-Ponty, in particular, places the body at the center of his phenomenology. We are bodies that perceive the world. Scientific measurements and experiments can disclose the world in a particular way, but they can never reveal my perception of the world. In a way, Merleau-Ponty points us to the cave that science has created for us: "the real world is not this world of light and colour; it is not this fleshy spectacle which passes before my eyes. It consists, rather, of the waves and particles which science tells us lies behind these sensory illusions" (Merleau-Ponty 2004, 41). Plato told us that we indeed have to look beyond the visible realm, and beyond the bodily, to find the real truth. Science has taken Plato's cue and, indeed, claims that our sense perceptions are mostly invaluable illusions, and that our bodies deceive us. In Chapter 4 we will return to this idea through Bruno Latour, who argues that science claims to have left the cave behind, i.e., scientists create an image that the social sciences and humanities deal with shadows (social constructs and stories), while the natural sciences deal with truth. Latour, Heidegger, Husserl and Merleau-Ponty all question this distinction, albeit in different ways. For Heidegger, science is immersed in language – that world-forming instrument that is not a neutral medium, but a way of opening up the world, always involved in active interpretation and the creation of truth. This creation of truth is what makes us feel at home in the world. To dwell in the world as knowers means to own it.

Dwelling and being lost in language

For Heidegger, perhaps the most important home that we dwell in is language. As already mentioned, the significance of language is that it creates truth: to speak, or to use words, means to engage with the world, to be in the world and even to create that world. Language is not a neutral instrument in this endeavor; it opens up the world to us. Thus the language that we have available determines how we understand the world, what meaning the world has, and which parts of the world we grasp (as well as which parts are left out as not having a meaning). Medical discourse is a helpful example. Learning disabilities such as ADHD and ADD are today widely recognized, whereas these named conditions (or any other childhood mental disorders, for that matter) did not even exist 50 years ago. The symptoms of disorderly behavior, difficulty focusing, and lack of academic achievement have probably existed since the advent of school systems, but were not recognized as symptoms of a certain disability. Once the disability was conceptualized it created a new reality, in a sense bringing these disabilities into existence, to our social conscience. In other words, language creates or forms our world, to which doctors, students, teachers, and parents react.

We can then wonder if language perhaps creates fictions. Indeed, the issue is sometimes raised with ADHD and ADD, as some have called it a fictitious disease. A more subtle approach is that certain clinical pictures such as attention deficit disorders often lead to over diagnosing. As child psychologist Jeremy Kagan stated in an interview with the *Spiegel Online International* on August 2, 2012, "if a drug is available to doctors, they'll make the corresponding diagnosis." The very name of the disorder and its corresponding symptoms, as well as the available drug to treat the disorder, thus create a reality in which patients and medical doctors think, act, and react, or as Heidegger would say, the names create a world in which we dwell.

This significant relationship between language and reality or truth encourages Heidegger to create a new language to express his own thinking. Heidegger's language is notoriously opaque. He often builds worlds out of words that seem common, but are given an unfamiliar meaning. While many academics, philosophers, and others, seem to hide in their jargon in order to protect their field (or themselves), for Heidegger the use of language has an important philosophical meaning since it is the only way to create a new truth, a new way in which the world opens up to us. He certainly has important reasons to create a new language, as our old language gets us stuck in old ways of thinking, in a way of thinking that for Heidegger is highly problematic and that creates a sense of home, ignoring the fact that we are ultimately homeless. We *are* at home in the world; it is my world and this world is constituted through language. Our being in the world is rooted in language. Thus, we dwell in language. In the *Letter on Humanism*, Heidegger writes, "Language is the house (*Haus*) of being. In its home (*Behausung*) man dwells. Those who think and those who create with words are the guardians (*Wächter*) of this home" (Heidegger 1977b, 217). Heidegger creates an image that is as powerful as it is puzzling. What does it mean that this is the house of being? Is being dwelling in this house? Or is being the landlord, who rents the house out to us? The image of the guardians is likewise puzzling: what kind of house needs guardians? Is language perhaps a prison in which we lock being (or ourselves) away? Presumably, "the guardian" refers to philosophers: "those who think and those who create with words" (Heidegger 1977b, 217). Yet, why is such a thinker and creator a guardian, and not a rebel who tries to break out of this house? Or, if breaking out is impossible, s/he might try to remodel, or deconstruct, the house. The latter seems to be exactly Heidegger's aim in re-inventing language.

While Heidegger in particular argues that language has lost its ties to being, we can also suggest that language has lost its ties to the natural world and to ourselves as natural beings. Emerson argues that language has its origins in nature, citing ethical concepts such as right and wrong that come from natural shapes such as twisted and straight (Emerson and Thoreau 1994, 23). David Abram argues that natural sounds are often the source for our spoken language. Language comes out of nature: we speak with our bodies, imitating the sounds of the natural phenomena we observe. We hear a river rushing and use a word ("'rush', 'splash,' 'gush,' 'wash'") that sounds like it (Abram 1996, 82). Nonetheless, language today has become increasingly technological, as have we. As Abram argues, language becomes more and more influenced by technology, and loses its relationship with nature. "As technological civilization diminishes the biotic diversity of the earth, language itself is diminished. As there are fewer and fewer songbirds in the air, due to the destruction of their forests and wetlands, human speech loses more and more of its evocative powers" (Abram 1996, 86).

Also for Heidegger, language constitutes the way human beings relate to the world. The oblivion of being is rooted in the diminishing of language. As indicated, Heidegger's image of language as the house of being, in which man dwells and which has guardians, raises many questions, such as what is the relationship between language and being, between human and being, and between language and human? Starting with the latter, it is helpful to pay attention to the German. *Wächter*, as well as the English guard, is a person who is waiting. A guard is not necessarily passive, but mostly reacts to what comes. The guard does not actively invite, and is not the host. His or her task is to make sure things run in an orderly fashion. S/he is not fully passive or fully active, but somewhere in between, i.e., both active and passive. This might seem to be a strange task for a philosopher. Yet, Plato already provides us the image of the philosopher as a midwife, someone who does not produce anything, but assists others. In using the image of the guard, Heidegger's task is to help us understand that action is not merely a cause that produces an effect, but it is rather an "accomplishment [*Vollbringen*]" (Heidegger 1977b, 217). The word "Vollbringen" means "to bring full" or "full bringing," and the closest translation would be "fulfillment." That the expression of language is an accomplishment or fulfillment indicates that we do not find mere passivity in that which is expressed in language. What is expressed in this case is that being is active; it manifests itself. The guardianship (*Ihr Wachen*) of the philosopher "accomplishes the manifestation of Being insofar as they bring the manifestation to language and maintain it in language through their speech" (Heidegger 1977b, 217).

Thinking is the connecting activity here, not as an activity that is either an effect or a cause. Instead, "in thinking Being comes to language" (Heidegger 1977b, 217). Thinking takes on an interestingly somewhat passive role: thinking "does not make or cause the relation [of Being to the essence of man]. Thinking brings this relation to Being solely as something handed over to it from Being" (Heidegger 1977b, 217). In other words, thinking is a medium, with being as the active part handing itself over to man. It does so by coming to language: "in thinking Being comes to language" and thinking "lets itself be claimed [*in den Anspruch nehmen*] by Being so that it can say the truth of Being" (Heidegger 1977a, 217). Thus, the triad of language, being, and man is connected through the activity of thinking, not simply as an activity of man, but rather as an expression, or a claim made (or more literally a being spoken to) by being. I will hint here at a term developed in the last chapter of this book, where I discuss this activity on the side of what is mostly considered as passive as "reactivity." The human being is not the only active part in its observations of the world of passive objects. Rather, we exist in a reactive relationship with the world, mediated through language.

Later on in the "Letter on Humanism," Heidegger states this phenomenon as a "bringing to language." He then writes, "Being comes, clearing itself to language" (Heidegger 1977a, 262). And earlier he states: "Language lets itself be claimed by being so that it can say the truth of Being" (Heidegger 1977a, 218). Both language and being (including human being) take the side of cause and effect simultaneously. Language speaks by letting itself be spoken to; it is an expression, or effect of the expression of being. Being comes to or clears itself to language, the effect. Language, also takes the role of the cause, by "saying the truth of being," thus taking a more active role. Thinking accompanies this process as a guard. Returning, then, to the image of the house, one can argue that language, as the house of being, is a dwelling place claimed by being, but only insofar as thinking allows itself to be spoken to by being. We are living in this house, but often without realizing it. Without such realization, being is kept at bay; we lock her out, and with that we are lost at home.

In addition to the metaphor of the guardian, Heidegger also uses the image of the shepherd (*der Hirt*), apparently the human being "whose dignity consist in being called by Being itself into the preservation of Being's truth" (Heidegger 1977a, 245). Interestingly, the human being now dwells in the nearness of being: "Man is the neighbor of Being" (Heidegger 1977a, 245).

It might be helpful at this point to recall that being is not some mystic abstraction. Being is always mine, which can become the true recognition of one's self if one grasps this being as temporal in nature, i.e., as finite. Our limit or finitude is always, at least potentially, near. Thus we live next to it, and we are being called by it. We can and we often do ignore it, but in our role as a shepherd we cannot but listen to this call. The shepherd is without technology, without the "they," and thrown back upon him or herself. The shepherd is also a figure who is homeless in the sense that s/he does not have a home that is a structure specifically built for dwelling. The home of the shepherd is language, where s/he resides close to being.

Still, today we are far removed from the shepherd and with that increasingly homeless in a different, negative, sense. We might live in sophisticated and technological dwellings, but we have lost our essence by abandoning being. Heidegger bases this sense of homelessness partly on Marx's analysis of alienation, in which we are strangers in the world and to ourselves. This inauthenticity is specifically tied to the oblivion of being, the fact that we fail to recognize the fact that we are and that this being is temporary. It is the opposite of the existential homelessness: it is a being lost without the recognition that one is lost.

Da-sein, being-there is "nearness 'of' being," a nearness that we often forget (Heidegger 1977a, 241). Homecoming, a return to being, occurs through thinking, which can bring being to language, and "builds upon the house of being" (Heidegger 1977a, 259). What that means is that "Being comes, clearing itself, to language. It is perpetually under way to language" (Heidegger 1977a, 262). This is the "essential unfolding of Being itself to language" (Heidegger 1977a, 263).

In *Being and Time* the return home is the return to ourselves as utmost possibility, i.e., we recognize ourselves as temporal beings that, in a Nietzschean vein, have to make the most of our time. As we have seen, Nietzsche argues that we are lost in the ideas of an afterlife, and an original sin that will never allow us to be fully present in this life. For Heidegger, we are lost in the everyday, in the gossip and idle talk as well as our concerns about what others might think of us. We are at home in this perpetual state of homelessness – a ground without a ground, a homelessness that is not recognized. We find ourselves at home in utterly homeless places such as the shopping mall or the coffee shop replicated all over the world. The fact that the mall is the same everywhere or that I can drink a cup of coffee that tastes exactly the same wherever I am in the world might make me feel at home on a superficial level. Yet, such experiences are ultimately without ground, without a foundation, since the everywhere of these places is also a nowhere. This groundlessness of the everyday is only realized when things fall apart.

Notions of home

We do our utmost to not let things fall apart; we feel at home in our body, and in the world by knowing it, observing it, monitoring it, and manipulating it. It is our world. And yet, Heidegger identifies this being at home as inauthentic (*Uneigentlichkeit*). Even in our knowing we are too often concerned with what others think of us, with gossip and idle talk. We busy ourselves in our everyday engagements with the world. Following Nietzsche, Heidegger argues that we are not ourselves and he ties it to our very being; we forget about our being and specifically that our being is temporal. This forgetting of who we truly are as mortal beings occurs when immersed in what Heidegger calls the "they," *das Man*. It is the anonymous structure in which everyone is a no one, in which we lose ourselves entirely. Yet, it is in this structure that we believe we are at home.

The lack of knowledge of our environment, of the places in which we live, results in a lack of knowledge of ourselves. The places where we are born and in which we live determine us, first of all because they provide us with an identity. Different places come with different identities. "We are unknown to ourselves," Nietzsche writes; Heidegger, accordingly, suggests that "[t]hat which is ontically closest and well known, is ontologically the farthest and not known at all" (Heidegger 1962, 69). While in *Being and Time* Heidegger does not specifically identify our place as what is ontologically important, the metaphors of homelessness, neighborhood, being at home, and nearness all emphasize spatiality and place. In a later essay, entitled "Building Dwelling Thinking," Heidegger emphasizes the correlation between thinking and place. Our places determine who we are, how we think, and how we act. In *Being and Time* he articulates this as a negative kind of determination; in our "everyday everydayness," we flee to the things around us, without ever noticing what is truly important.

This constitutes the contradictory reality of our lives – we know so much, and yet we are far removed from ourselves and do not truly know who we are. We are at home everywhere, "ontically," i.e., on a factual level. Yet, we are not at home "ontologically," i.e., at the level in which we understand ourselves in terms of being. The inauthentic part of who we are, the not being our own self (*Uneigentlichkeit*) is a form of not being at home. It is the ontic understanding in which we are at home by being familiar with the beings around us. We know these beings and we are in the world, alongside these familiar beings. In *Being and Time*, Heidegger explains being-in-the-world as "'to reside', 'habitare', 'to dwell'" (Heidegger 1962, 54). Being-in-the-world is then a "residing alongside [*Wohnen bei*]" (Heidegger 1962, 188), which means to be familiar with the world.

However, familiarity does not mean being truly at home; to know, to be familiar with and reside alongside, provides a certainty and sense of security. Heidegger interprets this as a fleeing. We keep escaping the ontological question of what it means to be. "Dasein's absorption in the 'they' and its absorption in the 'world' of its concern, make manifest something of a *fleeing* of Dasein in the face of itself – of itself as an authentic potentiality-for-Being-its-Self" (Heidegger 1962, 184). Here Heidegger reflects on one of the biggest contradictions of our modern world. Despite our invented machines and equipment that should, in theory, reduce the amount and intensity of labor required to maintain a comfortable world, and therefore should create more leisure time, the opposite is true. We are constantly busy, working long days, often including parts of the weekend, and have little time to spend with our family, friends, or just with ourselves. In other words, we characterize the way we are in the world by being busy, by occupying ourselves with the things around us. We can blame the boss, the manager, or the system, but ultimately we all contribute to keeping this structure in place. Despite our complaints and efforts to change, there seems to be a part in us that is happy to be busy. In our leisure time, when we are not asleep, we spend most of our time behind electronic media that occupy us, and these activities can also be regarded as a fleeing away from ourselves. Thus, we are not at home with ourselves, but merely at home in residing with other beings. In the contemporary world this translates into a being-in social media, television, and Internet, while not being with our self. The very word "Internet" indicates a "being in" or "being inter," immersed in a World Wide Web or network. The Internet creates a world of its own and changes the world at large. Social media, for example, take on their own life. It is a reality that constitutes a large part of our "being-in." Again, this is ultimately a removal from ourselves that can only be reversed in a fundamental and life-changing experience, in which we recognize that our being at home everywhere is fundamentally a not being at home. We will find then a different kind of "being-in," not determined by "the they" but by more authentic structures.

Disruptions of home

While we desperately hold on to the structures of "the they," things do fall apart around us. The melting of icecaps, droughts, floods, intense storms, arctic vortexes, and so forth are troubling events. Until such radical changes in our environment affect us immediately, we mostly ignore the environment that provides us with the very opportunity to be in the first place. In Heidegger's analysis, we understand our world as equipment. This attitude makes us forget about the equipment as long as it works. In that regard, we are proficient at taking for granted that everything is fine. Heidegger famously describes the hammer as a piece of equipment used to build a house. A carpenter uses the hammer to drive in nail after nail and forgets about the piece of equipment. Similar to how I currently have forgotten about the keyboard that I am using, how you have forgotten about the paper these words are printed on, the hammer has blended into the user's "lifeworld." When we are in tune with the equipment we utilize, we forget about it. This changes when the hammer (or the keyboard) breaks (or when one spills a cup of coffee over the book). Suddenly, one is very aware of the equipment, as it becomes a thing standing out by virtue of its no longer working. Likewise, as long as the equipment that is the earth still provides us with resources, it "works" and we can ignore any troubling signs, such as the warnings of scientists, the continuing growth of corporations, widespread deforestations, or air and water pollution. As long as the stock market provides profits and the Dow Jones keeps going up, we are in a trouble-free world, or rather we are troubled only about ultimately insignificant things such as the stock market.

As Heidegger's carpenter takes the hammer for granted, we take our natural surroundings for granted. We breathe the air without noticing the air or our activity of breathing. Only when the air is so polluted that breathing becomes difficult do we recognize the air and our respiration. Only then do we recognize our dependence on clean air, which is a hint at our own mortality. Of course we already knew all this, but we fail to secure an understanding of our mortality, a necessary condition for our very being. For Heidegger, time in terms of mortality is the essence of our being. While living our daily lives we constantly forget this simple fact that our time is limited.

Such recognition occurs in what Heidegger describes as a fundamental attunement (*Stimmung*).[4] *Dasein* is always in a mood or attunement. Our attunements determine the way we relate to the world, to our environment. The same place, let's say a shopping mall, might appear attractive or disgusting, depending on our attunement. If we are in the mood for shopping, the mall is a heavenly place. Conversely, when we really need to purchase a new item (instead of just wanting it) and we cannot quite find what we need, the mall, the other shoppers, the salespeople, the building, as well as the very premises of capitalism, all start to overwhelm and annoy. We are then in what we call a bad mood. In *Being and Time*, Heidegger argues that because of our moods or attunements our world is "never the same from day to day" (Heidegger 1962, 177). The world opens up through these attunements. While we often think of scientific research as objective since it works with data that should be the same regardless of our moods, it certainly does not know reality in an absolute manner, as we have seen in our discussion of Nietzsche. For Heidegger, the researcher's attunement opens up the world she investigates: "even the purest τηθερια [theory] has not left all moods behind it" (Heidegger 1962, 177). The famous "eureka moment" often occurs at a moment when the scientist takes a break. Archimedes famously found a solution to measure the mass of gold when he took a break, drew a bath, and made the tub overflow as he stepped into it. Likewise, data might be the same from day to day, but how we interpret it and whether or not we are actually able to discover anything significant in the data changes from day to day and is determined by how rested and focused, and moreover how creative we are at the moment. Thus, it is not only a poet or creative writer whose world is determined and opened up through attunements, but all science, even in its most pure forms, is determined in a similar fashion. This is part of what it means to be human and to be in the world. This perhaps appears as a limitation. However, our attunements actually make the world accessible in the first place; they open up the world to us.[5]

Attunements play an important role, together with language and our theoretical understanding, in our engagements with the world, and they help determine how things open up to us. We find here with Heidegger that the world, the places in which we find ourselves, are not consistently the same thing. Similar to Nietzsche, Heidegger describes a perspectival notion of truth: the shopper and the philosopher (who could be one and the same person) interpret the world very differently. From day to day, even from hour to hour, the world also appears differently depending on how we are attuned. Behind all this is not a true (or True) world that is somehow hidden or obscured from our views. In fact, the world is that which is disclosed in our theories and our attunements – the world is our interpretation.

In his lecture course "The Fundamental Concepts of Metaphysics," Heidegger describes our relation to the world as world-formation. Language, knowledge, and attunements form the world. Heidegger juxtaposes this interpretation, or opening up of the world, with the poverty in the world that characterizes the being of the (non-human) animal (Heidegger 1995).[6] The animal is poor in world; namely, it can only behave toward the objects that it encounters and it lacks the kind of opening up of the world that is made possible through our (human) attunements.[7] The animal possesses less – "less in respect of what is accessible to it, of whatever as an animal it can deal with, of whatever it can be affected by as an animal, of whatever it can relate to as a living being" (Heidegger 1995, 193). The world of the animal is poor or limited. The bee's world, for example, is limited to its hive, blossom, and other bees. It is not only that the domain of the animal is quite small, but also "the extent and manner in which an animal is able to penetrate whatever is accessible to it is also limited" (Heidegger 1995, 193). The animal is not able "to know" the things around it.

Heidegger argues that the human animal has a world that is much richer; its world is greater in range, and it is able to extend this range. Despite Heidegger's critical assessment of contemporary *Dasein*, the human being has the potential to explore and know, and while I am critical of over-emphasizing the significance of human knowledge, Heidegger regards the wide and deep range of human knowledge as positive. Compared to the animal's range, the human being's range is not only fundamentally different in the sense of this accessibility of beings as beings, i.e., to understand a being on an ontological level, but is also larger and can be extended – it can "penetrate ever more deeply in this penetrability" (Heidegger 1995, 193). This is the world-formation of the human, "the extendibility of everything that he relates to"

(Heidegger 1995, 193). In other words, both horizontal (a wider range) and vertical (deeper penetration) expansion is possible. This might pose a problem for Heidegger's philosophy: the human being as a former of the world feels at home in the world, through the act of formation. We create the world, first of all, through language, and second through our physical manipulation. The former impels the latter. It is here that I am mostly critical of Heidegger, since his thinking leads to prioritizing the human over other beings. Even while he claims that the human can fall much farther than any animal, his suggestion of world-formation excludes all animals and rocks from having a valid perspective.

For Heidegger, the notion of world formation is important in order to think through the issue of our relationship to our world. Nature – the animal, the plant, and the ecosystem – is created or formed. Following Heidegger, we can say that we do not simply grasp an animal as food, or as a pet, but we can understand it on many different levels. We have a name for the animal; we group it with other animals of the same sort, and understand it in the context of broader categories (such as pet or predator). We understand the animal's importance for the ecosystem it lives in; we know it is "poor in world," and so on. All of this is problematic, since – as seen in the Nietzsche chapter – classifications, names, and ideas of native and non-native are highly problematic.

The poverty of the animal is opposed to our world-formation, which is one of the ways we are at home in the world, by creating our home through meaning, by grasping and manipulating the things around us. Thus we are at home – at least until we are not. The negation can be found in the fundamental attunement, which is a disruptive and significant event. It disrupts our being at home, resulting in an uncanny feeling. The first and best-known fundamental attunement is being-toward-death; the realization that I am finite and someday will die. With the recognition that one day I will not be anymore, I feel lost: homeless (*unheimlich*) or not at home (*das Un-zuhause*). This experience, as Heidegger describes it in *Being and Time*, is the fundamental attunement of anxiety. In this attunement we experience not-being at home: "anxiety brings [Dasein] back from its absorption in the world. Everyday familiarity collapses" (Heidegger 1962, 189). At this point in the text Heidegger introduces "not-at-home" (*Un-zuhause*) and "uncanniness" (*Unheimlichkeit*), perhaps better translated as "homesickness." We feel at home in "the they" characterized by gossip and idle talk. We also feel at home in the "entities" of the world, such as our possessions; we flee toward these entities and the structure of the they, and we flee away from feeling "not-at-home." This fleeing is ultimately "a fleeing in the face of one's own most Being-towards-death" (Heidegger 1962, 252). It is the recognition of one's mortality, that one's being has a beginning and an end. We are not at home with our own mortality, the very essence of our own being, and thus we flee away in the everyday and flee toward those beings around us whom we feel comfortable with, and make us feel at home again.

In the *Fundamental Concepts*, Heidegger uses the example of profound boredom as a fundamental attunement that takes us out of our captivation with the everyday. This experience also ties us to our temporality, and throws us back upon ourselves. Though we have dreaded boredom since childhood, Heidegger describes it as an attunement that can have very positive connotations. Although I will not discuss his analysis of boredom here in detail, the fear of becoming bored relates to how we live in our contemporary world, always without a dull moment, constantly connected and entertained. In a world that is increasingly determined through technology, no one needs to be bored. Heidegger's analysis seems particularly accurate in a review of the iPad, written by Peter Bregman on June 16, 2010 in the *Harvard Business Review* soon after the sleek tablet first came out. The author of "Why I Returned My iPad" enjoyed his iPad. The problem is that Bregman enjoyed it a bit too much, and spent every single minute of his "free" time on it. He writes, "Sure I might *want* to watch an episode of Weeds before going to sleep. But should I? It really is hard to stop after just one episode. And two hours later, I'm entertained and tired, but am I really better off?" (Bregman 2010). This seems to be the problem not only with the iPad, but also with many devices, including the television. One can watch TV all night, but is one really better off? While TV seems rather passive (although I have seen and heard people yell at the set, I am confident that all of them knew this did not have an impact on whatever or whoever they are yelling at), the iPad creates a sense of being active, and with that a sense of productivity. Bregman complains that the device is, in fact, unproductive, because it does not leave us with a moment of boredom:

> Being bored is a precious thing, a state of mind we should pursue. Once boredom sets in, our minds begin to wander, looking for something exciting, something interesting to land on. And that's where creativity arises. My best ideas come to me when I am *un*productive. [. . .] They are the moments in which we, often unconsciously, organize our minds, make sense of our lives, and connect the dots. They're the moments in which we talk to ourselves. And listen.
>
> (Bregman 2010)

Bregman argues that with the iPad such moments are lost; this is the reason he returned the tablet to the store.

Most of us experience comfort in not having to talk and listen to ourselves. We might hear or say something unpleasant, and so we start to fear the moments of boredom, the moments of emptiness and nothingness that might throw us back at ourselves. This is the picture that Heidegger presents us with: we want to be in a world with familiar beings. We are close to these beings, while we are far removed from ourselves. We are not at home with ourselves, with our ultimate possibility, or the end of possibilities – our mortality. Again, this is inauthentic homelessness, opposed to the existential homelessness that both Heidegger and Nietzsche identify as a necessary condition for authenticity or becoming oneself. What we can learn from Heidegger in this regard, then, is that maybe in our daily lives we are not looking for something new, but we are constantly escaping. We go somewhere new, we move somewhere else, we buy something new, etc. In each case we seem to seek a new identity in what we are not: the new place, or the things we own. We are literally moving around, but in our thinking we lack an existential homelessness, a freedom of thought, since we flee away from thinking.

Enframing

In the introduction I discussed our homelessness as a new nomadism in which we are less tied to particular places and move around. At the same time, we also turn the places around us into homogeneous land. One of the ways in which this happens is through technology. I have already mentioned social media and gadgets, but the technological understanding of the world extends far beyond this. Heidegger's critique of technology is important in understanding that we are not using it as a tool to do what we want with it; technology creates a world of its own in which it tells us what to do and how to engage with the world. Technology tells us how to appropriate the world. While language creates a feeling of home since our words take possession of the things we name, technology takes this act a step further by manipulating the things that we appropriated through language. The world becomes a place that is ours as something to be manipulated.

In *The Question Concerning Technology*, Heidegger claims that we make a mistake when we regard modern technology as a neutral tool; in fact, technology actively changes the way we engage with and understand the world. Through the notion of "enframing" (*Gestell*), Heidegger argues that technology enframes the world so that everything in it becomes a "standing reserve." In a way, enframing is the context in which we make sense of the world and determine our actions. In the example of technology, enframing provides us with a technological understanding. Thus, the river is actually not perceived as a river, but as the potential to become a hydroelectric plant. When the engineer sees the river, s/he sees the river through the eyes of technology. Thus the river becomes a potential for energy, a standing reserve. Today, we can add the ever-increasing use of smartphones, tablets, and computers with which to communicate and be in the world. These technologies are not neutral tools; they change the world in a radical way, determining how we relate to one another and how we behave in public spaces, walking (or driving!) with our eyes glued to a gadget, missing most of our environment even while we think we are fully aware of everything around us and able to "multitask."

Modern technology adds to what Heidegger describes in *Being and Time* as our absorption in what others think of us, and our immersion in idle talk instead of the more philosophical thoughts of which we are capable. We mostly do not think about who we are, what we can and should do, or what it means to be in the first place (see, for example, Heidegger 1977b, 38).

Heidegger criticizes contemporary *Dasein* for constantly occupying itself with the beings that surround it, within which – one could say – *Dasein* forgets itself. *Dasein* is absorbed with all kinds of responsibilities, tasks, and appointments. In completing these, we have become an indifferent one, a no one, because we busy ourselves with the "present-at-hand" and the "ready-to-hand." We occupy ourselves with those things that we can handle with our acquired skills. We are, one could say, lost in the things. Our identity has been lost in the beings with which we occupy ourselves. We have become an "undetermined I" (Heidegger 1995, 143).

Our technological engagement with the world partly constitutes the "undetermined I," in which we all think and act in the same way, as determined through the technology that is at hand and the technological attitude. The whole world becomes a resource at our disposal. Places have lost their meaning outside of this resource. It is probably too radical to say that we are no longer attached to any place, but as we care less about particular places, it becomes easier to change landscapes. Heidegger's notion of enframing is important here – technology is a tool through which our view of and engagement with the world changes. The earlier example of the river that becomes a source of energy, the potential for a hydroelectric plant (that will effectively change the river into a reservoir), is an example of how such enframing has tremendous influence on our environment. Dams radically alter ecosystems, destroying the habitat of wildlife both above and below the dam. The soil that used to wash down the river and contribute to a healthy environment for many species now collects in the reservoir, creating problems rather than benefits. Salmon and other fish cannot swim past the dam, unless a nifty (and expensive) ladder is created next to the dam. While reservoirs have many benefits, mainly in terms of water and energy supplies, dams destroy ecosystems (and sometimes human communities that used to live there) simply by changing a valley into a reservoir (or lake). Using Heidegger's analysis, I argue that we have come to a point in which we no longer measure such benefits and costs. In fact, when we think of costs we mostly think of costs in terms of dollars, not in terms of environmental costs (cf. Orr 1994). Often, we are simply reasoning without applying any analysis: oil should be drilled, water should be stored, coal should be mined, etc.

For Heidegger, technology does enframe nature so that everything becomes a standing reserve. Technology challenges nature; it challenges the landscape. It does so by making us ask the question, what can we do with this mountain, with this river, with this field? What resources can we mine, what can it grow, what can it carry, etc. More specifically, in "The Question Concerning Technology" Heidegger discusses the idea that nature becomes a supply of energy. Modern technology claims nature as such a resource, "which puts to nature the unreasonable demand that it supply energy that can be extracted and stored as such. [. . .] The earth now reveals itself as a coal mining district, the soil as a mineral deposit" (Heidegger 1977b, 14). In other words, our technological enframing of a place turns it into a resource that has to be challenged as a source of energy, and hence as a coal-mining district.

Further, after nature, technological tools also become a standing reserve. Heidegger provides the example of the airliner that "stands on the taxi strip only as a standing-reserve, inasmuch as it is ordered to ensure the possibility of transportation" (Heidegger 1977b, 17). The machine is then not an autonomous thing, but is rather ordered within the technological frame-work. Hence the machine itself is challenged or claimed by the enframing of technology: the machine, too, becomes a standing reserve. Perhaps Heidegger hints here at the more complex issue of the airliner as well as other pieces of technology – unless we think about the individual plane (as Heidegger does), air travel is not just ordered or challenged by our technological framework, it also changes our way of thinking and living, further enhancing, or entrenching, our technological being in the world. The airplane creates the possibility of air travel and, as such, challenges us to travel further. Thus, the possibility to travel fast distances in short times and for relatively little money orders us to do so. Air travel also contributes to our inauthentic homelessness, since it makes it easier to move to a different part of the world. We can always return if needed, usually within a day. In short, the airplane as set up in the larger framework of technology then asks us to challenge it, to use it, to move, and so forth. Thus, attending conferences all over the country is not merely a possibility, but becomes an expectation.

Third, we ourselves become a standing reserve:

> As soon as what is unconcealed no longer concerns man even as object, but does so, rather, exclusively as standing-reserve, and man in the midst of objectivelessness is nothing but the orderer of the standing-reserve, then he comes to the brink of a precipitous fall; that is, he comes to the point where he himself has to be taken as a standing-reserve.
>
> (Heidegger 1977b, 26–7)

Heidegger's point here is along the lines of the Marxist analysis of alienation in which we ourselves become part of a machine, which functions within a system that determines all players. Worker and capitalist are equally determined by external forces, and in both Marx's and Heidegger's understandings we have lost our freedom and ourselves. For Marx this means that we have lost our ability to enjoy our very basic and natural capacity to work. For Heidegger it means that we have lost the very sense of our own being, of who we are as human beings. We are so lost in the world of "the they" and tied to our technology, we even fail to notice that it is ordering us and that our essence has been reduced to a standing reserve, ready to be used for the economic purposes of our society. Heidegger provides the (romantic) example of the forester, who today also has become a standing reserve: the forester "is today commanded by profit-making in the industry, whether he knows it or not.

He is made subordinate to the orderability of cellulose, which for its part is challenged by the need for paper, which is then delivered to newspapers and illustrated magazines. The latter, in their turn, set public opinion to swallowing what is printed, so that a set configuration of opinion becomes available upon demand" (Heidegger 1977b, 18). Thus, we are not unlike the landscape that has been reduced to a mining district; we are human beings reduced to human resources. Yet, the human being takes on a more active role than the landscape: "he takes part in ordering as a way of revealing" (Heidegger 1977b, 18). Still, it is questionable how active the role of the individual is in this act of ordering. We will return to this issue in more detail in the chapter on Foucault, but it should be clear that Heidegger uses passive forms to describe the individual – the forester, for example, is ordered and the descriptions of the illustrated magazines are reminiscent of the they, the anonymous structure in which every one is a no one.

The last important insight regarding our contemporary view of nature and how we relate to the world comes from another important essay by Heidegger, "Modern Science, Metaphysics, and Mathematics." Similar to the notion of "enframing," in this work Heidegger uses "the mathematical" as the framework through which we understand the world. The Greek *ta mathēmata* he argues, "means what can be learned and thus, at the same time, what can be taught" (Heidegger 1977b, 274). It provides a certain structure of understanding through which we then grasp things. He explains it is "what we already know them [the things] to be in advance: the body as the bodily, the plant-like of the plant, the animal-like of the animal, the thingness of the thing, and so on" (Heidegger 1977b, 277).[8] The mathematical provides the very possibility for learning and teaching. True teaching and knowledge engage with these foundations.

In "Modern science, metaphysics, and mathematics," Heidegger argues through the notion of the mathematical, that with the introduction of natural laws that are external to natural objects, a notion of violence – the very idea that we can do something violent to nature – has disappeared. He argues for this by analyzing some changes in the foundations of scientific knowledge, by recalling the ways in which we know natural bodies, or phenomena. "The way in which we know" is the role of the mathematical. In particular, he compares the modern with the ancient Greek understanding of movement as a relationship between an object and place. For the Greeks, natural objects were determined out of themselves – there is a proper relation to place for an object that is determined by the object itself. As Heidegger assesses Aristotle, the "kind of motion of the body and its relation to its place depends upon the nature of the body" (Heidegger 1977b, 262). Movement is part of the *phusis*, the nature of the body, or the natural body. Thus, a rock itself falls to the earth, as opposed to the Newtonian notion that gravity, an external force, pulls the rock toward the earth. For Aristotle, this also means that violence can occur: "if a rock is thrown upward by a sling, this motion is essentially against the nature of the rock, *para physin*. All motions against nature are *biai*, violent" (Heidegger 1977b, 263). Heidegger claims that with modern science the very possibility of violence, of doing something against the nature of a natural body, disappears. There is no longer a natural force that determines the proper relationship of a natural body to a place, and so throwing (or blowing) up a rock is not exercising violence against it. The rock's relationship to place is already determined as external, and so there is no essential difference between gravity pulling a rock down and a human being throwing it up or blowing it up. There is no inherent proper place for a thing, and thus moving it, removing it, changing it into something else, etc. are all to be considered acts without violence.

Today this notion that we cannot exercise violence over a natural body often drives our understanding of nature. For example, in the discussion of hydraulic fracturing (better known as "fracking") we hear many arguments for and against the practice, but none of those arguments state that the procedure is extremely violent toward rock formations deep under the ground, which are "fractured" by pressurized fluids. Thus, we hear that fracking might solve our dependence on foreign oil or that it pollutes drinking water, but we do not hear that the practice violates nature by fracturing rocks and pumping up what should be down. The disappearance of violence in our understanding of natural bodies indicates that science is itself a phenomenon. It appears differently over time and appears differently for different people. Historically, science tells different stories in relation to nature as a place that we inhabit, that we are a part of, or that we can manipulate and change. Science does not simply collect data. It tells us ethical narratives about what to do and what not to do with nature. It also enframes political discourse and informs our general attitude toward nature – points that I return to in the last chapter.

In a way, phenomenology draws us back into the cave, not to avoid the truth or to educate those left behind (which is, as we know from Socrates, a suicidal mission), but to show that only caves or shadows exist. Furthermore, phenomenology shows that the shadow has no source beyond what we have made out of it. We are looking at our own shadows. This does not mean that we should give up, but rather recognize that every "truth" is a perspective structured by categorizations, language, past experiences, and pre-conceived ideas of what is true and what is false. The body is not the only medium with which we perceive: thinking is also a medium – one that can change over time and never provides direct access to the world. Merleau-Ponty takes this notion a step further by turning around, and eventually overcoming, the subject–object relationship that has so dominated modern philosophy. The very idea that the human subject is active, determining the things around it, and the related conclusion that truth lies in the subject, not in the object, has, arguably, led to us further distancing ourselves from nature and from the place(s) in which we live, our environment. If truth lies in us, it seems to suggest that natural objects lose their value and are no longer true or false, do not belong to a particular place and, in fact, start to belong wherever we see fit.

In "Modern science, metaphysics, and mathematics" Heidegger, interestingly, demonstrates how science is itself a phenomenon: something that we experience. We might be tempted to contrast phenomena and the natural sciences as two opposites, as a "soft" and "hard" understanding of the world. In such a contrast disciplines like philosophy, literature, poetry, and painting can be appreciated as creative and original, but lack the exactness that the data and facts of science present. Yet, science is itself an approximation through creativity. Data and facts are constructions. We have just seen how natural laws have replaced other stories that used notions of violence. Thus, science is a phenomenon that lacks exactness and is merely one way of looking at the world, and not *the* way of looking at the world. As discussed in the Nietzsche chapter, science is not free of storytelling, and it has not reached the realm outside of the cave, which according to Latour, science claims to have done. Heidegger makes a similar point in describing science as a phenomenon, placing science in the cave, not as a discipline studying shadows, but as a shadow itself to be observed and studied by, among others, philosophers. Phenomenology provides, then, not a "soft" story as opposed to the "hard" facts of science. Both are rationalities, and whereas science uses data to tell its story, phenomenology uses experience and our bodily immersion along with other beings in the world to tell its story.

David Abram provides a very interesting and compelling reading of Merleau-Ponty and Husserl as proto-ecologist-philosophers. Abram puts the human back into the environment and in doing so he turns things "inside out." As opposed to our traditional way of thinking in which we are the only beings with intelligence, he writes, "Intelligence is no longer ours alone but is a property of the earth; we are in it, of it, immersed in its depths" (Abram 1996, 262). First, Abram reminds us of a simple fact we often seem to forget: we cannot exist without the earth. It is our home. A home is more than a shelter. Our intelligence is a part of, or comes from the intelligence of the earth. This does not mean that the earth has a brain, or that it is created by a divine intelligence. Rather, the earth has a thinking, a reasoning, more basic and, at the same time, more profound than ours: the "rationality" that makes life possible in the first place. Technology makes us forget the interconnectedness of the earth and our lives. As Abram writes:

> [O]ur reflective intellects inhabit a global field of information, pondering the latest scenario for the origin of the universe as we absently fork food into our mouths, composing presentations for the next board meeting while we sip our coffee or cappuccino, clicking on the computer and slipping into cyberspace in order to network with other bodiless minds, exchanging information about gene sequences and military coups, "conferencing" to solve global environmental problems while oblivious to the moon rising above the rooftops.
>
> (Abram 1996, 265)

The conflict between knowing so much and being such great political animals on the one hand, and not being aware of our environment as the greater political arena on the other hand, forms the foundation for our problems today. I share Abram's idea that we cannot solve our environmental crisis from a distance, i.e., from behind our desk, or from the boardroom. We have to step outside of our technological world to reconnect and retrieve a sense of who we are.

One of the problems Abram identifies is that modern language and thinking tend to separate our existence from other animals as well as from nature. Abram and Heidegger suggest that the separation between nature and the human originated from language. Language is an artificial boundary created and maintained by human logos. We return here to the idea that we are at home everywhere, in the sense that we know everything, yet we are utterly homeless in that being at home; we fail to grasp the most basic aspects of our existence, like our dependence on the earth. Abram now argues that our very being in the world is a sharing in the intelligence of the earth. Merleau-Ponty plays an important role in reaching such a strange but important conclusion. He points out that we are first of all with our bodies in the world, and more-over that we are involved in an intricate relationship, in which subjectivity and objectivity, as well as activity and passivity, are blurred. The world is not experienced as a quantifiable and/or measurable quality observed through instruments and mathematical formulas. We actually experience the world through our bodies. He explores the relationship between object and subject, for example, through the experience of the painter Paul Klee as expressed by André Marchand, "In a forest, I have felt many times over that it was not I who looked at the forest. Some days I felt that the trees were looking at me, were speaking to me. . . I was there, listening. . . .I expect to be inwardly submerged, buried. Perhaps I paint to break out" (Merleau-Ponty 1964, 167).

Merleau-Ponty (or Klee) does not argue that trees have eyes, or minds, so one could ask why he refers to such an obviously absurd idea. The point, rather, is that we have taken for granted that we are the knowers, the observers, measurers, and theorizers. All the activity of scientific observation lies on the side of the human subject. We tend to think that whatever we observe is passive in this process and let's itself be observed "objectively." The phenomenological tradition challenges this commonplace understanding in the most extreme way possible; not only is the tree active in showing itself to us, *it* is watching us, while we become the passive, observed party. Without the trees, the observable reality, our experience is entirely empty and is, in fact, not at all. Thus, without an activity from the side of the object we observe, in letting itself be observed, we do not observe. Interestingly, this theoretical idea is captured in the intimate relationship Klee developed with the objects he tried to paint, suggesting that if we are truly open to the objects around us (a situation that is, perhaps, best obtained in practices such as painting), we will find that we are not merely active while the object is passively letting itself be observed.

Merleau-Ponty and Abram, thus, bring us back from a state in which we have, in a sense, become our technology. We forget our bodily being in the world, our embodied engagement with the things around us, and instead observe through scientific equipment in such a way that we fail to distinguish between our technology and ourselves. This is another form of homelessness: we have abandoned our experiencing bodies, an illusion that arguably started with Descartes' definition of the human being as a thinking thing rather than an embodied being.

Conclusion

Heidegger's philosophy brings to the fore how we understand the world through language, science, technology, and attunements. Phenomena, thus, never appear "purely" as the things themselves, but they are always our experiences, and therefore mediated through these structures. Thus, Heidegger characterizes our existence as world forming; we create the places around us and make them "ours." We form the world, first of all, by inhabiting it, by dwelling in it, by building, by changing landscapes, by constructing and so on. We also form the world by naming all we find in it: we categorize, group, and institute boundaries. Even those places that we explicitly do not inhabit are formed by us; we call those places "wilderness," a human and particularly American invention that creates an artificial boundary between the human and the natural world – one of the many ways in which we form the world.

Despite all this ownership through the formation of the places around us, Heidegger claims that we are utterly lost. We fail to recognize our own limitations, including our ultimate limitation: death. Our forming of the world, our enframing of the landscape, and our homeless dwelling in the language of the they, are all ways of fleeing away from our approaching destiny and the responsibility that our own mortality presents to us. Despite Heidegger's own mistakes, which continue to haunt his legacy into the twenty-first century, we should not forget that Heidegger is a Nietzschean at heart. Nietzsche's idea of the eternal recurrence of the same seems to have influenced Heidegger's notion of being toward death and its ethical implications: live your life in such a way that you want to live it again and again. By living inauthentically we are lost, homeless in a negative way. However, we need at least moments of existential homelessness that provide opportunities to change who we are and how we are in the world.

As discussed in the Introduction, Odysseus responds to his being lost when returning to his own home with an act of violence. Odysseus has traveled for years and feels displaced at his own place. He appropriates the household, restores his authority, and "comes home" by killing those who, supposedly, had acted in improper ways during his absence. It should be familiar to us: the whole world has been conquered through acts of violence, such as killings, as well as displacements. We feel at home by displacing others. In addition, we displace natural resources by bringing them to our home, our cars, and our life-styles. The whole earth has turned into a resource that we have to use. Preservation is not part of immediate economic growth and thus it is deemed worthless. Ultimately, this is a result of our being lost and our need to be at home in the world. Not unlike Odysseus we do this violently, often without even recognizing the violence. When we fill the tanks of our cars we do not see the blood that was involved in securing the oil (cf. Klare 2008). Nor do we see the environmental destruction, and the violence to rocks deep under the surface of the earth. In fact, we do not even see the gas; we might smell it at best. The only thing we really see is the amount of money that we have to pay in exchange for the black gold. We might complain about rising gas prices, but whatever monetary price we pay, it is never going to reflect the true cost of gas. The transfer of money creates the illusion that it is now mine and that I have paid my share in order to enjoy burning it over the next couple of hundred miles.

Heidegger relates themes of appropriation and violence, in which we fail to recognize the violence in acts of appropriation. We experience being at home in the world very comfortably: science, technology, and language make us feel safe and secure. Yet, for Heidegger we are utterly lost, homeless in the world, not in the positive sense of a transitional thinking that we found in Nietzsche, but rather as a being lost in what Nietzsche describes as the herd. Only a fundamental attunement can pull us away from this fleeing into "the they" and return us to questions about what we are and what it means to be. The inauthentic life is simply taking our home, the earth, for granted as a resource we can exploit. We are then lost at home in a negative way, while a fundamental attunement can create a homelessness or homesickness that can help us to start to think. There is thus again a double meaning to homelessness, as being lost in the they, or being pulled away from this inauthentic structure in which we are confronted with a feeling of existential homelessness as the condition in which we can start to philosophize.

Notes

1   Some of the criticism will be discussed in more detail in Chapter 4 in the discussion of Watsuji.
2   A related pressing question is why we feel the need to build borders, fences, and walls around a country. If we would truly be at home in the world would we need borders? Is the act of declaring certain others to be foreigners perhaps an act in which we most of all establish our own identity, and with that a sense of being at home?
3   The theme of homelessness and homecoming is at work throughout Heidegger's work as explored by Robert Mugerauer in his thorough study *Heidegger and Homecoming*. The book has been extremely helpful in thinking through the issue of home in Heidegger, even while I only take up a few of his ideas of homelessness, dwelling, and homecoming. I have focused mostly on those occurrences that are relevant to the topic of this book, and in particular to the

idea that we assume we are at home everywhere without actually ever truly being at home (Mugerauer 2008).

4   *Die stimmung* first of all refers to the tuning of a musical instrument, and *die Stimme* is the human voice. For this reason, I prefer the translation "attunement" above "mood." Heidegger sometimes uses the term in conjunction with *bestimmen* (to decide, determine, or ascertain), or *Die Bestimmung* (determination, destination, or vocation). As we will see, one's attunement can contain a certain call that can determine one's destination.

5   In this sense, attunement is perhaps a harmony or tuning with the world. It is also worth mentioning that in his lecture course, Heidegger does not use the concept *Befindlichkeit*, which in *Being and Time* seems to be equated with *Stimmung*.

6   I have discussed Heidegger's assessment of the animal in much more detail in (Kuperus 2007).

7   The animal is a "poverty in mood [Ar-mut]" (Heidegger 1995, 195). In his interpretation of Heidegger's lecture course, Alasdair MacIntyre misses this point entirely when he takes the poverty of world of the animal as a lack of possibility to grasp the world as a whole (MacIntyre 1999, 47). McIntyre ties the notion of "poverty in world" to the non-language-possessing animal (MacIntyre 1999, 50). Yet, in describing Dasein as a being always attuned, Heidegger attempts to overcome the traditional way of thinking the human animal as an animal with language, or reason. Poverty in world is, therefore, not (as McIntyre suggests) a poverty in language or reason, but a poverty in mood, or attunement. That means that the animal cannot experience different moods. For Heidegger the animal always has one and the same: a drive through instinct.

8   In the essay "The age of the world picture," Heidegger explains the mathematical as "that which man knows in advance in his observation of whatever is and in his intercourse with things: the corporeality of bodies, the vegetable character of plants, the animality of animals, the humanness of man" (Heidegger 1977b, 118).

References

Abram, David. 1996. *The Spell of the Sensuous: Perception and Language in a More-than-Human World*. New York: Pantheon Books.

Bregman, Peter. 2010. *Harvard Business Review*. June 16.

Cazeaux, Clive. 2011. *The Continental Aesthetics Reader*. London and New York: Routledge.

Emerson, Ralph Waldo, and Henry David Thoreau. 1994. *Nature Walking*. Boston, MA: Beacon Press.

Heidegger, Martin. 1962. *Being and Time*. New York: Harper & Row.

——. 1977a. *Basic Writings*. San Francisco: Harper & Row.

——. 1977b. *The Question Concerning Technology, and Other Essays*. New York: Harper & Row.

——. 1995. *The Fundamental Concepts of Metaphysics: World, Finitude, Solitude*. Bloomington: Indiana University Press.

Husserl, Edmund. 1970. *The Crisis of European Sciences and Transcendental Phenomenology: An Introduction to Phenomenological Philosophy*. Evanston: Northwestern University Press.

Klare, Michael T. 2008. *Blood and Oil*. Northampton, MA: Media Education Foundation.

Kuperus, Gerard. 2007. "Heidegger and animality." In Corinne Michelle Painter and Christian Lotz (eds.) *Phenomenology and the Non-Human Animal at the Limits of Experience*. Dordrecht: Springer.

MacIntyre, Alasdair C. 1999. *Dependent Rational Animals: Why Human Beings Need the Virtues*. Chicago: Open Court.

Merleau-Ponty, Maurice. 2004. *The World of Perception*. London and New York: Routledge.

——— . 1964. "Eye and mind." In *The Primacy of Perception*. Evanston: Northwestern University Press.

Mugerauer, Robert. 2008. *Heidegger and Homecoming: The Leitmotif in the Later Writings*. Toronto: University of Toronto Press.

Muir, John. 1961. *The Mountains of California*. Garden City: Doubleday.

Nietzsche, Friedrich Wilhelm. 1968. *Basic Writings of Nietzsche*. New York: Modern Library.

Novalis. 1923. *Schriften*. Jena: Diederichs.

Orr, David W. 1994. *Earth in Mind: On Education, Environment, and the Human Prospect*. Washington: Island Press.

3 Plastic places, settled nomads

An analysis of our sense of place through Foucault and Deleuze

Introduction

How do we relate to place today? What is an acceptable or "normal" relationship to place and home, and how are these norms established? What do laws, norms, and practices tell us about our relationship to place(s)? What does it mean to be "at home," "out of place," or how should we feel "at home"? What should our relationship be according to our values, and how have these values historically changed? This chapter seeks to answer these questions by partly providing a genealogy of our contemporary relationship to place, a relationship that is characterized by a sense of mobility.

Experiences of places depend on a number of factors. One's class and race determine and limit possibilities. They determine where one feels at home and where one is welcomed or kept out. Certain places are off-limits. Our sense of place also depends on our culture. Having grown up in the Netherlands, in which all wilderness is gone, I have always experienced places as continuously changing.[1] Changes to the landscape are not merely historical (most of the land is reclaimed and two-thirds of the country sits below sea level), but continue to evolve. One of the places where I grew up has changed dramatically in just the past 20 years – from green pastures with cows and sheep to an industrial area with a canal, docks, a yacht harbor, and newly created wetlands. Although the contrast is quite dramatic, this is not an uncommon story in the Netherlands, which created a freshwater lake by building a dike, and added a whole province in 1986 after reclaiming more land. Arguably, such rapid and ever-changing landscapes seem to create a "plastic" (i.e., moldable) sense of place. A place is not x or y, but can become (almost) anything.

In this book I mostly focus on the USA, where the landscape has also undergone huge changes in terms of deforestation (over 95 percent of forests are gone), the railroad, the car, roads, the continuing expansion of cities and new suburbs, architecture and infrastructures built around cars, irrigation canals, mining, oil exploitation, landfills, etc. This chapter partly traces the history of our relation to or sense of place in the USA and relates it to the migration from places all over the world, but in particular Europe. It in addition also relates to globalization or the migration of the "American sense of place." I address in particular in what ways places have become entities that can be constantly transformed. In the previous chapter I argued through Heidegger that in our technological mindset we care little about preservation of the places that make us able to live. Technology determines our thinking and acting towards places.

Beside the idea of changeable, moldable, or what I will call "plastic" places, we find not only that places transform, but people as well, by virtue of increased mobility. This chapter focuses on this mobility, our nomadism. It maintains the opposition between wandering and transitional thinking defined as an existential homelessness and the inauthentic homelessness of the herd, or "the they." In the following that distinction is played out between Deleuze's nomadic thinking (inspired by Nietzsche) and the modern nomadism that has developed since the Industrial Revolution. In the latter, with inauthentic homelessness, we frequently move across the country or the globe, we travel virtually everywhere, and we commute long distances on a daily basis. In order to think through how this (inauthentic) nomadic existence has developed, I trace some of the most important changes of the last two centuries regarding our experience of place.

In order to analyze our current understanding of place, I discuss our notions of belonging to a place, and how places belong to us, by relating to a few pivotal historical changes. In doing so, I will borrow a method developed by Nietzsche and Foucault: the genealogy. Nietzsche most famously uses this method in *The Genealogy of Morals*, a work in which he traces the history of Christian values. He uses notions of slave and master moralities – both failing moralities since they lack authenticity and rely on oppression of, or being oppressed by, some other power (Nietzsche 1996). Foucault uses the genealogical method fairly consistently (and rigorously) in analyzing sexuality, the birth of the prison, and the clinic. He is interested in how norms have been established and have changed over time, as well as the particular forces that have been instrumental in making those changes.

Foucault's analysis of discipline is helpful in order to grasp the radical changes in terms of power that occurred first in Europe and later in the USA. The analysis in this chapter traces the history of our current norms regarding place in order to better understand how we treat places. Foucault also uses the notion of heterotopias, places that are not really places, somehow outside of what we consider to be a place. Foucault describes these as "sites." I argue that our contemporary experience of place can be understood within this concept of the heterotopia.

In order to oppose this inauthentic relationship to place that is largely nomadic or homeless to the possibility of a more authentic relationship I will use some of the work of Deleuze and Guattari. They speak about nomadology, a notion inspired by Nietzsche's appeal to think freely, outside of the established concepts, norms, values, and truths. Deleuze argues that in our thinking we lack a particular mobility, a way to transcend limitations, boundaries, or borders. He thus calls for nomad thought, which for him means to become Nietzscheans.

The work of Deleuze, Guattari, and Foucault clarify how today's nomad existence is in many ways the opposite of what Deleuze and Guattari call "nomadology." Today's tendency to never settle down, to remain on the move, to be nomadic, is unique in both the history of the human being, as well as in the animal realm. This nomadic existence comes without a particular place, but with the moldable places that I described before. We move, but the places that we move between are the same, or are made into the same. Thus, I argue, first, that we have become "settled nomads." Second, I oppose this to the nomadology proposed by Deleuze.

Discipline and biopolitics in Foucault

Today, places have become "plastic" or moldable. A forest can become a city, an arid area can become green, the sea can become land, and a valley can become a reservoir or lake. Urban spaces constantly transform as well. Buildings are torn down, new ones take their place; a cemetery can become a university (as is the case of the University of San Francisco); bike lanes are added to streets; green spaces are constructed; businesses disappear and are replaced by new ones, etc. The main question in this regard is: how are we able to change places so rapidly? This is not a technological question, but rather a question about the lack of attachment to existing places.

I argue that the key to answering this question is closely related to contemporary human beings' lack of a long-term relationship to particular places, what one could call our "nomadism." It could be argued that we have always been nomads, or at least started as such. However, every nomadic tribe moves cyclically, with the seasons, between different places. They are not freely moving, or moving at random. Only catastrophic events would change patterns of movement on a large scale.

In the first chapter I discussed how, for Nietzsche, humans construct norms and values, as well as all meaning. In the second chapter I discussed how, for Heidegger, this construction occurs through language. Language creates meaning and unites what is different, and tells us what should and what should not be. Language also constructs places. No single individual creates standards or places. Michel Foucault is particularly interested in how standards and ideas of what is normal and abnormal are constructed and maintained. His analysis focuses on the relationship between power and knowledge, and largely deals with political power. However, in doing so he does not simply focus on politicians and powers that traditionally have been associated with politics. Instead, Foucault identifies political power in places where one would not expect it, such as the prison, the clinic, and the school. His analysis, in a way, reverses the dictum "knowledge is power," since it pivots around the question "who, or what, has the power to determine knowledge?" In other words, in which powers (such as institutions) do we find the creation and maintenance of knowledge that determines what is normal and what is abnormal?

Examples of such political power structures include: parental relationships that tell a child about gender relationships, such as who is supposed to be the breadwinner; who can marry whom; what is sane, or what is insane behavior; what schools instruct students (and their families) about being on time; etc. An overarching question is how do we determine what is normal and what is abnormal, and what do we do with the abnormal or insane? Foucault points out that abnormal behavior is increasingly excluded from society. The insane used to be part of society. Today they are either in a psychiatric institution, outside of normal life, or in a prison, together with those other so-called abnormal people.

Within the context of normalization in *Discipline and Punish*, Foucault discusses the origins and development of the modern penal system (Foucault 1977). The subtitle of the book – "the Birth of the Prison" – hints at the investigation into the changes that shifted from a punishment of the body to that of the soul. The public spectacle during which a criminal was tortured in the market place was replaced by punishing the criminal by removing them from society. Punishment thus changed from taking place in the most public place to the least accessible. Incarceration is a way of punishment in which those who do not fit in society are literally taken out of it, displaced. In prison, inmates are, ideally, normalized and corrected. Throughout his book, Foucault argues how this correction has always failed. Prisons create delinquents who do not have a choice but to return to criminal behavior after they leave prison.

The prison is, certainly, a very strange place. Prisons are hard to get out of, for all the obvious reasons, but also extremely difficult to visit. Organizing a tour for a class means navigating a bureaucracy that involves, among other things, a background check of all students (and the instructor). Once one gets to the prison one has to go through several security measures, including searches, metal detectors, and security measures involving, among others, numerous gates.[2] The point of this impenetrability – the impossibility to get in – could be attributed to the fact that one wants to avoid contraband and communications between prisoners and the outside world. Yet, more importantly, Foucault makes the point that by being inaccessible the prison becomes a non-place, something outside of our society that plays with our imagination and turns punishment away from the body toward the soul (Foucault 1977, 9, 16).

In combination with this analysis of the penal system, Foucault makes a more fundamental analysis of our society. He suggests that the prison is a more radical or exaggerated model of society. All the structures that we find in the prison can also be found outside of it. The well-known prison model of the panopticon draws, for Foucault, the best parallel. In this structure, designed by Jeremy Bentham, the inmates can be observed continuously, while they are not able to see those who observe them. The basic idea that drives the system is that since one *can* be observed, the observation is internalized. One behaves *as if* one is being observed, even if actual observation does not take place. The model of the panopticon can be found everywhere in our society. Surveillance cameras, police patrols, and the monitoring of computer activities in the workplace are some of the more obvious examples of how the panopticon works: the idea of the panoptic structure is that a continuous *possibility* of observation exists. The result is that individuals behave well in public and in the workplace, for the simple reason that someone could be watching. In the end, the actual observation does not matter any more, since the individual has internalized this observation and starts to observe him or herself as an object. The lack of freedom here consists in "being placed" within a structure that one ultimately absorbs in such a way that it is contained within the self.

More subtle panoptic structures are at work as well. The school is aimed at creating normal citizens, who have to perform according to certain standards. From a very young age, children learn to live according to the clock. We are punished when we are late; there is a particular time for a particular activity. At the time when we join the workforce we do not protest, but celebrate the fact that we are asked to work from nine to five. We expect to be told to start with a certain activity, followed by another one, with a lunch break from twelve to one, and so forth. Our education, for which we, or our parents, have paid a high price, has prepared us for such an exact partitioning of time and space, to such a degree that we would, actually, feel uncomfortable without such a clear structure. The panoptic structure is complete when guilt arises if we arrive late for work, or if we read our personal email while we should be working. At that point we have internalized the structure to such an extent that no one needs to punish us; we already punish ourselves by feeling guilt.

Ultimately, Foucault's analysis of our society can be interpreted as a Marxist critique in which we are coerced to conform to the standards of capitalism. The previous chapter examined how, for Heidegger, our thinking is enframed, for example by technology. We are not free thinkers, but our thoughts are "coerced" by seeing everything as a standing reserve. Foucault finds a similar structure in conforming to the standards of capitalism, which means quite concretely that we produce as disciplined workers (Foucault 1977, in particular 85ff.). The interesting aspect of this coercion under capitalism is that we regard work as our destiny. Following Foucault, this can be explained as follows: we are led to believe that the sole purpose of our existence is to find a job and to partake in producing. When one does not succeed in finding a job, no one needs to tell that person that she has failed as a human being. She knows it herself.

According to Foucault, the capitalist system works through normalization, in which the standard is to produce. Within this coercive system the human subject has become an object of knowledge (Foucault 1977, 29, 200). Records are kept of each human subject within the education, health, financial, and legal systems, all aimed at reaching conformity. Speeding tickets, bad grades, and behavioral or credit problems are all recorded. We correct abnormalities through a punishment for aberrant behavior, but moreover these systems of knowledge already constitute a structure that works in a corrective way. For, everyone wants to be normal. There is thus a particular place or placement that one wants to achieve, and this means that one wants good grades, good credit reports, to be healthy, and to stay out of legal problems. It might seem to be a good idea to obtain all of this, yet, for Foucault freedom is lacking. When the human subject (the knower) is seen and sees itself as an object of knowledge (among other things through the panoptic structure), it will constantly attempt to match a norm, to either maintain or strive for a better place within the hierarchical structures of economy and society. The institution of the human being as an object of knowledge, thus, works as a coercive force. Yet, such coercion is not an external corrective force, but rather an internal self-correction (Foucault 1977, 177, 195ff.).

How this form of discipline is exercised and experienced is in a few different ways tied to place. First of all, we find the architectural idea of the panopticon, in which human subjects are placed within a structure of observation that turns into a self-observation (Foucault 1977, 195–228). This use of norms and values is exercised everywhere: all the places that we occupy and in which we act are, in our experience, observable places. Even virtual places such as the Internet are potentially observed by employers or government institutions. This is a positive insofar as we want those agencies to observe those who do extensive online searches for how to make a bomb. Yet, surveillance also brings far-reaching limitations to our freedoms. Even without direct observation, we have internalized the panoptic structure and bring it to all places. There is, in other words, no place outside of norms. In terms of home and homelessness this means that to be at home means to act normally.

Foucault's description of the workplace is helpful here. He claims that the power structures of education, and the medical and legal fields are directed toward training subjects correctly. That means that they become good workers and thus become an economic means for the capitalist. Foucault describes docile bodies (Foucault 1977, 135ff.). Our bodies are "moldable homes," like the places in which we exist. The ideal example is that of the soldier, a body that is completely docile in its movements, its posture, and its behavior. The body of the soldier has been trained to such an extent that it has become an extension of the machine it operates, the weapon. Similar trainings and docility can be found in all human beings. In school, teachers train us to sit straight and still, to hold the pen correctly – all practices that contribute to productivity.[3] The body itself is a place or home that finds itself at home only in certain places. This is what the docile body is, at home in a particular space at a certain time for a particular activity: space is partitioned, creating places. In school and in the workplace a particular space, a place, is assigned to a particular individual – or each individual is assigned to a particular space. This creates an easy observation of presence and absence, and makes it possible to establish necessary communications and to avoid those communications that could disrupt production. The workplace becomes a functional site in which, as Foucault writes, supervision takes place that is both "general and individual" (Foucault 1977, 145). One can observe at once both the productivity and skill of each individual and the "successive stages of the production process."[4] Problems are quickly identified. This coercive machine creates docile bodies that become extensions of machines in what Foucault calls a "body-weapon, body-tool, body machine complex" (Foucault 1977, 153). Similar to the soldier and the student, the factory worker, the office worker, and the teacher are all trained to posture and move their body as a factory worker, an office worker, or a teacher.[5] While we often feel uncomfortable in our bodies since it does not match standards of beauty, as a student, a teacher, or an employee we feel at home. This is the comfort and home that such placement provides.

In relation to place, normalization through training works, for Foucault, on different levels. He writes, among other things, about: the architecture of the school and the hospital that aim at transforming the individual (Foucault 1977, 172); how individuals are distributed in space; and how we are tied to particular places (Foucault 1977, 141–2). In relation to factories he discusses the isolation and mapping of individuals, as well as spatial arrangements (Foucault 1977, 144). These structures make observations possible both in a general as well as an individual sense. When the whole process is disturbed or someone is not in the right place it is immediately obvious. In short, capitalism ties people and particular activities to particular places within a network of relations.

In order to summarize Foucault's position regarding discipline, we can say that our society in its entirety is a coercive force that sets certain standards or norms, to which all individuals are forced to comply. This force is not coercive in a violent manner – at least not in a visible or physical manner – but rather through a training that *seems* to aim at the interest of the individual. For Foucault, however, the training, standards, and norms have numerous consequences that destroy our individuality. In terms of home and homelessness, it means that in order "to be at home" one must conform to norms, which are – as witnessed in Nietzsche and Heidegger – not our own.

In *Discipline and Power* Foucault, thus, describes the mechanism of discipline in the prison, the school, and the workplace. This mechanism of power is expressed, among other things, in the development of the prison as the main means of punishment, controlling individuals in its entirety. The school and the workplace also use mechanisms that are not unlike the prison in how it controls individuals. In *The Birth of the Clinic*, Foucault, likewise, discusses how our health is monitored and recorded. This might not seem like a bad idea in the case of, for example, infectious diseases. Yet, as Foucault points out, the clinic also constructs ideas about health and, with that, norms. He himself was judged to be abnormal and sick, by experiencing homosexual feelings. The clinic is not merely an institution that promotes health, but is also political in the sense that it determines, polices, and attempts to correct abnormal behaviors.

Therefore, the prison, the clinic, the workplace, and the school are considered structures of power through which norms are created and maintained. We have seen that such norms constitute a productive workforce that functions well within, among other things, factories. Without such discipline the steam engine would never have had the impact it had.

While in the works just mentioned Foucault uses the idea of discipline, in *Society Must be Defended* he uses the additional structure of biopolitics, often in conjunction with biopower, which in contrast to discipline "exists at a different level, on a different scale, and [. . .] has a different bearing area" (Foucault 2003, 242). Discipline addresses bodies, whereas biopolitics applies "to the living man, to man-as-living-being; ultimately, if you like, to man-as-species" (Foucault 2003, 242). While discipline uses the techniques of surveillance, training, and punishment of individual bodies, biopolitics addresses human beings as "a global mass that is affected by overall processes characteristic of birth, death, production, illness, and so on" (Foucault 2003, 242–3). This shift is then from "individualizing" to "massifying," from "man-as-body" to "man-as-species" (Foucault 2003, 242–3). More concretely, this means to gain knowledge and control of life as "processes such as the ratio of births to deaths, the rate of reproduction, the fertility of a population, and so on" (Foucault 2003, 242–3). Biopolitics is a "technology of power" that emerged in "the second half of the eighteenth century" (Foucault 2003, 242) that seeks to understand population, with the ultimate goal to control it.

Discipline and biopolitics lie very close together and intersect. The differences might at times seem subtle. Discipline focuses on training individuals in order to normalize behavior. The ultimate purpose is not to normalize but to create "efficient and productive workers" (Foucault 2003, 242–3). Biopolitics creates structures that direct the population at large. It manages population. The purpose is close to the purpose of discipline: "to ensure a healthy workforce" (Foucault 2003, 242–3). Biopolitics is no longer discipline, since it becomes a structure that allows the state to govern less; the population starts to govern itself. Foucault describes the panopticon in his book on discipline, where he is already moving in the direction of biopolitics. It is, namely, a structure that controls the whole population. Biopolitics thus finds its roots in discipline, but becomes a self-governing principle. Yet, it remains a principle that requires training in order to be established, and surveillance itself remains a principle of discipline. Biopolitics, on the other hand, consists in the structures that are so engrained in our society that no one can escape them as we live within, for example, financial institutions. These structures tie us to particular places. Quite literally it provides a home since most of us who own a home are paying mortgages. Our debts tie us even more to the need to work. We cannot afford to lose our job. Biopolitics at that point is biopower, a self-regulating force that creates and maintains what the state needs: a healthy workforce that does not simply want to work but needs work.

One of the main factors that Foucault identifies as the instigator for the emergence of biopolitics is the attempt to control illnesses, which "sapped the population's strength, shortened the working week, wasted energy, and cost money, both because they led to a fall in production and because treating them was expensive" (Foucault 2003, 244). Biopolitics, for that reason, prioritizes public hygiene in an attempt to diminish the amount and spread of illnesses. While these intentions arguably have a positive effect on both society as well as individuals, Foucault seeks to point out the far-reaching consequences of such a politics that attempts to control the human species in its entirety. We can call these unintended consequences. Some of these include

> control over relations between the human race, or human being as they are a species, insofar as they are living beings, and their environment, the milieu in which they live. [. . .] This includes the direct effects of the geographical, climatic, or hydrographic environment.
>
> (Foucault 2003, 245)

I argue that biopolitics, together with discipline, also controls and creates environments in which people can move around.

Displacements: toward a mobile workforce

Foucault's analysis of discipline provides an interesting explanation for why people were enticed to move to cities, to take part in the process of production, to become part of a machine. It was not a free choice, Foucault argues. Vagabonds, nomadism, and undisciplined behavior were systematically rooted out. Those who did not contribute to the capitalist machine were trained in order to fit this new reality.

We thus find an opposition between the state that seeks productive bodies and what Deleuze calls nomadology. *Nomad* in the original Greek meaning is first of all "the allocation of pasture to the tribe" (Braidotti 2011, 62); it is also translated as "to roam about for pasture" (Liddell and Scott 1940). Such roaming for pastures involves a herdsman (*nomeus*) and animals. They were not necessarily dedicated to one place in terms of a geographical location; however, their roaming took place within a certain range and involved points that they would return to every year. Spots that provided good shelter and pasture were on their radar. Even while gatherers and hunters were roaming about for something other than pastures, their nomadism also followed similar patterns. All animals, including the human, do move from point to point, never without aim. In fact, virtually all nomadic cultures return to the same places again and again. Nomadism is, thus, not a free and open roaming for pasture, wherever it can be found. In roaming around, stability can be found. It is only in rare circumstances that nomadic cultures (or animals) change their patterns of migration.

However, even if a nomadic existence follows certain patterns, this does not contribute to the kind of discipline required to run a factory. The period that Foucault describes in terms of discipline coincides with the start of the Industrial Revolution. This was a time in Europe in which people either moved away from the rural places where they had lived for generations, or were forced out of their nomadic existence. It is certainly true that movements of population occurred throughout history in terms of crisis or adventure, and mostly on a small scale (after all, consider the way *Homo sapiens* spread around the world through migrating). Yet, when in Europe the population started to expand, more and more agricultural land was needed. This resulted in more people moving, as well as in deforestation.

While these initial changes were gradual, the Industrial Revolution created entirely new forms of existence, re-determining what it means to be human. It generated extremely different places, since industrialization forced people to conglomerate. Cities had existed for millennia, but up to this point cities had been determined as political centers. Although manual labor had always happened in cities, they did not exist by virtue of it. With the industrialization of the Western world, cities came into existence that were identified by and built around industry.

Three significant consequences in relationship to place occurred at this time. First, as Foucault describes, the vagabonds and nomads became illegal, and were forced and trained to settle down. Second, people were displaced on a massive scale, and lost their connection to places where they had grown up, worked, and lived. Furthermore, they were displaced from places where their families had lived for generations. They knew these places well through practices as well as through stories (which often informed their practices). This knowledge contributed to a sustainable way of living. It provided insights in growing food and maintaining the land – insights that had been developed over hundreds, or even thousands, of years of farming and caring for the land. All this knowledge disappeared.[6] Third, human beings lost their connection with natural places. While today's European and American cities make a true effort to include green spaces, this was far from a priority at the height of the Industrial Revolution.[7]

Thus, we find at this moment in history a (forced) detachment from the natural world, as people used to experience it either in a nomadic or in a sedentary manner, as well as the loss of a sense of place. Identities of families and communities were seriously disrupted. Living according to natural cycles was replaced with a strict regime determined by mechanical cycles. While I am on the verge of romanticizing the pre-industrial era, it should be mentioned that a rather quiet world of farming and outdoor labor was replaced with a violently loud world that took place indoors.

Besides displacements of people within Europe, the Europeans also settled the New World, which started another history of displacement, from Europe and eventually other parts of the world, as well as within what is now the USA. With a few exceptions the inhabitants of the USA have all been displaced over the last centuries: Native Americans were either killed or lost their land; immigrants came initially from Europe and later from all other continents; indentured servitude was in place as early as 1620; slaves were brought from Africa; fortune seekers flocked to California in 1849; Jews fled Europe during the Holocaust, followed by political refugees from all over the world. The history of the New World is an ongoing trend of displacements.

These displacements were partly voluntary, partly involuntary; sometimes the difference between voluntary and involuntary is hard to tell. Some of the movements certainly involved discipline as discussed by Foucault, in the sense that people were behaving according to patterns of discipline or forced into such patterns. It became a norm that moving toward opportunity is positive and that it is abnormal to not participate in this movement.

Such a norm is also an excluding norm in the sense that the opposite of the ability to move constitutes an abnormality. In fact, exclusion of the norm or standard occurs in having no ability to move. We can find this exclusion, first, in the fact that the borders of the USA are closed today. For centuries people had been forced to the USA through different techniques. Yet at the end of the nineteenth century the country started to impose limitations, excluding many from the land of freedom and opportunity. Furthermore, within the USA, it is predominantly white people who can move to and feel welcome in any city or town. The lack of availability of loans for both cars and houses, realtors keeping people of color out of certain areas, and people of color not feeling welcomed and thus not even wanting to live in certain areas, all create a disadvantage of mobility for people of color (Cole and Foster 2001). When poor areas, mostly inhabited by minorities, are targeted by waste facilities (such as incinerators), industry, harbors, and other polluting facilities, housing prices drop as a result and people become truly stuck. City and county boards, with little representation of people of color, make these decisions for so-called Locally Undesired Land Use (LULU). Strategies to pass these decisions and to exclude these communities from the decision-making process include providing little to no information to the communities concerning the issue and holding meetings in places that are difficult to access for these communities. In a particularly upsetting instance in 1984, the California Waste Board paid a consulting firm to define communities that will provide the least resistance to the siting of LULUs. The resulting "Cerrell Report" suggests avoiding housewives and going for people in rural communities without college degrees, with a low income, and who are open to a promise of economic benefits (Cole and Foster 2001, 71ff.). While the report is, arguably, not necessarily racist, it does suggest targeting lower-class communities that tend to be populated predominantly by people of color. In California this translates in particular to small rural Latin American communities, who indeed repeatedly have been victim to the siting of LULUs. One of the better-known examples of a town that fits all the criteria of the Cerrell report is Kettleman City, CA, a small (1,500 residents), low-income, and mostly Latino community in the San Joaquin Valley. A hazardous waste facility was built in the area and while state agencies are unable to link the facility to any health issues, since the time the waste facility moved to the area a cluster of infant deaths and birth defects has occurred in the community (*Mother Jones* 2010; Cole and Foster 2001). A governmental report concluded: "No specific environmental exposure was identified as a likely cause of the increase in birth defects" (California Department of Public Health 2010, 36). The grouping of birth defects was not linked to the waste facility and, according to the lack of scientific findings, apparently just happened by chance. While any person with the means to move away from this area has done so, the people who are left are poor and have no other option – a true lack of mobility. It is, perhaps, the ultimate consequence of a society that is constantly mobile, both in terms of class and in terms of place. Not everyone can participate in this mobility and those left behind become victims tied to places that make them sick and kill them.

The people left behind are often tied to the place where they live because they cannot afford to live in a healthy area. They are also tied to the place because of their jobs. This is another way in which many people of color have been left behind; the car and public transportation created a new way of living that separated workplace from living place. It could be argued that public transportation is available to everyone and thus would create the possibility of mobility for everyone. Yet, public transportation is another instrument we can grasp in terms of biopolitics. It controls the movement of the different parts of the population. White middle-class areas will typically have commuter buses available that take them to financial districts. Silicon Valley is famous for its "Google Buses," which take employees directly to their job, leaving behind everyone else. Such a divide in accessible transportation could be explained in terms of demand. However, it does not only keep the status quo in place, it also solidifies the class differences, controlling the divisions in population in terms of class and race. Those who work together, commute together, and live in the same communities.

While some are solidified in their place because there is nowhere else to go, the story of forced migration, or displacements, keeps repeating itself. People are forced out of a place when others are attracted to this place, such as today's "Silicon Valley." In the latter example we find two migration patterns: those who seek fortune in the industry and those who are driven out by new wealth arriving and growing on a large scale. Housing prices in most of the San Francisco Bay Area were, first of all, barely hit by the 2008 financial crisis, and are today at an unprecedented height. Areas that were formerly defined by violence and poverty are experiencing rapid gentrification. Poverty, however, does not disappear. With the influx of money, poverty is merely moved elsewhere. Likewise, many people who consider themselves native San Franciscans cannot afford to live in their city any longer, or the next generation is unable to buy a house (cf. Tracy 2014). Similar trends can be found in Napa, where property prices have been driven up because of the wine industry and the tourism associated with it (Gmelch and Gmelch 2011). While the double meaning of the Greek word *Krisis* seems to indicate that a crisis brings opportunity, it can also mean (as becomes clear in Napa and the Silicon Valley) that opportunity brings crisis.

Within Foucault's analysis of discipline this lack of mobility constitutes an abnormality, which excludes certain people from the trend that determines our own being in the world. The message we receive is that it is normal and good to be mobile. It is abnormal to not move. By locking certain groups either out, or within a place, they by definition are not part of our world.

Some have attributed the radical economic change of industry to the invention of the steam engine in 1712 (McKibben 2007). The Industrial Revolution could not have occurred without this machine. However, not everything can be explained simply by the invention of a machine. The bigger question in this regard is why people were willing to cooperate in this system that produced machines that had replaced them in agriculture, and how people were even able to live in a setting with a completely different sense of place.

Starting with the latter, the Industrial Revolution and its consequences created a new sense of place. Instead of historically, culturally or socially defined places, we moved to an economic model that creates spaces according to principles of efficiency (which itself became a social norm). We have seen in Foucault's analysis of discipline that people were moved out of their nomadic or vagabond existence and were trained to work in factories. This partly explains why people were willing to work in factories and why labor itself became increasingly mobile, eventually resulting in a workforce ready to move wherever opportunity can be found. Cars and airplanes make mobility possible, but the availability of these machines does not explain the scale of our usage. Heidegger explains technology itself as something that is a standing reserve. The airplane is not simply something that we can use, but something that we should use. Likewise, nothing keeps us tied to our places: we do not only have the possibility to move, but we should move. Foucault's notion of biopolitics, understood as a power that aims to force the movement of population, can be a helpful way to explain these phenomena: where people move and who moves become controllable factors. The aim here is not the individual, but the group.

In order to understand the kind of power at work in today's senses of place, let us consider where we work in opposition to where we live. Today, it's hard to imagine that in the past people either lived at work or in close proximity, in walking distance, from their job. Up to the Industrial Revolution, and even during the first part of it, living and working had always been tied together. Farmers housed their laborers, and factory workers initially lived on the factory grounds. People had to live within walking distance of their job and in most cases this meant that people lived at the site of their job. Work was, therefore, not just one aspect of one's life: it determined all other aspects, including family and leisure time. Economically and socially, work was completely integrated. In essence, one's whole life was determined by one's job. The two could not be separated. How did the separation of one's job and the rest of one's life come into existence in the first place? The American construction of places and how it has created a healthy – i.e., reliable and mobile – workforce can be explained in terms of discipline and biopolitics. I trace this history, in order to better understand how the dynamics of class, place, and mobility intersect.

Today, we tend to not work where we live, and actually crave some spatial separation between our profession and the rest of our lives. This separation seems very natural now, but it only became a real possibility when transportation developed in the second half of the nineteenth century. The separation of work and the rest of who we are and what we do (and how this separation is experienced as natural) can be called the ultimate consequence of the Industrial Revolution. If we take Marx's word for it, this revolution, and the capitalist machine that drives it, has created human beings who hate to do what they naturally are inclined to do: to produce (Marx and Engels 1972; Marx 1955, 1994). For Marx this is one of the essential forms in which alienation expresses itself. The problems are well-known: the factory workers (or today's office workers) who are doing the same activity over and over again, fail to recognize their selves in the product, and often do not even recognize the product. The whole activity of production does not seem to contribute in any way to an affirmation of the producer or consumer. While for Adam Smith the circumstances of capitalism spurred creativity and inventions for workers (precisely because they were focusing on just one activity), for Marx the opposite is true. As Charlie Chaplin so masterfully depicts in *Modern Times*, the worker has become a cog in a machine. The human is the squeaky part, the part that causes the problems. The human also turns out to be the part that can be replaced most easily. A broken part in the machine shuts down the process of production; a sick employee is quickly replaced. And while the machine becomes more valuable as it produces more, the opposite is true for the human being. Ironically, as the human works harder and produces more, she makes herself less valuable. The human being is also the part of the production process that feels miserable. It has turned into "the most miserable commodity" (Marx 1994, 58). It might seem that this is the opposite of what Foucault describes as the goals of biopolitics, consisting of creating a healthy workforce. Yet, the only solution to the misery experienced as a worker is to find a better job, or to find work in the first place. The workforce is healthy precisely in its misery insofar as the goals of capitalism are concerned: to produce as much as possible as cheaply as possible. Happiness is not its goal, since content human beings will become inefficient or lazy.

While today in the USA few people work in factories and very few people produce tangible products, alienation seems to not have subsided. Perhaps it is our inability to recognize what we produce, and thus a failure to constitute an identity as a producer of x, which makes us hate our jobs, and collectively exclaim, "Thank God it's Friday!" Jobs are an inconvenient thing we just have to do in order to make a living.[8] We would not want to imagine living on the grounds of these jobs that we so despise. Friday, the day to leave this place, would never come.

Considering the way people generally relate to their jobs today and the amount of alienation that exists, it can be argued that the separation between the place where one works and the place where one lives was a very welcome one when the car and public transportation (ironically, produced by alienating labor) took off at the beginning of the twentieth century. The eventual development of suburbs accentuates this need to separate: the further one lives from work, the better. The artificially created threshold (the highway full of others trying to get to a similar destination) is a representation of the separation that in our minds should exist between the two. It should not be easy to move from family to work.

It could be argued that deep down people have always wanted to separate work from the rest of their lives, and that this was only realizable when the car and public transportation developed. It is certainly possible that people never liked to live close to their work and that without a car they never had the ability to change their situation and thus could not but accept this unhappy marriage of work and life. Yet, people seemed to have jumped on this possibility rather enthusiastically, and agree to commute long distances, taking away time from other, more enjoyable, activities. We should recognize that leisure time is a modern invention, certainly for the working class. The creation of a life apart from work is a part of the creation of the middle class: people who make enough money to not only buy a house, but also some other extras and who can, thus, separate themselves physically, in terms of location as well as activities, from their jobs. Part of this new reality can be traced to the circumstances that made workers feel horrible about every aspect of who they were and left them with a lack of identity. The remedy was to separate this horrible part of one's life spatially, and to create an additional part of one's existence entirely separate from one's work.[9]

Another way to understand the development of (1) the separation of work and other parts of one's life, (2) the very idea that there is a life outside of work, and (3) the middle class that came into existence in this new reality is that it was again part of a biopolitical attempt to control population. The biggest threat to the capitalist economy was that workers would rise up against their horrible existence. The solution was to create another part of their lives that kept them busy with more enjoyable activities. Not only did it keep people happy, it also aided in avoiding strikes and other disturbances of production since workers were busy with living their own lives. Labor meetings and planning of strikes took them away from the part of their lives that actually made them feel alive again.

Since this development also created a third class, another aspect of population control emerged: by having a middle class and a poor class, those in the middle class actually had something to lose. In a two-class system, the upper class was under a constant threat by a majority that was unhappy. In a system with three classes the threat of falling into poverty by losing one's job instituted an important incentive for working hard and being mobile in times of crisis. This is again a mechanism of biopolitics: the control of the population in terms of a workforce that wants to work.

Furthermore, when workers lived next to or on the factory grounds they would naturally live with everyone else who worked there. This was certainly a dangerous situation for those trying to maintain power. Strikes in the USA were violent and costly. Several strikes involved police and state militia. Labor reform eventually provided more rights to workers. The changes came slowly since companies fought back vigorously. Yet, in retrospect they could see the many benefits. Through better salaries and working conditions, workers eventually changed from laborers (who could turn violent) into consumers who had something to lose rather than to gain from unrest.

To return to Marx's idea of the worker as the most miserable commodity, we see that leisure time, time spent particularly in a different place than work, changed the happiness of the worker, not at work, but outside of work. On a biopolitical level this separation of work and the rest of life seems to work well: work is not to be enjoyed, but has become necessary in order to enjoy oneself when one is not working. One's wages are not simply paying for basic needs, such as food and shelter, but provide for luxury products. It is these products that one wants and can only have by working hard. Thus, the healthy workforce consisting of workers who consume is a reality. In the following I will discuss some aspects of consumption by specifically addressing the credit system.

Consumption

The question of why people were willing to spend money and take out loans for goods that were considered luxury, or non-essential, takes us to the car. The car was the first luxury good that got people hooked on consuming as well as credit. The thrill of driving a car that could take you anywhere lifted people into a different class. It arguably created the middle class, consisting of those people who could afford a car and thus buy freedom of mobility. The crucial part is that they actually could not afford it. The invention of the assembly line had created a "luxury problem," since it provided the possibility to produce many more cars than the market demanded. Cars were very cheap because of the assembly line, but not cheap enough to reach a wide market. Thus, we again find strategies at the biopolitical level – strategies that changed the buying power of a particular part of the population. Instead of reducing the number of cars, the market was changed. Most people did not have enough cash to buy a car. General Motors offered the possibility to buy a car with a down payment if consumers provided proof of a steady income, so they could make a monthly payment. This system of financing a car became available as early as 1919. A car quickly became essential to the newly adopted lifestyle that came with the freedom of mobility, but the car and the lifestyle were a luxury nonetheless. As such it provided, arguably, a stepping stone to taking out loans on other luxury items. Advertisements certainly helped, but something had already changed in consumers' mindsets for them to buy into this new reality.

For the (white) population things kept changing, despite the crisis and the war.[10] Even while World War II stopped the production of the car temporarily, mass production of consumer goods quickly became the country's new paradigm. Consciously, or subconsciously, people recognized that one could transform the world, or at least how one experiences it, by buying a mass-produced good, a product that is affordable, well made, and a true convenience.

This recognition was further used after World War II in rebuilding and strengthening the economy. While Europe was recovering and rebuilding following this war, the USA had to rebuild in its own way. The end of the war meant the end of the production of weapons and war machinery. To fill the gap in production and the subsequent loss of jobs, an answer was sought and found in consumer goods. The workforce and capital were present, but the question remains how a market was created and how people could afford it. With the car the answer of interest is fairly straightforward and widely discussed: cars could take you places. People preferred cars above more basic needs such as decent plumbing. None of the other consumer goods had such a transformative force. In fact, most goods seemed to have the opposite effect: items such as the radio and television (and later the computer) connected one to the world from one's home. Initially only a few families owned these new media, and listening and watching were communal events, but over time it tied one more to one's home and disconnected one from the community. Being connected to the world came with a loss of contact with one's neighbor. These technologies did not take you places; they rather recreated the home as the center, with the world streaming into it.

The credit system was a true stroke of genius. It created markets that were necessary to keep the economy growing.[11] It also created people who were in debt, and, thus, inherently tied to the economy. They needed to keep working in order to pay back loans, and they were rewarded by being able to take out larger loans, often in order to pay back other loans. At this point people are no longer merely workers who might get into a conflict with their employer. Their work is tied to a network of financial relationships.[12] This was initially a case not so much of biopolitics, but certainly of discipline at work: problems such as strikes are avoided. Losing one's job is no longer an inconvenience, but a threat to one's financial well-being and with that to one's happiness. Not being able to buy the products that one wants is a failure in life.

Today's credit scores do more than discipline people. Credit is a biopolitical mechanism insofar as it affects all aspects of our lives: credit scores determine if and what kind of loan one can be offered, and thus it controls one's buying power and with that one's class. Credit has created a new reality that values people in terms of how many loans they have taken out and paid back. To be a good citizen means to be a good, reliable consumer. It creates a place for us in the economy. Marx already speculated that the credit system turns us into money. Today an important part of one's economic status is the credit score. Interestingly, one can only score well by taking out loans in the first place; one has to prove that one is able to pay back a loan. Thus, in order to buy a house with a reasonable mortgage rate, one already needs a history of loans. This means, in essence, that one can only be counted as good – an honest and trustworthy person – if one has purchased consumer goods that one could not afford without a loan. In an extreme turn of events, even some contemporary dating websites ask for credit scores, since the revelation of a low credit score can, apparently, be a real turndown on a first date. It affirms Marx, who told us that marriage under capitalism has turned into a form of prostitution.[13] One site even states: "Good credit is sexy."[14] To be a good and attractive human being, one thus needs to consume and do so in the right way. Let us not forget that this is a type of placement (as well as dis-placement), namely the determination of one's place in society in terms of class. For class can be regarded as a place, as well. It places one in a hierarchy and makes a judgment not only about one's financial health, but also about one's ethical status. This place or placement and our good credit score can be lost if we lose our job.

One's place in society is certainly obvious in many other visible ways, such as fashion, the gadgets one caries around, the kind of car one drives, and so forth. Shopping itself is not experienced as a torturous experience; it is part of our holiday schedule, in which the rituals of eating together with family and friends are complemented with trips to the mall and the exchange of consumer goods. Scores of consumers walk through malls and downtown shopping areas advertising the places where they bought their stuff on the bags they carry around. The department store name that appears on one's bag affirms one's place in society.

What kind of effect did consumerism have on the USA as a place and the American experience of place? Within the new reality of consumption, Americans finally, truly united: they quickly turned from a hotchpotch of different backgrounds with different histories and ideologies into a society of consumers. Consuming, the freedom to buy, became the new ideology. With this new reality America as a place was redefined. The car made people more mobile and thus made people experience different places. On the other hand, the building of roads and the movement of people also made these different places more and more the same. Companies started franchises slowly in the 1950s – a development that took off in the 1960s and 1970s, developing a unity of stores and restaurants across the country.

Consuming itself has developed into a ritual, and it is this ritual that unites the country in terms of their behavior. The Jew in New York City, the Muslim in Los Angeles, and the Christian in Alabama all go shopping on Black Friday in stores that have the same name and offer the same items for the same price. While different Americans might practice different religions and vehemently disagree about how to interpret basic rights and values, all, except for a few cynics, recognize the value and goodness of consuming. In terms of this value and ritual there is no essential difference between the plains, the Midwest, the East, the South, and the West. Not being able to participate in this ritual is an embarrassment of sorts. It affirms that one's place in American society is marginal.

The development of this ritual that translates into a short-lived happiness, we have seen, started with turning the automobile into a consumer product that could be bought on credit and, thus, became widely available. That the car has united this country seems unlikely today, since we predominantly see single drivers isolated in their vehicles – monads instead of nomads. As a result, the car has not only united the people living in this country, it has also contributed to an idea of individualism, albeit a false one: the make of a car affirms one's class and status; the commute is an expression of herd behavior, rather than individualism. Furthermore, the fact that one has a car is, for a middle-class American, taken for granted. Not having a car, or sharing a car, even with one's partner, is exceptional (the average number of cars is 2.28 per American household).

Plastic places: settled nomads

We have seen how people have been displaced and how in the twentieth century people have become a flexible workforce. In addition, the car provided mobility and was a first step for Americans to become consumers, i.e., the American identity started to become one of consumers, a middle class that did not fight the upper class, and that did well for itself, as well as for the economy. The unifying ritual of consuming developed because of franchises that spread the same stores and restaurants across the country. The first step happened fairly quickly, although momentarily interrupted by the economic crisis of the 1930s and World War II. The unification of places through commercialization took longer, starting slowly with franchises in the 1960s. It was again the car industry that functioned as an example, in this regard with dealerships, which sold one particular make of car. Although the concept of the dealership is somewhat different than a box-store (dealers just sell one brand of one expensive product) the idea of brand recognition and a commercial enterprise that sells the same product with the same financing options across the nation is similar in principle. The results were identical "universal" or "uniform" places across the USA – places that were experienced in the same way.

Interestingly, around the same time that commercial enterprises started to turn public spaces into uniform places across the country, people again started to move. In the second half of the twentieth century people became extremely mobile, often packing up and moving with the family across the country. As people started to move more and more, they encountered more of the same places. A few centuries ago Omaha, Nebraska must have looked very different from Sacramento, California. Today, both will provide the same restaurants and box-stores as well as a capitol building. In the downtown area one will find either the same or very similar financial institutions, in buildings that are modern architectural expressions of a fortress. The American place has become uniform through commerce and our spiritual connection is one that involves money, or preferably credit cards.

It could be argued that the homogenization of American places comes from a need for identity across a country that consists of people who have been and are continually on the move. I have argued that people are in need of a place with which they can identify. Cultures, even the most nomadic ones, have always been tied to particular places. The American population consists of displaced people who constantly move around. Commercial and public spaces that look alike and that are experienced in the same way across the country provide a sense of security, belonging, and identity. These places make it possible to move without moving. It seems almost as if one is not moving at all, and we have become what I call "settled nomads."

This nomadism is the opposite of the homelessness that I have argued for through Nietzsche and Heidegger, who argue for an existential wandering in which we attempt to find ourselves or become who we are. The settled nomadism is much closer to their respective notion of "the herd" or "the they," inauthentic modes of existence in which one acts in conformity with the norms of society, without thinking for oneself. As settled nomads people are flexible to move wherever work can be found. They find a sense of home anywhere, and are defined through the places that are the same everywhere. While this is, arguably, an inauthentic being-in-the-world, it provides for a perfectly flexible workforce. In terms of Foucault's biopolitics it means that the population is controllable by virtue of where they are. People will move anywhere they are needed and move away from those places where they are not needed. Politics can care less about creating jobs at particular places, since people will move wherever they can find work.

The trend of changing places and the development of these settled nomads started much earlier. Many of the first immigrants recreated a place that resembled home, sometimes using the name of their home country or even the town where they used to live. When people move around today the job of changing the place to conform to known norms has already been done by corporate America. Every place in the USA feels like home. It is an ideal model for the capitalist system that requires loyal consumers who could be tracked down in order to pay their debt (and their taxes), but that also needs flexibility in terms of the location of workers. When the demand rises in one area, workers will flux toward it. For Adam Smith this is the "natural" way in which capitalism regulates the market. Smith and most proponents of capitalism argue that this system functions best when left to itself (Smith 1976, 456). Perhaps it is the system itself that then created identical places that make it easy for certain people to be on the move without feeling displaced. As already suggested, the creation of these identical places can also be seen as a biopolitical device that was a welcome development. Since no single individual or group of people is solely responsible for these developments, we could see it as a development of the market itself, driven by self-interest. However, at many points people intervened in this system, manipulated and encouraged it to develop in certain directions. The system itself did not invent credit, franchises, or cars. Security is provided through a network of banks, insurance companies, pharmacies, grocery stores, hardware stores, and department stores that provide loyalty rewards cards and credit cards that contribute to one's credit score. Furthermore, a social security number (understood by many as equal to one's identity) is necessary in order to work legally. It tells whether one has a place in a society or not, and even if one has a place, one can still be an "alien." Furthermore, a social security number is a great tool to keep track of a person's financial history. It is also used to determine whether one can be issued a loan, or whether one has paid sufficient taxes, etc. In many ways, the social security number does constitute one's identity – it places one in a network of relationships that determine the individual. As Foucault argues, we are no longer subjects (as autonomous beings), but we have become objects of knowledge (Foucault 1973, 1977). Where our health, our grades and behavior in school, our criminal behavior, or our financial responsibility are concerned, we are constantly being tracked, charted, objectified, and known. In a large country such as the USA, one is traceable, partly because of our social security number and recordkeeping. Such recordkeeping only functions because the same institutions and corporations exist across the country, which share information with one another in order to generate knowledge of us.

What we have learned from Heidegger in Chapter 2 is that in looking for something new we are escaping or fleeing away from ourselves. When we buy something new or move somewhere else we seek a new identity in what we are not, the place, the things we own, and so forth. In the analysis of the universal plastic places we find that people are following a similar pattern: even when they move, they will not be confronted with their own being, or face some other existential crisis. Since every place is the same we will feel fine.

Yet, we also have to question this feeling at home everywhere in which everything mostly *seems* fine. In his book *Risk Society*, Ulrich Beck provides some valuable insights into the individualization and lack of stability in today's society. While our place in society, environments, and family relationships used to be stable, today we are facing a different reality. We are living in uncertainty. With high divorce rates, the family has lost its status as being a stable and reliable factor in one's life. Likewise, jobs for life have become very rare. People lose their jobs, or find better jobs, constantly. In fact, in many fields staying too long with the same company might hurt one's career. Moreover, in order to create a career one no longer just obtains a degree and finds a job. One needs, Beck argues, to individualize oneself by creating a biography (Beck 1992, 92). A BA in Philosophy is just a small part of a biography. It needs to be supplemented with internships, extracurricular activities, a study abroad, a minor, if not a second major, a research project, a second degree, evidence of certain skills, and so forth. Interestingly, "individualization" by biography creation is, first of all, not a voluntary choice, but rather demanded by the job market of individuals. Second, the process of individualization becomes a mass movement: everyone takes part in this. The consequence is that those who fail to create an interesting and compelling biography fail to find a job.

This idea of "the risk society" provides a way to conceive of our place in society and how the powers of this society are constantly putting us in risky situations. We have to worry about career opportunities, family, and our environment. Particularly for working women, the balancing act of family and work presents a tremendous challenge: society demands they do both well. Lastly, the American educational system creates workers who have been well trained to participate in the capitalist process. This training comes with a high price tag for graduating students, who start their careers in a risky situation, with a loan that often takes many more than the proposed ten years to pay back. Such a force can also be understood within Foucault's biopolitics; the student loan seemingly constructs the possibility for every person to get a college degree, while in reality it is creating a healthy workforce, that is well-educated and willing, even desperate, to work since they need to pay back the price paid for this education. It is a system that creates a self-governing population.

Heterotopias

We have seen that the history of the USA is characterized by displacements, from natives to slaves, from the jobless and the poor to the adventurous. Have we, inhabitants of this vast country, been able to maintain some sense of place? Is the USA equivalent to artifacts like the Statue of Liberty, the skyscraper, Mount Rushmore, the Hoover Dam, and the Golden Gate Bridge? Do we identify, rather, with more natural places such as Niagara Falls and the Grand Canyon? Or, do commercial spaces conglomerated in strip malls define our sense of place? After all, natural (or historic) and artificial sites are mostly only visited, not inhabited. In fact, it seems that such places are, indeed, sites rather than places: one visits them temporarily, passing through as visitors, rather than inhabiting these as actual places. Laws prohibit permanent residence in national or state parks, or historical sites. The same could perhaps be said of commercial places such as a Walgreens, a Starbucks, and a Home Depot. Regardless, visiting a store is very different in nature from visiting a natural phenomenon. While it might be a stretch to call a store our home, we do in a sense inhabit these places by visiting them so frequently. While we marvel during a visit to Old Faithful in Yellowstone, we will find few (if any) surprises at the local Walmart in nearby Bozeman, Montana, even if it is our first time in that particular store. In fact, even the layout of the area in which we find this store will be familiar. We know these commercial places as a part of, or an extension of our home. While a natural park, a museum, or some landmark is a temporary site that we pass through, the drugstore is a place where transactions occur that are integral to our domestic lives.

We can understand our experiences of American places, both the iconic places and the commercial places, through Foucault's notion of the "heterotopia," a place that is a non-place as discussed in his essay "Of other spaces" (Dehaene and De Cauter 2008). The earlier examples of the prison and the mental institution are such non-places; places that, simultaneously, do and do not exist; places that are outside social norms. We find that insanity does not exist in our society, not because there is no insanity, but because we displace it outside of society. In order to explain the heterotopia, Foucault refers, among other things, to the loss of virginity that traditionally takes place in a non-place: a honeymoon hotel. Today this might be an outdated practice, but the first experience of sexuality for the American teenager still usually does not take place, by taking place outside of the home (unless the parents are gone, who can then assume it did not take place). In places that lack reality and fall outside the realm of known places such as the university campus (where genders are divided in the dorms, in order to suggest sexual acts are not possible), or the car. Cars themselves are heterotopias, not in the sense that they are outside of social norms, but because they are places that are always somewhere else. The car also placed the worker in the category of consumer. The twentieth century started with the mass production of cars, and the building of roads. By 1927, 15 million Ford Model T cars had been produced and 23 million cars were owned across the nation. Interestingly, over 50 percent of those cars were located in rural areas. While transportation also radically changed life in the city, the effects the car had on rural living were truly transforming. People who lived miles away from their neighbors, far away from cities and villages, were suddenly taken out of their isolated existence. The car immediately connected them to local communities. Thus, while people at this point still lived in rural areas, the very essence of rural life changed with the introduction of the car. The gap dividing rural and urban life grew significantly smaller.

Since the car bridged the gap between urban and rural lives it was immediately something more than a means of transportation, and arguably a heterotopia, since it connected places that had been so radically different. Today, a car is a place where people spend a significant amount of their day, not only driving, but drinking their coffee, eating their meals, listening to the news, applying make-up and shaving. The car is a place, or site, without one location. It is an extension of the home, or ties work and home, a place that does not really exist. Similar to Foucault's honeymoon hotel, it is the ideal non-place for the first sexual encounter of the American teenager. Something that is not supposed to happen happens in this heterotopia and can as such be denied or ignored.

Heterotopias are prominent in our modern world that is largely constituted by digital media. For example, new media, such as social media, have created a new reality, a place that does not really exist. This new reality consists, for example, in shallow, brief messages, which create the world for many. In that sense technology claims the opposite of what a heterotopia is: it is not a place that does not exist in one's perception. In fact it creates places by playing on people's perceptions and, *de facto*, it creates the world. With that creation it excludes everything else from this world. To state it in a simplified form, if events are not tweeted they do not exist. Such media thus create a place or space in which certain events and things are included and others excluded. Along these lines, one can spend hours on the Internet, a place or non-place that one can take everywhere and that takes one everywhere, while not physically going anywhere. We have seen in Heidegger's analysis of technology that we tend to view technological devices as neutral tools. In reality, Heidegger argues, technology enframes the world (Heidegger 1977b). A place, as we have seen in his analysis, can turn from a landscape into a coal-mining district, in which we see a place only in terms of its potential for energy. Technology, furthermore, changes our very sense of place. Walking around with our eyes (and mind) glued to a screen certainly alters our experience of the places that we occupy.

Historically, Foucault distinguishes three notions of place. First, the medieval notion of space as one of localization of things and people.[15] In both the ancient and medieval conception of place, things can be out of their place, but not without violence. Second, with Galileo place becomes extension: "The place of a thing was nothing but a point in its movement, just as the rest of a thing was only its movement indefinitely slowed down" (Dehaene and De Cauter 2008, 15). Third, today, Foucault claims, places are determined as emplacement (*l'emplacements*), i.e., as places determined through relationships to other places, as "relation of proximity between points or elements" (Dehaene and De Cauter 2008, 16). He provides the technological example of the storage of data and the more concrete example of demography. Populations are related to the storage and transportation of materials, food, water, and energy. Thus, place "is given to us in the form of relations between emplacements" (Dehaene and De Cauter 2008, 16).

This idea of place takes us beyond Heidegger's notion of place as enframed and a standing reserve, although it does not exclude these notions. Relations between places, or sites, are determined with the idea that nature provides us with resources. Heidegger's coal-mining district is, thus, determined as such a resource. Yet, today it is not a district around the corner but in distant places, such as the Third World. Ever since the Europeans started to colonize, places all over the world have been used as resources and a network of relationships has been in place since that time, further advanced by economies of scale that make transportation (one of the relationships that turns places into sites) more efficient.

It is important to note that Foucault's notion of "heterotopia" is not specific to our time. We find them in "primitive societies" as sacred or forbidden places. He identifies today's heterotopias as places of deviation, for those who do not fit the norms, such as criminals (the prison) or those with severe mental issues (the psychiatric hospital). Foucault's panopticon – the internalization of observation and the subsequent normalization – has been called (and I believe rightly) a heterotopia (cf. Dumm 1996, 106). Foucault emphasizes the internalization of the observation, which amounts to the true effectiveness of the panopticon; it does not matter whether or not one is actually observed, one observes oneself as if one is observed. Thus, the watchtower of Bentham's model does not actually have to exist in order to exercise its power. It is a place that exists in our mind even if it does not actually exist. It can only function in this ambivalent existence.

To return to the current American place, while it might be tempting to draw this conclusion the stores and other commercial spaces are not our heterotopias. Rather, I suggest that the places that iconically represent the USA are quite close to what Foucault determines as heterotopias. The Golden Gate Bridge is one of the most photographed spots in the world. Yet, it is a non-place. Just like the Eiffel Tower, it represents human ingenuity, the capacity of a nation to do great and beautiful things. It is a site full of meaning, symbolism, and beauty – in short, a representation of a place rather than a real place. It is also a site of tragedy with a high rate of suicides, representing the darker places that this icon represents. In another tragic way, the World Trade Center as a symbol of the strength of the US economy created the perfect target for a terrorist attack. The 9/11 events turned the site into "ground zero," a place that in its very name ceased to be a place.

In terms of natural locations, we find the same kind of iconic and symbolic element. Everyone visits the Grand Canyon, and marvels at it, but not merely as a place. The Grand Canyon represents "America the beautiful," its greatness not only in terms of breathtaking sceneries, but also by virtue of the vastness of the land and the possibilities this vastness presents. The Grand Canyon is, in Foucault's terms, a site in relation to other sites or places. It is known from posters and films, it represents the geological history of this country, the beauty that was once all around, and the greatness of the country.

While I might be stretching Foucault's definition of the heterotopia to some degree, as already mentioned, he does identify heterotopias in sacred and forbidden places. Sites such as the Grand Canyon or Yosemite do have a certain element of being sacred. They are protected from commercialization and permanent human presence and, as such, have a forbidden aspect. Landmarks like these are treated as things that need to be protected. Likewise the Statue of Liberty is heavily secured. The Golden Gate Bridge is not accessible for pedestrians after sunset (bicyclists have to pass a gate that opens only for bicyclists, adding to the sacred character of the site). After sunset, one can only be on the Golden Gate Bridge if one is on the move.

The difficulty of accessing these iconic sites, the parts that are off-limits, and the many activities that are forbidden, each contribute to their symbolic value. This works, presumably, in a similar way to how ancient sacred places created a deity or divine meaning. In fact, inventing the notion of sacredness lies in the forbidden aspect.[16]

Our access to the most majestic places in the country is, therefore, limited. The experience of these places is perhaps sublime, but the sublimity does not merely lie in the experience of the site, but also in what is not experienced: the restricted access and temporary character of the visit creates a symbolic sense of greatness. The reverse is true for commercial places. During the hours that most people are awake one has unlimited access to anything from cereals and bananas to electric sanders and paint. Some stores are open around the clock. This juxtaposes the sacred or forbidden heterotopia. The store and the possibility to consume are always available – even in the middle of the night. Through this accessibility, these commercial places have truly become an extension of our homes. These commercial places are today real places in which we dwell, in which we find a home. They provide security, anywhere, since they can be found everywhere. While we might be tempted to think that these commercial places are heterotopias, they are in, in fact, constituting the most prominent experience of place and with that they define our sense of place. Icons such as Half Dome in Yosemite constitute the other place, while the commercial spaces are the same. No matter how far we travel in the USA, the box store will always provide comfort and identity. This place is who we are and we are this place. We, thus, do not identify with the iconic and sacred heterotopias, but rather with the commercialized public places, places where the public in fact has been privatized. The iconic heterotopias might provide a perfect background for a film, or a family vacation picture, and as such they represent the greatness of this country, but only by not presenting. For these are sites that can only temporarily be visited and do not provide a daily experience of place as does the freeway, the office, or the grocery store.

Nomadology: Deleuze and Guattari

Plastic places and settled nomads indicate the opposite of what Heidegger and Nietzsche describe as an existential homelessness. While the latter experience makes one uncomfortable, the settled nomad can feel comfort everywhere. Within Foucault's analysis I have framed this in terms of capitalism in which we find the mechanism of discipline and biopolitics creating a workforce that is willing to move wherever they are needed. The opposition to this capitalist and state mechanism, which ties people to particular places (even while those places can be anywhere), can be understood in terms of Deleuze's idea of the nomad, nomadology, or nomad thought. This is the resistance to settling or to sedentary thinking that ties people down. I contrast our contemporary nomadism – which I coined "settled nomadism" – with the one described by Deleuze and Guattari. This last part will tie this chapter back to the earlier chapters of the book.

Deleuze himself is a nomadic thinker, highly influenced by Nietzsche.[17] His later thinking, partly in collaboration with Guattari, is especially nomadic by calling for a different way of thinking, of being a philosopher. This call is partly political, partly ethical, and partly ontological.

The idea of the nomad or nomadology is a recurring theme in Deleuze's thinking and yet little attention has been paid to it. This is surprising considering that the term is closely related to rhizomes and other well-researched Deleuzian concepts. The term "nomad" is used throughout his works, beginning with *Difference and Repetition* and culminating in the twelfth plateau in a *Thousand Plateau's*, entitled "Nomadism: the war machine." What nomadology entails is the questioning of everything (including itself).

The development of nomadology is initiated in *Difference and Repetition* as nomadic distribution. Deleuze finds nomadic distribution in open space: a space without limits. This distribution is "without property, enclosure or measure" (Deleuze 2001, 36). It is opposed to models of distribution that divide and set limits as we find it, among other things, in the agrarian world, or as Deleuze phrases it, in "the agrarian question." What this question is exactly is not explained, but since it opposes the nomadic, it seems fair to assume that Deleuze is considering the need to secure land as property. Agriculture changes the land through one's labor, and by that same token it changes the nomad into a farmer who is now tied to a place as property owner. We find an opposition between a nomad, who is in Deleuze's words "without property enclosure or measure," and a model of distribution defined through limits and divisions. There is a shift from a model in which everything and everyone is moving and changing, to a model in which everything is solidified – a change toward no change.

This model is also tied to the political, and in particular to the origin of the state. Rousseau, in his *Discourse on Inequality*, locates the creation of the social contract exactly at the point in time when landowners felt a need to secure their property, and to transform their wealth into power. This transformation solidifies everything, even making nomadism illegal. We have already seen that Foucault, in *Discipline and Punish*, analyzes the distribution of space in this new model, in which vagabonds and other nomads were trained, disciplined, and punished in order to become members of an apparatus that found its goal in producing rather than roaming. By, among other things, producing wage-earning workers the "aim is to derive the maximum advantages and to neutralize the inconveniences (thefts, interruptions of work, disturbances and 'cabals')" (Foucault 1977, 142).

The distribution model that Deleuze identifies as nomadic is not a model of the past; it is supposed to be the future model. It is not necessarily nomadic in the sense that one would roam around from one place to the next, or more radically in an open space without limitations and demarcations. Rather, for Deleuze nomadology is philosophical in nature, i.e., one should be able to think without borders, without limitations. Nomadism frees our thought, not simply in the sense that we can think whatever we want, but more so in that we can think in whatever way we want. Thinking itself might very well become something else. This is the opposite of the settled nomadism discussed in the previous section: the settled nomad moves around constantly without ever experiencing anything new. His thinking has been solidified; his thoughts have already been thought, constructed by the capitalist structures of consumption and work.

One of the few scholars who have analyzed and used Deleuze's nomad thinking is Rosi Braidotti. She provides a feminist approach in her book *Nomadic Subjects*, in which she proposes an alternative subjectivity: "to learn to think differently about the subject, to invent new frameworks, new images, new modes of thought. This entails a move beyond the dualistic conceptual constraints and the perversely monological mental habits of phallocentrism" (Braidotti 2011, 1–2). With this emphasis, Braidotti analyzes and rethinks the "bodily roots of subjectivity."

Similar to Deleuze, she emphasizes that nomadism does not necessarily involve travel: "some of the greatest trips can take place without physically moving from one's habitat." Nomadism is, instead, "the kind of critical attitude that resists settling into socially coded modes of thought and behavior" (Braidotti 2011, 1–2).

In order to unpack these ideas of changing thinking and behavior, advocated by Deleuze and Braidotti, the further development of Deleuze's thoughts on the nomad are helpful. In *A Thousand Plateaus*, written together with Guattari, he utilizes the term "nomadology." The term is tied, loosely, to the rhizomatic, which represents "another way of travelling and moving: proceeding from the middle, through the middle, coming and going rather than starting and finishing" (Deleuze and Guattari 1987, 25). In order to follow this nomadic rhizomatic direction we need to learn "how to move between things, establish a logic of the AND, overthrow ontology, do away with foundations, nullify endings and beginnings" (Deleuze and Guattari 1987, 25). The rhizome provides, like the nomad, a different model of distribution, one that is without *telos* and without *arche*. It just goes.

Where does it go, then, and *how* does it go? The nomad becomes female (or moves beyond gender dualism), it becomes child, it becomes animal, as well as molecular or non-human, or the body without organs, the plane of immanence or consistency, or any of these other concepts that baffle and often irritate any first-time reader of Deleuze and Guattari. We can see here how Deleuze and Guattari's nomadology is Nietzschean in nature, since it asks us to step beyond categories, limits, fixed points, and so forth. To understand their notion of becoming it is helpful to unpack the distinction between nomadology and the state.

The state partly relates to the kind of institution that Rousseau and others describe. It is the institution that stops movements, and that forces everyone to settle down. The state also represents philosophy, particularly those in the tradition of Western thinking, who can be called rationalists, who think in terms of absolutes, of truths, of limitations, borders, hierarchies, and so forth.

Deleuze finds relief in nomad thinkers: those who want to transition, who cannot and do not want to be pinned down to a position or place, who define existence in terms of becoming rather than being. One of these thinkers is Nietzsche. Beside his longer monograph on Nietzsche, Deleuze wrote several essays on him. Among those is the essay entitled "Nomad thought." The essay appears five years after he introduced the term "nomad" in *Difference and Repetition*. It is an essential essay to understanding Deleuze's distinction between the state and nomad thinking. The first are the defenders of property. The latter are the warriors, or the war machine, those who think nomadic. In fact, it is Nietzsche who uses the word "state" to describe "some pack of blond predatory animals, a race of conquerors and masters [. . .] which [. . .] sets its terrifying paws on a subordinate population which may perhaps be vast in numbers but is still without any form, is still wandering about" (Nietzsche 1996, "Essay II," 17). Deleuze quotes from these pages, where Nietzsche writes about the founders of the state as coming "like fate, without reason, consideration or pretext" (Nietzsche 1996, "Essay II," 17). Both Nietzsche and Deleuze fight against these animals, possibly by becoming animals themselves, by reinventing nomadism – to leave any form and to wander. Nietzsche argues that we recognize our animal being, and question the superiority of our rationality. He also asks for a transition into something else, a beyond or *über*. Deleuze and Guattari focus on the transitional aspect itself, in which it is not so much about what one becomes (another identity, limitation, boundary, and so forth). It is for them about the act of becoming itself: nomadism without a destination or goal.

Part of Nietzsche's nomadic thought is that he transforms his readers. Thus we find that, although Deleuze transforms Nietzsche, it is most of all Deleuze who is transformed by Nietzsche, as presumably any reader of Nietzsche is going to be transformed by his writings. Krell speaks in this regard of the infectious Nietzsche (Krell 1996). Being infected is arguably occurring when reading any philosopher. As Heidegger writes, one does not simply toy around with some ideas. One takes them in, and such taking in, as Socrates already warned us, can be dangerous. One cannot inspect ideas or thoughts in any other way than by taking them in, which means that one is going to be infected by them (Plato 1992, 313–14).

Such infection occurs when reading Nietzsche, but something else, a reverse movement, an infection of Nietzsche, also occurs. In the essay "Nomad thought," Deleuze explains Nietzsche in this regard as

> transmitting something that does not and will not allow itself to be codified. To transmit it to a new body, to invent a body that can receive it and spill it forth; a body that would be our own, the earth's, or even something written.
>
> (Deleuze 1985, 142)

Deleuze's Nietzsche is, as such, nomadic. However, it is not just the thought that is nomadic. The body that reads and thinks these thoughts is becoming something else: A new body, perhaps not our own body (or our body that becomes the earth's) or a body that is the text. In this sense, it is, indeed, Nietzsche's reader who is infected.

Deleuze finds a different movement of infection in the form of exteriority. While philosophical systems function by interiority (mediation, the inner essence of the concept, etc.) Nietzsche's aphoristic style of writing is run by exteriority, an intrusion from the outside. Since "an aphorism means nothing" (Deleuze 1985, 145), it is an invitation to transform Nietzsche. Paraphrasing Nietzsche, Deleuze states: "if you want to know what I mean, then find the force that gives a new sense to what I say, and hang the text upon it." Thus, Deleuze concludes, "there is no problem of interpreting Nietzsche" (Deleuze 1985, 145).[18]

The idea that one can be infected by an idea, thought, or way of thinking finds here a reversal; a reader is also able to infect a text, to "hack" it and run it as some external force. Deleuze points out that the exteriority of the meaning, in the sense that the text does not have a fixed meaning but is rather a meaning in flux, has an intensity. This intensity is exactly its nomadic aspect, as a displacement or even a lack of placement. In this regard, Deleuze then calls nomadism a machine of war; a precursor to what in a *Thousand Plateaus* is called "nomadology, the war machine."

We have already learned that nomadism does not necessarily involve movement: Nomadism or nomadology can happen on the spot, motionless. One way to understand this motionless nomadism is through the notion of exteriority, in which one never knows what is coming next. Such an exteriority is full of danger, as exemplified in Deleuze's citation of Kafka's soldiers who are "nomads from the north" (Deleuze 1985, 145).[19] You don't know how they got here, you cannot speak with them, they miraculously grow in numbers, they camp under the open sky, and even their horses are carnivorous. It is, arguably, partly through Kafka that Deleuze develops the idea of the war machine, the nomad thinker who challenges everything and who welcomes otherness.

Braidotti associates this aspect of nomadism with violence. Nomads can be trained armed bands: "The raids, the sacking of cities, the looting, the killing of the sedentary population are the nomad's answer to agriculture" (Braidotti 2011, 25). The violence of saboteurs, revolutionaries, and terrorists then opposes the violence of the state. This is not, on Braidotti's, Deleuze's, or my part, a call to literally take up arms. It is, first of all, an acknowledgment of the fact that the nomad is often placed in positions in which they face violence. Braidotti provides the example of the killing of Gypsies in Nazi concentration camps. Second, the sabotage, revolutions, and terror created are philosophical in nature. They undermine the authority of phallocentrism, of philosophy, of thinking as such, and of the human being.

Along these lines Deleuze finishes "Nomad Thought" by describing Nietzsche as follows:

He made thought into a machine of war – a battering ram – into a nomadic force. And even if the journey is a motionless one, even if it occurs on the spot, imperceptible, unexpected, and subterranean, we must ask ourselves, "who are our nomads today, our real Nietzscheans?"

(Deleuze 1985, 149)

He ends the essay in the form of this question. The ensuing silence seems to suggest that we do not have any true nomad thinkers. The essay, thus, challenges the reader to become nomadic.

In the previous sections I have discussed our settled nomadism. Using Deleuze's and Guattari's ideas of nomadology, one could say that we are today stuck in a "bad nomadology." We move from one place to the next, living where we find work, instead of working where we want to live. Still, working and living are artificially separated by a commute that we prefer to make in the confines of our cars. Traveling itself, the movement from one point to the next, has become a point of being, either in the form of the car, the airplane, or the cruise ship. As I have argued, movement itself has solidified even further because the places or points that we move between are identical, each with their own strip mall full of the same restaurants and box stores. Or we move from anonymous hotel to anonymous hotel, wiped clean of all traces of previous visitors. The suggestion is that nothing ever happens and no one moves. Movement has been reduced to a commercialized transition between identically commercialized places. This movement, I have argued, is the opposite of Heidegger's homelessness as fundamental attunement or Nietzsche's wandering toward the *Übermensch*. Likewise, we can say that it is bad nomadism since movement itself has become part of the state as a commercialized and solidifying institution, and as a mode of solid thinking. In addition, we change everything around us to make it match our ideals of a place. We change the landscape, build structures and infrastructures, and become what I would like to call "settled nomads." We are moving between the places that are the same, and if they are not the same we will change them to be so. This plasticity of the places that we inhabit further feeds the pre-Copernican idea that everything still revolves around us.[20] We also come to the strange conclusion that places change, while movement has become stationary. The consequence is the ambiguous notion of the settled nomad, who travels to and from the same place.

Nomadology fights against borders, rigidity, solidification, and so forth.[21] The nomad thinker as a war machine targets borders, barriers, and limitations that create points. One fights existing topologies, for example the kind of plastic places that I have analyzed in this chapter. Yet, what lies beyond the merely reactionary process, the movement beyond points and movement? How can thinking become nomadic in a positive way? Deleuze provides a few suggestions in the form of the earth, the body, and the text.

Let me start with the earth. Deleuze might implicitly refer here to Zarathustra's prescription to be true or faithful to the earth. Instead of escaping the earth, we now have to embrace the earth, our life, and the body.

To turn away from all fixed and dogmatic ideas of the afterlife and (original) sin, is nomad thought, which the philosopher should embrace.

Our relationship to the earth is one of the body. Deleuze writes about Nietzsche's body, and about all kinds of different bodies. We can also think about Deleuze's own body. Towards the end of his life this was a sick body, so sick that Deleuze could not write any longer; presumably, he had grown so weak that he could no longer hold a pen. He committed suicide by jumping out of his apartment window. Thus, we have another body in its ultimate act of falling toward the earth and to its death – a body that stops becoming.

The non-writing body was a body Deleuze did not want to become, a body that in this sense failed to become. Writing seems for Deleuze the ultimate act of becoming.[22] Writing itself has its shortcomings. For Deleuze personally this can be found in the fact that both Deleuze and Guattari considered their first collaborative work, *Anti-Oedipus*, a failure. Still, for Deleuze, a body that could not write at all cannot become any longer – it cannot produce nomad thought, or think nomadically. Nietzsche also ended up in a state in which he was unable to write. He, also, was often disappointed in his own writing. *Ecce Homo* might be an exception to this, but when Nietzsche states, "Why I write such great books," it is not entirely clear who this "I" is – possibly a Nietzsche of the future, an I still to come. It certainly does not seem to be the Nietzsche who finishes *Beyond Good and Evil* with the following words:

> Alas, what are you after all, my written and painted thoughts! It was not long ago that you were still so colorful, young and malicious, full of thorns and secret spices – you made me sneeze and laugh – and now? You have already taken off your novelty, and some of you are ready, I fear, to become truths: they already look so immortal, so pathetically decent, so dull!
>
> (Nietzsche 1998, 236)

How can it be that such a great book seems to disappoint its author? Perhaps these words are the ultimate nomadic move, and thus make the book great. It is making the exact appeal to the reader that Deleuze identifies: to find a force that one can use to give the text new meaning. It is the ultimate exteriority that intensifies the whole work. The intensity and exteriority exist not in what has been said, but about what failed to be said, what still needs to become. It is the nomad thought that evades documentation – that cannot become a truth, but is out there. The nomad thought penetrates the work from the outside as some alien force that is both dangerous and funny.

The exteriority and silence can result in the heterotopia: the text, or the iconic site, represents something beyond representation. While it is important to bear witness to the fact that not everything can be said, the same structure can also create an illusion if it takes the form of a secret that only a small group may access. Nomad thought should not be mistaken for such a secret.

Its purpose is rather the opposite: to say, or try to say, the unsayable; to think, or try to think, the unthinkable; to disclose the oppressive nature of any secret.

Today, we lack such nomad thought and writing. Our writing moves across the world in a matter of seconds, yet is not only shallow; it also solidifies. What can be said in a tweet is the opposite of what it means to be nomadic. It is state thinking that represents and further affirms boundaries. Likewise, it is true that we move, but from point to point. Often these places are identical and any act of becoming is impossible. For Deleuze and Guattari, physical movement is not essential, yet if we move from identical point to identical point all our becoming is fixed by the homogeneous places that have already shaped us into consumers. As such it affirms whom we already are and denies the very possibility of becoming.

Conclusion

Both our thinking and being today lack the kind of nomadism described by Deleuze, the wandering search of Nietzsche, or the existential homelessness described by Heidegger. Nomadism, we have seen, is the transformation of ourselves, the becoming something other. Perhaps such transformations are told best by Kafka, for example in the *Metamorphosis*. The transformation of Gregor into an insect symbolizes a change that he, in a way, already underwent: the metamorphosis into something less than human, a worker who supported his family but who is not appreciated beyond the economic aspect of his life. In other words, his transformation into something less than human had already occurred before he became a giant insect. Many humans are facing Gregor's situation, in which they are tied to their jobs and tied to their family only through their financial support as breadwinners. Mortgages, loans, college funds, and other financial obligations tie one down. This solidification often requires movement, since one needs a better job, but as argued in this chapter, such movement lacks a true becoming and only solidifies people further. Any true nomadism is lacking, since one is economically bound.

Our nomadic existence today is certainly not the nomadism that Deleuze and Guattari had in mind. Their nomadism involves an actual becoming of something else, a change in our thinking, our bodies, our writing – in our whole existence. Today's nomadism does not so much seek a transformation of ourselves, but rather a transformation of the places that we move to and from. All these places have been commercialized, and express economy. Even the movement between these points is solidified in terms of economy. We might move from one point to the next, but the points turn out to be equal.

America's (and the world's) history of displacements and capitalism has moved us away from the iconic places, which have merely become sites we temporarily visit, rather than places that we inhabit. We are defined by what I have called "plastic places," the strip mall, the Main Street identified by financial institutions, the chain restaurant or coffee shop, the housing development with homogeneous homes, and so forth. We move between places that are so similar that we are, more or less, stationary. We do not become and enrich our lives by moving across the country. Our thoughts only become solidified when they are affirmed. Different places turn out to be the same in the sense that they confirm what we already know. Such places tell us to think in the same way we were thinking in the previous place. None of the plastic places will ever challenge us and as such they have, I have argued, created settled nomads. For our capitalist society this population creates a healthy workforce, in the sense that it is flexible. Labor will freely move to any place where work can be found without a threat and without adjustments needed. As such, it can be understood in terms of Foucault's biopolitics, which aims at the control of the population.

What works for capitalism, however, does not always work for us. By constantly being displaced between plastic places, we only know the same, i.e., the places that are shaped through commerce. We do not know the places beyond this façade. What foods to eat and grow are utter mysteries; when wildlife appears we experience a threat; and even the weather and the seasons take us by surprise. What kinds of signs of nature we entirely miss, we cannot even guess, since such knowledge has been destroyed.

The first three chapters, and in particular this one, have been highly critical of who we are today, of where we are and how we relate to the places around us and the places that determine us. Nietzsche, Heidegger, and Deleuze provide potential trajectories for our thinking and becoming, for re-placing ourselves. Yet, it seems that we are mostly moving in the opposite direction, solidifying and commercializing the places around us, and with that we solidify and commercialize ourselves. In the last two chapters I provide some alternative approaches and argue for a different direction to take. In the upcoming chapter I will discuss some ways to rethink our relationship to nature, the natural places around us without which we could not exist.

Notes

1 In a widely discussed development the Dutch have created a "wilderness" area on reclaimed land, called the Oostvaardersplassen. The area is literally only half a century old since it is reclaimed land, yet is engineered to mimic nature before humans. See Lorimer and Clemens (2014) and Colbert (2012).

2 Of all the senses it is probably hearing that is mostly overwhelmed in this experience, and guards have told me that if something is wrong in the prison, they first of all hear it.

3 In his description of the development of the school, Foucault writes, "[t]he school became a machine for learning, in which each pupil, each level and each moment, if correctly combined, were permanently utilized in the general process of teaching" (Foucault 1977, 165). The school disciplines and creates pliable bodies that will function within capitalism as efficient productive forces.

4 Hierarchy is essential within Foucault's panoptic model, in which the person at the top of the hierarchy can observe the complete operation by simply observing those that work directly under them. In the perfect hierarchical model each individual will attempt to reach the next level in the hierarchy, and this itself constitutes an internalization of the model of observation. Since each individual

is an object of knowledge, it will constantly attempt to create itself as a more positive object.

5   Another related structure is the normalizing judgment. Each individual needs to conform to a norm. In the school and the workplace alike, the individual needs to meet certain standards. The judgments institute a hierarchy in terms of grades, or productivity. Good grades (or stickers!) and bonuses affirm and create rules and norms.

6   In Europe, where the Industrial Revolution started, there had been some exceptions to this sedentary existence, mostly due to the growing population in Europe as well as some natural disasters, such as famines. Still, the general picture of Europe before the Industrial Revolution is one of relative stability in terms of the places where people lived. Nomadism also constituted a relatively stable way of living. Even while on the move, the places nomads moved between were solid points. Both stabilities were radically dismantled with the Industrial Revolution.

7   Furthermore, today's cities in Europe and the USA are a lot greener because industry has moved overseas, relocating pollution along with it. The city of the Industrial Revolution was a gray and unhealthy place to live, not unlike today's Chinese cities.

8   As David Schweickart discusses, alienation does not merely relate to who owns the means of production. In his analysis of Mondragon, a cooperative multinational in the Basque region of Spain, he still detects different levels of alienation in the hierarchies of the enterprise. Even while all workers are owners and while anyone can move into a management position, receive training for new positions, or propose plans to develop a new product or service, levels of alienation from the products and the means of production correlate to one's place in the system. Low-skilled workers feel much more distanced and objectified than managers (Schweickart 2002, 65–70).

9   Of course, the ultimate step toward the separation of work and life consisted in the development of suburbs. After the Second World War many people who worked in the city started to live outside of that place. The car and public transportation systems made this development possible. This development had many disastrous consequences in terms of continued segregation, impoverishing cities, and a detachment from particular places by living in generic suburbs lacking any kind of particular identity. The topic of suburbs is complex and widely discussed. I do not have the space here to develop a full analysis of this other place.

10 Race created a different reality. The Great Migration of African-Americans started around 1914, who moved from the Jim Crow-era South to urban areas in the North, predominantly ending up in segregated areas that came to be known as ghettos. The cars that produced mobility for the white population created jobs that attracted blacks to the cities. Yet they did not face the same reality as whites, who became more and more mobile. While African-Americans moved across the country, they still remained in a position of oppression, facing poverty that included poor education for their children, poor housing and infrastructure, violence, and so forth.

11 I cannot discuss the details here, but economic growth became the new paradigm around World War II. The crash of 1929 had created widespread poverty that hit virtually all Americans, both in the cities and in rural settings. The economy seemed a disaster, yet while Franklin D. Roosevelt had been convinced that the economy could not grow any further, World War II brought a different reality. The war was economically advantageous to the USA. The suffering and hardship that occurred due to the loss of family members, and the impact of various rationed goods (including gasoline), must not be underestimated, but the war industry created many jobs. Millions of people found work and since many men

were enlisted in the army, women took positions that were formerly occupied by men, ranging from grocery clerks to manufacturing jobs.

12 In an insightful analysis of the influence of modern life on Eskimo cultures in the Northern parts of Alaska, Nick Jans describes how communities that used to live off the land today use modern tools such as snowmobiles and rifles. While such tools make hunting easier, it complicates their lives. Since they stepped into a monetary system, the expenses of gas, the replacements of snowmobiles, and the availability of Western foods force most families to use food stamps. We can understand the turn to credit systems in a similar way: when we use more than we can directly afford, our lives are going to be run by financial systems (Jans 1993).

13 Marx and Engels make this point in the second chapter "Proletarians and communists" of the *Communist Manifesto* (Marx 1994).

14 This is from www.goodcreditdating.com. The dating site uses the sentence as their slogan, without explaining it. On December 25, 2012, Jessica Silver-Greenberg published an article in the *New York Times* on the significance of credit scores: "Perfect 10? Never mind that. Ask her for her credit score."

15 Similarly, in "Modern science, metaphysics, and mathematics," Heidegger recalls the ancient Greek notion that the place of a thing is internally determined (Heidegger 1997a).

16 In speech figures we find a similar motive, as Derrida argues (Derrida 1989).

17 As has been argued by others, the early Deleuze finds nomad thinkers in the history of philosophy, such as Hume, Nietzsche, and Spinoza, and transforms their thinking. Robert Tally argues that the early Deleuze wrote mostly about "nomad" thinkers, such as Spinoza and Nietzsche, who challenged the tradition. In addition, Tally argues, Deleuze himself radically transformed these thinkers, forming the basis for his own thinking. This exercise itself is nomadic as it traces thoughts and ideas that are mostly not explicitly present in the texts that he reads. The philosophies Deleuze reads are transformed, becoming, something else. They are in transit (Tally 2010, 15–24).

18 Of course, in the next paragraph Deleuze mentions a problem with interpreting Nietzsche, in the form of fascist and anti-Semitic appropriations of Nietzsche. In this regard, Deleuze proposes to let fascist, bourgeois, and revolutionary forces meet head on.

19 Deleuze cites the "Great Wall of China," but the quote comes from "An old manuscript."

20 I would like to thank Peter Steeves, who introduced me to the term and idea of the agrarian as a "sedentary nomad." He used the idea to emphasize that we still think we are the center of the world. The modern agrarian, Steeves suggested in an email exchange, constantly changes the land on which they grow food, adding fertilizers, nutrients, water, and so forth. The farmer remains in one place while the land changes. I have somewhat reversed this idea by applying it to an actually moving person, who moves between identical places.

21 Likewise, our thinking about borders lacks any nomadic aspect. On one extreme we find walls, fences and patrol guards. The other "extreme" is immigration reform, which is certainly necessary in terms of justice and human rights, yet it is nowhere near nomadology. Instead of reforming who can stay and who should go, nomad thinkers open up all borders and think beyond any limitations.

22 Len Lawlor makes this suggestion in "Writing like a rat" in Lawlor (2007).

References

Beck, Ulrich. 1992. *Risk Society Towards a New Modernity*. London and Newbury Park: Sage Publications.

Braidotti, Rosi. 2011. *Nomadic Subjects Embodiment and Sexual Difference in Contemporary Feminist Theory*. New York: Columbia University Press.

California Department of Public Health. 2010. *Investigation of Birth Defects and Community Exposures in Kettleman City, Ca.*

Colbert, Elizabeth. 2012. "Recall of the wild: the quest to engineer a world before humans." *The New Yorker*. December 24.

Cole, Luke W., and Foster, Sheila R. 2001. *From the Ground Up: Environmental Racism and the Rise of the Environmental Justice Movement*. New York: New York University Press.

Dehaene, Michiel and De Cauter, Lieven (eds.) (2008) *Heterotopia and the City: Public Space in a Postcivil Society*. London and New York: Routledge.

Deleuze, Gilles. 1983. *Nietzsche and Philosophy*. New York: Columbia University Press.

—— . 1985. "Nomad thought." In: David B. Allison (ed.) *The New Nietzsche: Contemporary Styles of Interpretation*. Cambridge, MA: MIT Press.

—— . 2001. *Difference and Repetition*. London and New York: Continuum.

Deleuze, Gilles, and Guattari, Félix. 1987. *A Thousand Plateaus: Capitalism and Schizophrenia*. Minneapolis: University of Minnesota Press.

Derrida, Jacques. 1989. "How to avoid speaking: denials." In: Sanford Budick and Wolfgang Iser (eds) *Languages of the Unsayable: The Play of Negativity in Literature and Literary Theory*. New York: Columbia University Press.

Dumm, Thomas L. 1996. *Michel Foucault and the Politics of Freedom*. Thousand Oaks: Sage Publications.

Foucault, Michel. 1973. *The Birth of the Clinic: An Archaeology of Medical Perception*. New York: Pantheon Books.

—— . 1977. *Discipline and Punish: The Birth of the Prison*. New York: Pantheon Books.

—— . 2003. *Society Must Be Defended: Lectures at the Collège de France, 1975–76*. New York: Picador.

Gmelch, George, and Gmelch, Sharon. 2011. *Tasting the Good Life: Wine Tourism in the Napa Valley*. Bloomington: Indiana University Press.

Heidegger, Martin. 1977a. *Basic Writings*. San Francisco: Harper.

—— . 1977b. *The Question Concerning Technology, and Other Essays*. New York: Harper & Row.

Jans, Nick. 1993. *The Last Light Breaking: Living among Alaska's Inupiat Eskimos*. Anchorage: Alaska Northwest Books.

Krell, David Farrell. 1996. *Infectious Nietzsche*. Bloomington: Indiana University Press.

Lawlor, Leonard. 2007. *This is not Sufficient: An Essay on Animality and Human Nature in Derrida*. New York: Columbia University Press.

Liddell, Henry George and Scott, Robert. 1940. *A Greek–English Lexicon*. Oxford: Clarendon Press.

Lorimer, Jamie and Driessen, Clemens. 2014. "Wild experiments at the Oostvaardersplassen: rethinking environmentalism in the Anthropocene." *Transactions of the Institute of British Geographers*, 39 (2), 169–181.

McKibben, Bill. 2007. *Deep Economy: The Wealth of Communities and the Durable Future*. New York: Times Books.

Marx, Karl. 1955. *Capital*. Chicago: Encyclopædia Britannica.

—— . 1994. "Economical and philosophical manuscripts of 1844." In *Selected writings*. Indianapolis: Hackett.

Marx, Karl and Engels, Friedrich 1972. *The German Ideology*. New York: International Publishers.

Mother Jones. 2010. "What's killing the babies of Kettleman City?" June.

Nietzsche, Friedrich Wilhelm. 1996. *On the Genealogy of Morals: A Polemic by way of Clarification and Supplement to My Last Book, Beyond Good and Evil*. Oxford: Oxford University Press.

——— . 1998. *Beyond Good and Evil: Prelude to a Philosophy of the Future*. New York: Oxford University Press.

Plato. 1992. *Protagoras*. Indianapolis: Hackett.

Schweickart, David. 2002. *After Capitalism*. Lanham: Rowman & Littlefield Publishers.

Smith, Adam. 1976. *Wealth of Nations*. Oxford: Clarendon Press.

Tally, Robert T. Jr. 2010. "Nomadography." *Journal of Philosophy: A Cross-Disciplinary Inquiry*, 5 (11), 15–24.

Tracy, James. 2014. *Dispatches Against Displacement: Field Notes from San Francisco's Housing Wars*. San Francisco: AK Press.

4 Walking and thinking mountains

Dōgen, Leopold, and the Tlingit

So far, my approach to place has been one through Western thinkers. This is somewhat problematic, since it seems that the Western world is largely to blame for most environmental issues. Problems such as deforestation, pollution, and environmental destruction are arguably a consequence of the Western world's lack of a relationship to particular places. Why should we use the philosophical foundations of the Western world, which has always considered the human being as superior, to rethink our relationship to place?

The answer has, at least, two parts. First of all, thinkers such as Nietzsche, Heidegger, Foucault, and Deleuze fight the system from within. In different ways these philosophers challenge the Modern mindset that suggests we are on the path of continuous progress. Second, in order to fight this system we need to understand it: how it functions, what concepts it uses, where power and knowledge are found and created, and how it has historically shaped our thinking.

In addition to the fight-within notion, I bring in some alternative models of thinking. A number of rich and thought-provoking sources from other traditions are available. This chapter uses some of those sources, not necessarily as an alternative approach, but rather as a way to complement and strengthen the sources used thus far. That said, it should also be noted that, in particular, Nietzsche and Heidegger were influenced by some Buddhist traditions. Another preliminary remark relates to discrepancies between religious and philosophical ideas and environmental practices. For example, the Japanese appreciate nature, while their practices often contribute to environmental destruction.[1] Likewise, the longstanding idea that Native American cultures did not manage and engage in some destructive practices (and still do) has been challenged. These are important considerations that raise many questions about the correlation between practice and thinking, or the lack of thinking regarding some practices. It lies beyond the scope of this book to investigate such inconsistencies, but it is nonetheless important to keep in mind that we should not idealize any of these approaches as a clear solution. In addition, one should be careful to not simply consume some interesting ideas and appropriate them in inappropriate ways.

Though I wish I had a more original standpoint, the way I approach the non-Western discourses in this chapter is from a Western standpoint. It seems to me unrealistic to do otherwise. I was educated and have always lived, thought, and practiced in the Western world. Leaving those roots behind to study a non-Western tradition from the inside would take a complete transformation of who I am. I am not sure if I could do that, and any non-Western culture will always consider me an outsider. Instead, I think through these other traditions from my own standpoint – a standpoint that I presumably share with the average reader of this book. For that reason, I will also start the chapter in the Western tradition, with Aldo Leopold.

The second thinker is the thirteenth-century philosopher Dōgen, founder of the Soto Zen School, who greatly influenced Leopold. I then discuss the Japanese philosopher Watsuji and his text *Fudo*, translated as "A climate." Watsuji was the younger colleague of the better-known Nishitani (who studied with Heidegger). Watsuji, while heavily influenced by Heidegger (as well as Nietzsche and Kierkegaard), is critical of the philosopher for emphasizing temporality over place. Still, he applies Heidegger in interesting ways. His thinking is, in a sense, a marriage of Heidegger and Dōgen, providing a non-Western approach to Western thinking. Lastly, I discuss a way of thinking and practice that is closer to home: some of the American indigenous philosophies that persist today in Alaska.

Thinking and walking mountains

I approach Dōgen through Aldo Leopold's attempts to approach nature in a non-anthropocentric way. Leopold writes about "thinking like a mountain" using another human quality to reflect on the non-human world. His task, to think like a mountain, seems somewhat mundane compared to the task that Dōgen provides in his *Mountains and Waters Sutra*: study how the mountains are walking. The way mountains walk is apparently "just like human walking" (Dōgen 1985, 97). Dōgen invites us into an exercise that encourages us to step outside of our anthropocentric world.

I argue that both Dōgen and Leopold lead us away from a dichotomy of human and non-human, a move that Nietzsche was also seeking. The approach reflects Heidegger's notion of homelessness and home, in which we always appropriate different places. Dōgen arrives at some unprecedented ideas, including the idea that we should not appropriate a natural place such as a mountain, but let it appropriate us. What that exactly means may remain obscure, but his ideas lead us down some paths that will be worthwhile to walk.

Aldo Leopold's short essay "Thinking like a mountain" addresses a deep concern: we humans fail to think outside of the human realm. When we think about nature, we tend to frame our thoughts within certain economic models that command expediency. In Leopold's case, we fail to grasp the way an ecosystem, like a mountain, thinks. This can be understood as the most radical turn of Nietzsche's perspectivism. He argued for a multitude of perspectives. To add the perspective of the mountain is a significant and radical contribution to this multitude. The lack of this perspective and our belief that we can improve a mountain are fatal mistakes.

The most famous and transformative moment of Aldo Leopold's life involved the fierce green fire that he saw in the eyes of a dying wolf. Just a few minutes before this moment, Leopold, together with his buddies, shot the wolf and her pups. The young men are responsible for the slaughter, but moreover it is their mindset, full of trigger itch, that led them to act in this way. Wolves are predators, killers of deer. Thus, as Leopold writes, "I thought that because fewer wolves meant more deer, that no wolves would mean hunters' paradise. But after seeing the green fire die, I sensed that neither the wolf nor the mountain agreed with such a view" (Leopold 1968, 130). The green fire indicates that he has failed to think like a mountain.[2]

Leopold invites us to think like a mountain by thinking in terms of a community of all life and those things that make life possible: the land. His attempt to expand the already existing ethical community by including the land could be considered anthropomorphic. However, he takes an important additional step: the human being decentralizes itself. The individual becomes a community member and leaves behind the position of conqueror. Thus the individual steps beyond the young Leopold who shot the wolves, as he failed to be a part of the greater ethical community that is the earth. In that case he acted as a master who thinks he knows what makes the community thrive.

Within debates about invasive species, discussed in more detail in the final chapter, ecologists often take the exact same standpoint – although they frequently admit that they are still learning how ecosystems work, they still set certain parameters in the process of learning. The very idea that some species are native, while other species are non-native, is a set of knowledge in which all other knowledge takes shape – a structure that Heidegger calls the mathematical. This set of knowledge indicates that somewhere in history a static situation existed that constituted a balanced and healthy ecosystem. Sometimes the word "pristine" is used; mostly the word "native" is used, often without an explanation of what criteria are used to distinguish between native and non-native.

Leopold himself uses such language. In his time, a healthy ecosystem was a static system. Today, ecology has made significant progress in understanding ecosystems as fluid, without clear boundaries, evolving over time, and with influence from surrounding ecosystems. Leopold's philosophy, and more particularly his land ethics, could benefit from this insight. The community of the land ethic includes soil, plants, animals, and humans. This community is one that is constantly evolving; it is dynamic in the sense that it has shifting relationships between its members. Our planet started dead, and life appeared approximately 3.7 billion years ago, eventually leading to *Homo sapiens*, our own species that we ourselves (of course) consider to be the climax of evolution. The planet has gone through several climate changes such as ice ages that radically altered and destroyed ecosystems all over the globe. Over time, sometimes radically, sometimes slowly, plant and animal species were extinguished, moved to different parts of the earth, or lived together in other ecosystems. The moving and evolving of life has simply never stopped. This is not to say that humans do not do horrible things to the earth. We do. This is rather to say that since life started, things have been in flux. Indeed, one cannot step onto the same earth twice.

If we would be forced to choose a point in time that would reflect the most natural native circumstances, most people would choose a point before the influence of human beings, or before the influence of Western civilization.[3] This in itself reflects a problem, since we conceive of nature as an entity, a concept, without human beings. Native Americans, for example, do not fit in our picture of wild nature, as portrayed in their absence in most early American paintings of places like Yosemite. In US wilderness areas no one is allowed to reside permanently, a law that aims to protect a concept of nature that excludes human beings. I have discussed these sites in the previous chapter as heterotopias, places that are, in a sense, non-places, since we are excluded from them. These sites are defined as wild and natural only through this act of exclusion, in effect defining wildness as the non-human. This definition is not merely a philosophical matter: many Native American tribes, who lived in the wilderness long before the arrival of Columbus, have been displaced because of this definition and the Wilderness Act.

Leopold uses the metaphor of thinking like a mountain, without ever providing more than a few hints of what exactly this activity would include. With the word thinking he uses a very human category, a category that is mostly only associated with human beings. Leopold here, perhaps, falls into the trap of anthropomorphism that seems so hard to avoid when using language. It immediately assumes that a mountain has a rationality, and perhaps even a *telos*. It also assumes that there is a privilege to rationality.

In his famous "Mountains and waters sutra," Dōgen also uses a human category: walking. However, he appears to use this very anthropomorphic category in order to question our anthropocentrism. By pulling our category away from ourselves and giving it to the mountain instead, he, in fact, seems to set anthropomorphism up against itself. Dōgen sometimes falls into truisms, for example when he writes "[m]ountains do not lack the qualities of mountains" (Dōgen 1985, 97). In the very next sentence, he then states the opposite: "Therefore they always abide in ease and always walk" (Dōgen 1985, 97). And a few lines later he adds, "Mountains' walking is just like human walking" (Dōgen 1985, 97). Although it might seem that Dōgen ascribes human qualities to the mountains, the opposite is true. He explains a little later: "If you doubt mountains' walking, you do not know your own walking" (Dōgen 1985, 98). In other words, we should not understand the mountain as walking in a human sense, but we should understand our walking in a mountainous sense, i.e., in relationship to the mountain. We do not walk (or live) in a vacuum, but our walking can only occur because there is a place to walk in or on. We, thus, have to learn and study how to walk with (or along with) the mountain.[4] I admit that this is difficult, if at all possible, to grasp. It might be helpful to remember here that Zen Buddhism does not consist of easily obtainable truths, but of a life-long practice. I will attempt to make a few shortcuts here through Gary Snyder's interpretations.

In his analysis of Dōgen's "Mountains and waters sutra," Gary Snyder writes how there are different sorts of walking. He provides examples such as heading out across the desert in a straight line, weaving through undergrowth, or descending rocky ridges. One of the most famous essays on walking, Thoreau's "Walking", famously describes sauntering, the homeless walking without a clear destination (but away from society), and always without a map. By being homeless, one is at home everywhere. Dōgen and the Zen tradition embrace the idea of the homeless. For Snyder and Dōgen, homelessness means "being at home in the whole universe" or to practice in every place (Snyder 1990, 104). The latter means that one does not need to practice in a quiet room with candles and incense and one's favorite music playing. Nor do we need to practice in a church, or in nature, as the Transcendentalists suggest. By way of contrast with Thoreau, we can also think of Benjamin's "flaneur," the stroller in the streets of Paris (Benjamin 1999).[5] In Snyder's reading, Dōgen wants to overcome such oppositions between nature and city. Mountains, thus, stroll through the streets of Paris, or to give Snyder's American example, mountains "go [. . .] down to the Seven-11" (Snyder 1990, 103).

Snyder makes these comments on Dōgen within the context of "the practice of the wild," the title of his book. The practice of the wild is, on the one hand, our own practice, something we undertake, but it also means learning to recognize how the wild is itself a practice, how the natural world is not just there for us as a resource, but something that has a value in itself, like us. Snyder finds this in Dōgen: "His mountains and streams are the processes of this earth, all of existence, process, essence, action, absence; they roll being and non-being together. They are what we are, we are what they are" (Snyder 1990, 103). The idea is, on the one hand, so obvious: we are made out of the materials that the earth provides. When we die our bodies return to the earth. Even science confirms this story. Yet, on the other hand, it is so obscure, for we are trained to separate ourselves from animals and from the natural or wild world. We are rational and reasonable, whereas nature is untamed and wild. The point both Snyder and Dōgen make is that we are mountains, that we are wild and untamed – that we are nature.

Dōgen and Snyder indicate different sorts of walking. Returning to Leopold, we can first of all say the obvious: there are different sorts of thinking. Moreover, we can question what exactly is the difference between walking and thinking? The obvious answer seems to be that walking is a bodily activity, while thinking is supposedly not. Dōgen tells us to study and examine the mountain's walking, which is "just like human walking" (Dōgen 1985, 97). It is through our walking that we are, as Snyder says, with our bodies seeing the world (Snyder 1990, 99). Walking was the way for the Zen monks to travel, bringing them, arguably, closer to the thinking, or walking, of a mountain than the modern traveler in a car or airplane. Walking is not only a moving with your body through space. Moreover, it is an activity in which body and mind are immersed in the lifeworld.[6]

The more profound point that Dōgen makes, at the end of the "Mountains and waters sutra," is that the study, examination, or investigation itself "is the work of the mountains. Such mountains and waters of themselves become wise persons and sages" (Dōgen 1985, 107). While we desperately seek to understand nature and to appropriate different places, we fail to recognize the wisdom such places and nature have. This might sound obscure, and perhaps it is, but let us try not to dismiss it immediately as such. Mountains walk; they change and develop over time, geologically and ecologically. There is a certain wisdom that arises in these mountains, a wisdom that discourses such as geology and ecology seek to unravel. Dōgen quite literally understands this wisdom and practice of the mountain as a sutra. His "Mountains and rivers sutra" is thus not a discourse *about* but rather *by* the mountains and rivers. He starts the sutra by stating: "These mountains and waters of the present are the expression of the old buddhas" (Dōgen 1985, 97). More explicitly, he writes: "They passed eons living alone in the mountains and forests; only then did they unite with the Way and use mountains and rivers for words, raise the wind and rain for a tongue, and explain the great void" (Dōgen 1985, 97). The mountain and rivers, thus, speak wisely in their growth and maintenance of life, the soil and rocks that support that growth, the rivers that are fed by springs, rain, snow, and so forth.

The wise mountain can respond to disturbances, at least to a certain degree. It can mostly deal with humans, even when they dig mines and take out coal. In the extreme case of mountaintop removal, the mountain and its wisdom are all destroyed. What is left after the mining companies have blown up the mountain is a pile of rubble, a reconstructed mountain without wisdom: its fertile topsoil is gone, the rivers, springs, and creeks are gone. Virtually all life is gone. Maybe the human then overcomes the mountain by destroying some other wisdom. That in itself does not seem to be very wise, however. It indicates we are far removed from understanding our own walking along with the walking mountains. Rather, we seem to think we walk in a vacuum.

Wind and earth

A similar kind of approach can be found in Watsuji Tetsurō. He provides an interesting approach to both Heidegger and Dōgen. In the preface of his book *Fudo*, he writes: "It was in the early summer of 1927 when I was reading Heidegger's Sein und Zeit in Berlin that I first came to reflect on the problem of climate" (Watsuji 1988, v). He then immediately notes that Heidegger's emphasis on time left out another important constituent of our being: space. The problem is not so much that Heidegger does not discuss space (he does, for example, in the structure of "being-in-the-world," and the notion of "home" has an obvious spatial character). The problem, rather, is that he does not link time to space. Graham Mayeda puts it as follows: for Watsuji *Being and Time* lacks "an adequate understanding of existential spatiality" (Mayeda 2006, 37). For Watsuji, human existence involves time and space linked together to reveal history "in its true guise. And at the same time the connection between history and climate becomes evident" (Watsuji 1988, vi).

Fudo (pronounced as "food-o") means "wind and earth," or "wind and soil." It is derived from the ancient word *Sui-do* for "water and earth," which is often translated as "climate" (Watsuji 1988, 1).[7] Because of this, it might seem like the book is about our natural environment or climate, but *fudo* is far more; it also involves our social climate. I will use the translation of climate or environment, but it will have to be distinguished from our natural environment. In addition, the term is also closely tied to Dōgen's "Mountains and waters sutra," in Japanese *Sansui-Kyo*. Dōgen uses a similar opposition, and uses the ancient word *sui* (water), referred to by Watsuji (in the word *Sui-do*).

Watsuji's book describes how the human being relates to its environment: "All of us live on a given land and the natural environment of this land 'environs' us whether we like it or not" (Watsuji 1988, 1). This insight in many ways reverses the relationship to place that we found in the analysis of our contemporary being. We are not (passively) environed; we (actively) environ. Our environment is managed. The surrounding place is the passive aspect, adjusted to our needs and insights. We are active agents who have taken control of our surroundings, unwilling to accept that we are always already determined by our place.

In order to rethink our relationship with our environment, Watsuji provides an example of the phenomenon of cold. We could understand cold in an objective or subjective way, but Watsuji provides an alternative by understanding ourselves as "being out in the cold." "The basic essence of what is 'present outside' is not a thing or object such as the cold, but we ourselves" (Watsuji 1988, 4). Watsuji here redefines the self, which is not living independently of others and its environment, but is rather "the between" or, as McRae puts it, "a person within a context" (McRae 2014, 361). A self is defined in its culture, its history, and its environment. It does not reflect on these components from the outside in a subject–object relationship, but it is living in these phenomena. Likewise, the human being is not divided in spirit (or soul) and body, as this dualism maintains the individualistic approach and neglects the way the human being is socially and environmentally situated. Moreover, it regards the body as mere matter, and creates a sense of an absolute self. Both body and environment are, as such, written off as non-essential: "Climate too, as part of man's body, was regarded like the body as mere matter, and so came to be viewed objectively as mere natural environment" (Watsuji 1988, 11). Watsuji discusses how we dress and build to brace the cold; we also mine coal to provide heat. The cold is an example of how we are intrinsically tied to our environment, through our culture and history, for example in how we deal with the cold "individually and socially" (Watsuji 1988, 5).

Watsuji emphasizes the in-between-ness of the human being, effectively redefining who we are. A human being is not merely an individual, but socially and environmentally, the human being is interdependent. We exist in certain environments that are historically determined through the climate they provide. Temperature, humidity, earthquakes, and other natural components determine our society. By placing the human within this context of climate, Watsuji argues against human dominance over nature and puts our autonomy as individuals into question; we are nothing without our environment, and we are nothing without society. With the notion of in-betweenness, he also questions the divide between climate or environment and the human being. History and environment are intertwined. The human being changes its environment, and likewise does this environment change the human being. We, thus, do not find a dualism, but a symbiotic relationship in which environment is not the limitation of ourselves, where we end and something else begins. Rather, the environment is the possibility that embodies our existence.

Like Dōgen, Watsuji emphasizes that self-discovery occurs in our environment. Transcendence is not a turn inside, but outward, and it must include the entities of society, community, and climate. It is the discovery that we are our place and our climate. Dōgen wrote about the walking mountains that we must study in order to comprehend our own walking. Watsuji, likewise, encourages us to study our environment, how we changed it and how it has changed us historically. In both thinkers we find that we are not just in our environment but that we are our environment and cannot be separated from it.

Watsuji's critique of Heidegger emphasizes space, or environment, as intrinsically tied to time. While this is a radical change, he does not dismiss Heidegger's thinking. He uses, among other things, Heidegger's analysis of the tool and applies it to our environment. When we use hot and cold to grow or to freeze food, we use climate as a tool. As such we have to recognize ourselves as a part of our climate. As we have seen, Heidegger used the analysis of the technological mindset in a later essay, in which he criticizes the tool-like understanding of the natural world. Watsuji provides an interesting and more positive alternative to Heidegger's criticism. He moves us toward an understanding of nature and our environment as something more than a resource that we can use and manipulate. Instead, the environment or climate determines our essence, because it defines our existence. It determines who and how we are. We are who we are because of what our climate has to offer. He, thus, effectively places us in an integral relationship with our environment.

Native thinking

After our brief excursion across the Pacific through the Japanese thinkers Dōgen and Watsuji, let us now turn to a culture closer to home, at least in a physical sense. When we speak about Native American thinking we should speak about a multiplicity of philosophies. Although many tribes seem to have somewhat similar ideas and spiritualities, it would be a mistake (and upsetting to Native Americans) to speak about Native American thinking as if there is a unified philosophy that ties all tribes together. The stories, the meaning(s) particular animals have, and the connection to the land and sea are different for each tribe. There is a very obvious explanation for this: the places where these cultures developed informed their philosophies. In other words, a place abundant with water, ravens, and bears will develop different stories and connections than a desert with snakes. Underneath this obvious observation lies a deeper and more significant meaning: the culture and spirituality of a particular tribe is a direct consequence of and reflection on the place where they thrive. It reflects an understanding of the ecosystems that is immediately tied to a need to survive in, sometimes, harsh conditions and, more importantly, over time.

As already indicated in the introduction to this chapter, we should be careful with idealizing and romanticizing Native American cultures. Some have argued that American Indian tribes overhunted and burned forests extensively. Others argue that controlled burning was an important tool in keeping forests healthy (Dukeminier and Krier 1993). Today, ecologists and Native American tribes, such as the Tlingit, often have fundamental disagreements about healthy practices. Sometimes, disagreements stem from mistrust. Sometimes, the native ways are seen as destructive by today's ecological standards. Despite these reservations, we do find in most indigenous cultures a strong connection to places, as constituting an integral part of the identity of oneself and one's culture.

I focus here on the Tlingit tribe and the philosophy of nature their culture expresses, a philosophy that is immediately tied to the place this philosophy inhabits.[8] The Tlingit people consist of a group of tribes located in the Pacific Northwest, mostly around the inside passage in the southwestern tip of Alaska. The choice for focusing on this particular culture is not an arbitrary one; these tribes have done an extraordinary job in maintaining and retrieving their cultures, which has been partly possible because they live in Alaska, an area of the world that only became part of the New World in 1867, is difficult to access, and is the last frontier, with a very small population. Thus, Alaska has arguably not been fully settled by outsiders. Although the Russians did fight and kill some of the Tlingit, the tribe did not face the kind of mass killings that occurred in most other parts of North America. In their environment today, the "Western world" is certainly all around, but the natural habitat has been largely kept intact. By thinking through aspects of the Tlingit philosophy of nature and the norms and values that emerge from it,

I seek to provide a final supplement to our Western way of thinking and practicing regarding place.

What can we learn from other cultures, such as the Tlingit? For my purposes, I focus on the idea that cultures like the Tlingit are rooted in the place in which they live. The places that provide food and resources have over time established their cultural and social discourses. Since they live close to the water, many of their food practices are related to fishing, but berry picking and hunting are also essential parts of what is often called a subsistence economy. While subsistence is often understood as "producing" and harvesting merely for basic needs and support of life, for the Tlingit themselves it is "*haa kusteeyi*, 'our way of living,' 'real being,' an 'enriching existence'" (Thornton 2008, 117). The production of food and the use of natural resources are thus immediately tied to their being-in-the-world.

Both Thomas Thornton's *Being and Place Among the Tlingit* and Tim Ingold's *The Perception of the Environment: Essays on Livelihood, Dwelling and Skill* argue that the Tlingit sense of being in the world is tied to the place in which they live – where they produce their food and take their resources from. This is in radical juxtaposition to our own being in the world, in which resources and food are purchased from a store and thus lack a relationship to the places that actually provided these resources. For the Tlingit, places also have a significant presence in their culture in the form of stories. Both Thornton's and Ingold's work are very Heideggerian in orientation, relying in particular on *Building Dwelling Thinking*. Ingold's reading of Heidegger leads to his observation that "it is only because we live in an environment that we can think" (Ingold 2000, 60). Thornton specifically ties the notion of landscape, the place in which we dwell, to our sense of being: "In a fundamental sense the landscape is part of every individual's sense of being, not just that of Tlingits, or Native Americans, or indigenous peoples. [. . .] Place can be said to constitute a cultural system" (Thornton 2008, 4). The fact that place is significant across cultures does not mean, however, that place has the same significance in different cultural systems. In a striking and fitting example, Thornton quotes a middle-aged fisherman who spoke up at a public meeting about a proposed commercial timber harvest in Kelp Bay, an important place for the Tlingit. At the meeting, logging practices, resource management, and the concept of subsistence were discussed – all of which everyone involved could relate to. The meaning of the fisherman's comment was less obvious: "These lands are vital not only to our subsistence, but also to our *sense of being* as Tlingit people" (Thornton 2008, 3). While the Tlingit's sense of being might be the most significant and self-evident argument for the Tlingit, for the planners or the Forest Service the fisherman's words have no meaning. Even if one of the planners had majored in philosophy and had been able to get a sense of the meaning, the phrase "our sense of being" was not part of the discourse that determined what to do and what not to do in Kelp Bay. The fisherman might as well have chosen not to speak at all. The Tlingit voice is lost.

The guiding question for Thornton's work is, in fact, what the Tlingit sense of being is, how the places that they dwell in and that provide their resources and food, determine who and how they are. Within the Tlingit culture, important places are known, first of all, by their name. After the arrival of the Europeans or Euro-Americans, important landmarks, such as rivers, lakes, mountains, ranges, and valleys were renamed, sometimes using the name of the person who "discovered" it or the name of some person who needed to be honored. Gary Snyder writes how mapmakers renamed the hills and lakes in Alaska "after transient exploiters, or their own girlfriends, or home towns" (Snyder 1990, 7). The point is that these new names were now entirely unrelated to the place they named, in contrast to the "place-based stories the people tell, and the naming they've done, is their archeology, architecture, and *title* to the land" (Snyder 1990, 7). Returning to the Tlingit, we find indeed that from early on children hear the names and stories of the places where their fish and food comes from, as well as the places where they make camps. Some examples of place names or *Kwaan* (derived from the verb "to dwell") are "inhabitants of the Kaliakh river area," "inhabitants of the Area with Ice Inside," or "opening of the day people (sunlight through rocky pass)" (Thornton 2008, 44). Through learning these place names, which often bear a geographical description, a "cognitive mapping" of the terrain occurs that results in a sense that the places belong to them as a people. Sometimes this involves possessory rights to fishing grounds for a particular clan or even a side of a clan; clans are mostly named after the place with which they are affiliated.

This sense of property, in fact, determines their concept of subsistence, i.e., the places that they use provide them with a sense of their being. This is clearly opposed to commercial uses. It is not a surprise that commercial use of fishing grounds is especially threatening today, and it is probably also not surprising that the Tlingit are participating in modern capitalism, among other things, through fishing and tourism. It might seem that since this participation is voluntary it does not constitute a problem. Yet, cultures such as the Tlingit are undergoing the exact same changes we have undergone over the last centuries. We have become settled nomads who destroy every place. The only remaining place-based cultures with actual grounded knowledge of their environment are now threatened. The lure of modern technology, prosperity, sports, and Western education is destroying the knowledge that was passed on for generations. Despite these threats, their culture maintains an awareness of their intricate relationship to place, particularly to those places that are significant for food production and natural resources. Of course, as Thornton suggests, everyone is related to places. We can add in that regard, that we often fail to think and reflect about this relatedness.[9] Moreover, as we have seen in the previous chapters, Westerners tend to understand their environment as something separate from their identity. Evidence of this attitude was found in the ways we change the places around us. While it is impossible today to return to a model of subsistence, I do suggest that some subsistence practices and the notion that our places determine our sense of being, might actually tie us back to our place. In this regard, environment becomes something more, namely it becomes the place that determines who we are, described by Watsuji in terms of "in-betweenness."

The Tlingit have been able to maintain their culture, and with that their sense of being. Whereas *we* do not have a clue about the origins of our food, the Tlingit learn about these places through stories and names. By maintaining these stories they have been able to, at least partly, separate their own culture from capitalist influences. Our culture, on the other hand, is poor in maintaining its stories, always replacing them with new ones. Take, for example, two TV shows about brown bear hunting, both on Kodiak Island. The Discovery channel broadcasts "Kodiak," while The History Channel broadcasts "The Hunt," narrated by James Hetfield, singer of Metallica. The shows announce the hunt, brag about the kill, and show the desperation of some of the subjects to kill a brown bear. They use "traditional" hunting weapons: long/compound bow and black-powder, single-shot rifles. This often means that they wound, but not kill, the bear. To be fair, as often happens when animals are killed, the shows – and James Hetfield – have come under criticism. Yet, the show is part of a large number of TV series including *Alaskan Bushmen, Building Alaska, Alaska State Troopers, Deadliest Catch* and a variety of other "reality" shows that follow the extreme lives of the last frontier's inhabitants. What reality these series want to display is not entirely obvious, but it seems that they reinstitute a detached nature as something that is still out there somewhere. The paradigm of these shows is that we have all overcome nature, but these courageous and somewhat silly Alaskans are still trying to work in (and perhaps against) it.

Along with stories, we have done a poor job in maintaining our traditional ways of food production. For example, the so-called Green Revolution has transformed traditional organic agriculture into a huge chemistry experiment with enormous amounts of poisons (see, for example, Lyman and Merzer 1998). We are now re-inventing the old ways of farming, through new labels and certification agencies.

Returning to the Tlingit, I do not mean to suggest that the Tlingit subsistence model does not have its own problems; the clan structure is an obvious source for conflict and some of their practices have been deemed environmentally destructive. Nonetheless, it is impressive that the Tlingit, despite threats of commercial lumber enterprises, commercial fishing, and new technologies, have been able to maintain their culture so well and see themselves as a part of their natural surroundings, i.e., the place in which they live does provide their food and resources and, simultaneously, determines who they are.

Besides stories, the culture has been able to maintain its identity so well because it has existed for thousands of years in the same place. This continuity has created a sense of being that is in harmony with that place. In their religious beliefs and stories (often called "myths"), animals play a prominent role. Perhaps most notable is that an animal is the creator of the world. In Tlingit culture, as well as many other tribes in the Pacific Northwest, it is the raven (or "Raven") who created the world. Stories about Raven quickly reveal that he is not an altruistic character who acts out of an overflowing goodness. Raven steals, among other things, daylight, the moon, and water, and his actions always involve self-interest. This does not mean that he should not be respected. Raven reflects the idea that without tricking other animals, one will not survive. Hunting occurs out of self-interest (survival of oneself and one's family), and without tricking animals one will not be successful and survive. Raven's creation of creating the world involves violence and ruses. Light and water are not just created with the snap of a finger (or by flapping a wing). Likewise, food does not just appear on the table. Still, hunting and harvesting are to be done respectfully, since humans are sharing their place with other beings, brothers and sisters, who constitute the world in which and off which one lives. As such, the Tlingit practices and philosophies constitute a full sense of being: food, religion, place, cultural identity, individual identity, stories, and other beings are fully integrated.

In hunting practices, Tlingit pay attention to ravens. Ravens (or "Raven," indicating the spirit of the animal, shared by all ravens) might tell you where prey is. Again, ravens don't provide this information out of the goodness of their heart; they know that you will thank them by leaving a part of the animal. As is a common custom in many other Native American practices, Tlingit people also thank the animals whose lives they have taken. They will not brag about the size of the animal, how good of a hunter they are, nor will they ever announce that they are going to hunt. If one does brag in one way or another, the Tlingit suggest, one might upset the animal's spirit and you will not have much luck hunting next time. These ideas might be dismissed as superstitious practices, but more importantly the practices indicate what our place in nature should be: a humble member of the natural world, who should deeply respect anything that makes our life possible in the first place. The practice also indicates that we cannot always depend on having plenty of food. The balance in nature is fragile and easily disturbed.

The contrast with the natural understanding of the Western world is stark. We mostly do not know where our food comes from, and the animals that we eat are treated in the worst way possible. When we white people hunt or fish we do not hesitate to brag about our catch. Scores of people fly to places such as Sitka to fish for a weekend. On a Friday plane to Sitka one hears endless stories about fishing and hunting. These tourists take pictures of their biggest catches and brag about it at the local bar.

Both practices, the white tourist's bragging and the humble respect of the native person, reflect different relationships with our natural environments. For the tourists, the place is merely a place to fish. They travel thousands of miles to catch and kill an animal that they could have bought in the local grocery store. Their experience of the world contains food in abundance, as we all find abundance. Catching one's own fish is not a matter of survival; it is a sport.

Places in the Pacific Northwest, such as Sitka, have traditionally had an abundance of food. Because of this abundance, certain native families were able to become very wealthy. Many Tlingit stories reflect how good hunters became tribal leaders. However, greed, disrespectful behavior, and taking one's own place for granted lead to disaster. Being a good hunter implies being humble and respectful, understanding the natural world as potentially violent. It can and will turn against you without the proper practice.

Today, native people also have access to an abundance of Western food, and this has certainly had a significant impact on their cultures, resulting in, among other things, obesity and health issues. Yet, for many native cultures in Alaska, their tradition and the practices that are part of that tradition are still alive. It reflects their longstanding relationship with the place that they not only live in, but also live off. They are not the owners and conquerors of their place. They follow practices that place them in a very humble position in relation to animals, plants, trees and the earth itself.

While subsistence is attainable for a small population in Alaska, proposing such practices for the total population of the world, or even this country, would be utterly naive. Yet, the way in which Native American cultures, such as the Tlingit, relate to their place at least presents a guideline for more sustainable practices. Native American people have, for a long time, changed and managed the land. Yet, in those practices a humble position in which one recognized a different hierarchy than ours was in place. The very fact that the earth was created by an animal, Raven, is telling: divine power does not lie in a creature that has human characteristics (e.g. after whose image the human being was created), but in the animal realm. One could simply dismiss such stories as indeed "stories," or "myths," but what these stories ultimately tell us is that we humans are not all-knowing and that in fact we might know less than some of the animals do. While we walk slowly and have limited sight, hearing, smell and touch, animals such as ravens sense a lot more in the forest (and perhaps even in the city) than we do.[10]

It is our modern tendency to think that we can know (and solve) everything. This is, arguably, a deception in part created by the very instruments with which we gather data. We collect mostly visual information, and are able to peek into distant, young, parts of the universe. The images created by instruments such as the Hubble telescope are often amazingly beautiful. Yet, such images create, at best, a partial truth of the places we study. One of the well-known problems with Hubble images is that its camera takes black and white photos, and the colors are filled in by human beings. Thus, NASA uses some aesthetic capacities to create images that others will find beautiful, partly to keep people excited about these space explorations, and to ensure future funding. We find science thus immersed in politics, aesthetics, and economics.

I turn now to a well-known story in the Pacific Coast Athapaskan cultures. The story is titled *The Woman Who Marries a Bear*, and is discussed by Gary

Snyder in *The Practice of the Wild*, among others.[11] As the title suggests, the story is about a woman, a young woman of "about ten years old" who is tricked by a bear (Snyder 1990, 155).[12] The story reflects on our relationship (and in particular that of women) to nature. Many Native American cultures that share their environment with bears have clear rules and taboos about a woman's behavior in relationship to bears. She is not allowed to look at a bear, or even speak about a bear. She should not eat the meat of a bear, nor come close to its hide, which is often considered to be alive for many years after the bear was killed; it retains its spirit powers. Breaking any of these rules will bring bad luck.[13] Excrements are another taboo, as is discussed in the story: "Men could walk over them, but young girls had to walk around them." This young girl "loved to jump over the bear droppings, and kick them" (Snyder 1990, 155). Perhaps this is where the trouble started; perhaps this was a symptom of the trouble. Either way, while she is berry picking with her mother, sisters, and aunts she kicks some bear droppings and when at the end of the day she falls behind the group, she is approached by a man who tells her he knows a good spot with even better berries. While this seems like a classic trick of a child molester, this story is a bit more than that. The man is the bear in disguise, who knows another trick that will make her forget about home:

> The young woman talked about going home, about her father and her mother, and he said, "Don't be afraid. I will go home with you." Then he slapped his hand down right on top of her head and put a circle around the woman's head with his finger, the way the sun goes. Then she forgot and did not talk about home any more.
>
> (Snyder 1990, 156)

She slowly realizes that he is a bear and they spend the winter in a den, where she has two babies, a boy and a girl. In the spring, her brothers come. She asks her husband not to kill her brothers – "Just think of the kids" (Snyder 1990, 159). He, apparently, does listen – and instead the brothers kill him. This is not the end of the story. After returning to her family, the girl who married a bear actually turns into a bear when her brothers tease her and throw "bear hides over her and her little ones. She walked off on four legs! She shook herself just like a bear – it just happened! She was a Grizzly Bear. She couldn't do a thing." The story ends with a lesson: "So, a Grizzly Bear is partly human. Now people eat Black Bear meat, but still don't eat Grizzly meat, because Grizzlies are half human" (Snyder 1990, 161).

The story provides us with many other lessons regarding respectful behavior toward animals. Our relation to the bear is a close one. We should not kill it without acknowledging this closeness. We have to respect it, thank it, not make fun of, and not waste any of the parts of its body. Like many other aboriginal stories, it provides the message that a disrespectful relationship to animals and natural resources is going to haunt us. Taking too much, or taking things without proper care, is dangerous. *The Woman who Marries a Bear* challenges our place in nature. While the story is not factual (I assume), its metaphors are rich. It relates us to the beings with which we share food like berries, the beings that fertilize the soil on which this food grows, and the beings that have human appearances.[14]

The disrespect of the natural world in the mind and practice of the West has resulted in global environmental destruction, which has severe consequences for aboriginal tribes that are still tied to their place. Deforestation in the Amazon, for example, is not merely an environmental disaster; it also destroys tribes, who often do not just lose their culture, but also their lives. Displacements to lower elevations expose them to germs that can kill them. We are completely blind to these disasters. In addition, we have trouble understanding any way of thinking that does not place us on top of the hierarchy as the managers and controllers of nature. Dōgen and Watsuji, even Leopold, propose ways of thinking that are extremely hard for us to understand. We have learned that we are the measure of all things and in our practices we constantly change our environments. We use natural resources without ever thinking about the fact that we cannot replace those resources. We change the places around us constantly, so that it makes us feel at home. We even think that we know how ecosystems work and how we can improve them.

The politics of nature

Indigenous thinking, and the work of Dōgen and Watsuji, can perhaps be brought closer to home through the work of Bruno Latour, and in particular his work *The Politics of Nature*. Latour is famous for his actor–network theory, in which a collective of actors form a unity. Such a collective can consist of human beings, but non-human actors are also included. Along the lines of Heidegger's discussion of technology, Latour understands tools not as passive instruments, but rather as active agents within a network. Computers and cell phones play an essential part in our network today. Such technologies actively participate by changing the very network of which they are a part. It is true that humans make computers and cell phones, but these technologies also act independently of their makers; they change the nature of the network way beyond the intentions of the inventors of the technologies. Thus a social network consists of technologies and human beings in which the different parties are each recognized as actors.

In the *Politics of Nature* Latour takes a further step by including natural objects as well as animals in the collective or network. Trees, rivers, the weather, animals, etc. are not merely objects to be studied and manipulated by us. All these parts are, along with human beings, active participants within a network. Latour provides the example of toads for which a special tunnel has been built under a newly constructed highway. The toads are expected to follow their instinctual drive to return to their nesting site. Yet, the toads react differently: they refuse to use the tunnel and simply change their nesting site, defeating the knowledge we had of the nesting behavior of toads (Latour 2004, 87). They, thus, do not merely act, but re-act to the changed circumstances. We tend to think in terms of essences when it comes to non-human parts of the collective. Latour shows that it is not essential for toads to return to the same pond where they were born. Toads behave; they have habits which are not essential, but which they can change.

Animals and plants also react to climate change. The interbreeding of polar bears and grizzlies is one of those reactions in which we find a network consisting of the agency of weather, ice (or the lack thereof), different sorts of bears, and human beings, who possibly caused the climate change and who are disturbed by the interbreeding of two different species of bears. Similar to the toad, a polar bear is not essential as a species; it can interbreed and become a "grolar" or "prizzly bear."

Beyond the animal realm we can think about living and non-living things. Going back to Dōgen's and moreover to Heidegger's example of the river, we can think about what happens with our interactions with the river when we dam it up. The river is not just passively becoming a lake and a hydroelectric plant the way we want it to: it is, first of all, reacting to the damming. Silt or mud that used to be spread out down along the riverbanks now pile up behind the dam. Ecosystems are altered because fish cannot swim up the river anymore. We might seem to be the lone actors, but first of all, we did not make an intentional decision to change an ecosystem. It is mostly an unintended consequence. Second, hundreds of dams (in the USA alone) have collapsed under the pressure of a river. The river is then also an actant, one that refuses to be constrained by a dam. Humans, silt, fish, mud, water, and the dam are all actors, or actants, i.e., active participants in the collective.[15]

According to Latour, the metaphysics of nature as we find it at work in the natural sciences has been based upon Plato's cave, where we find on the one hand humans and on the other hand objective knowledge. Science presumes that it has either walked out of the cave, or has never been there. Nature is studied as a series of knowable objects, rather than shadows. In modern philosophy we find a distinction between subject and object in relation to freedom and necessity. Objects are necessary; they cannot be in any other way as they are passive and subject to causality. Only humans can be free (Latour 2004, 80).

While postmodernity has questioned what a subject is, Latour claims that postmodernity has failed to question objects and has failed to question the necessity of nature. Latour argues that, in fact, we need to get beyond dualistic thinking such as the oppositions of truth and appearance, necessity and freedom, and passive and active. Such oppositions only keep the cave intact. Overcoming the cave means overcoming the ignorant and arrogant idea that we can actually objectively study nature, as if the concept of an object is not a social construct, as if only human affairs are relative or socially constructed, whereas the truth with a capital T is to be found when we study nature. One could say that the humanities and social sciences try to drag people back into the cave in order to show the shadows of reality, while the natural sciences think they are entirely free of shadows and study the truth outside of the cave.

In his *Neale Wheeler Watson Lecture*, Latour provides the example of the *construction* of climate change, often criticized and used politically (Latour 2010). The criticism is that instead of objectively studying climate change, these scientists have fabricated a story. Latour's theory points out the (obvious) fact that scientists, indeed, do construct nature, instead of objectively studying it. Every theory, every law of nature, is constructed by humans, and so is the idea or concept of global warming or climate change.

Latour wants to move from matters of fact to matters of concern (Latour 2004, 66). There are no objective facts, but only matters with which we can concern ourselves. The world is composed through humans, and through language. Latour wants to argue that not only human agents, but also non-human parts of the collective, are able to speak. He interprets the whole enterprise of science as an attempt to let these non-human parts speak: "we all work constantly to make things relevant to what we say about them. If we stop working, they no longer say anything; but when they do speak, it is indeed they that speak and not we ourselves – otherwise, why the devil would we work night and day to make them speak?" (Latour 2004, 86).

Yet, within what kind of framework do we let things speak? It is crucial for Latour to step beyond the false opposition of nature and society, between nature and politics, so that we can establish an ecology in which we are part of a collective with the non-human parts. Latour makes three arguments or moves in order to reach this political ecology that consists of a collective involving human and non-human members. All three moves are related to the apportionment or distribution of certain capacities, such as the capacity to speak. While we have claimed reason or logos for ourselves, Latour redistributes this capacity. It is true we are more able to speak than non-humans, but it is not entirely impossible for them to speak and in fact the main goal of science is to let nature speak. This makes science political, since it makes things speak: "Scientists argue among themselves about things that they cause to speak, and they add their own debates to those of the politicians" (Latour 2004, 63). In addition, Latour uses the notion of a spokesperson.

> [W]ith the notion of the spokesperson, we are designating not the transparency of the speech in question, but the *entire gamut* running from complete doubt (I am a spokesperson, but I am speaking in my own name and not in the name of those I represent) to total confidence (when I speak, it is really those I represent who speak through my mouth).
>
> (Latour 2004, 64)

We always doubt any spokesperson in the field of politics: a spokesperson can always misrepresent and speak in their own name. Latour argues that the same is true for the scientist: "the lab coats are the spokespersons of the non-human, and, as is the case with all spokespersons, *we have to entertain serious but not definitive doubts* about their capacity to speak in the name of those they represent" (Latour 2004, 64–5). As with any spokesperson, we have to doubt their integrity as well as their authority. It would be naive to think that scientists have seen the truth that no one else has seen, that we cannot even see or comprehend. It is again the image of the cave that is implied here: too often science is regarded as an absolute truth that does not deal with shadows. In the everyday observation of the world's phenomena we are looking at shadows, while science claims to have stepped outside of this realm of shadows, and is presenting the truth, a truth the common person cannot understand or see. This is – for Latour – the use of the image of the cave against any philosophical attitude.

Instead, Latour emphasizes that scientists are politicians in the sense that they are spokespersons, speaking for non-humans. In their attempts to let the non-humans speak, we find the same problems we find in human politics. Things, or facts, do not speak for themselves, Latour emphasizes. "The most common of all clichés in the City of Science is that 'the facts speak for themselves.' But what does it mean for a fact to speak 'for itself'?" (Latour 2004, 67). It is precisely forgotten that the scientist is a spokesperson who translates, using instruments, methods, as well as ideologies and a "thirst for power" (Latour 2004, 67). The positive aspect is that science is already bringing nonhumans into the collective. However, we have to recognize that this is not factual reporting, but a political endeavor. "Lab coats have invented speech prostheses that allow nunhumans to participate in the discussions of humans" (Latour 2004, 67). By rethinking scientists as translators and providers of crutches or prostheses in the form of language, Latour forces us to think beyond the opposition between humans and divine knowledge as we find it in the cave. With this move science is brought into democracy. "Democracy can only be conceived if it can freely traverse the now dismantled border between science and politics, in order to add a series of new voices to the discussion, voices that have been inaudible up to now, although their clamor pretended to override the debate: *the voices of non-humans*" (Latour 2004, 69). While Latour's claim that a true democracy can only exist if we include non-humans might seem outrageous, he points out that we do already speak on behalf of collectives that are non-human, in phrases such as "France has decided," but also in a person's knowledge of the mass of the earth (Latour 2004, 70). A spokesperson for the collective can also speak of species being endangered, rivers polluted, ecosystems being altered, etc. Latour wants to bring our attention to the fact that this is not different from the political discourse, in which one might be speaking on behalf of the poor, the wealthy, or the middle class.

In this idea of a spokesperson and the notion of a democracy that consists of a collective that includes the non-human, we recognize that non-humans have a capacity to act. Non-humans are not merely passive, and their essence has not been determined. Freedom is not limited to the human realm, but can be witnessed in the behavior of animals and plants.

As already mentioned, we should understand Latour's politics of nature within his actor–network theory in which he places the human in a network of relations with human and non-human actors. An actor or actant, for him is a member of an association (or network). The acts of these members "modify other actors" (Latour 2004, 75). We human actors are not isolated subjects, or merely in inter-subjective relationships. Echoing Merleau-Ponty's attack on the subject–object divisions, Latour places us in a collective in which the division of subject and object is replaced by an association of humans and non-humans: "objects and subjects can never associate with one another; humans and non-humans can" (Latour 2004, 76). Within this association everything is redefined. Non-human and human actants are taken beyond divisions of freedom and necessity and are instead seen as recalcitrant. Non-humans are no longer objects that have to be this or that, since "the facts speak for them." Likewise humans are no longer free beings who can choose their lives without environmental constraints, but are instead situated within a network with other actants, including non-human ones. These actants modify human lives. All members will experience necessity and all members can and will disobey necessity.

In many ways, Latour's philosophy can be seen as a Western version of the traditions discussed in this chapter. His actor–network theory is an attempt to think outside of the human realm and in particular attacks the way in which science and politics have created two separate realms that he seeks to join. In fact, he argues that non-Western cultures "have never been interested in nature. They have never adopted it as a category; they have never found a use for it" (Latour 2004, 43). Nature is a category that institutes a reality, which Latour relates to the truth science has found outside of the cave. By joining science and politics he seeks to reverse that idea and bring Western thinking, science, and politics de facto closer to the non-Western ideas discussed above. Latour brings the mountain into the collective and places the human within the climate that determines who we are and how we act. From an isolated self we become an interrelated actant, related to the places around us. In that relationship place is not understood as merely a moldable and manipulative plastic entity. Place is also, and moreover, an actant, determining us at least as much as we determine it.

With this insight in mind, I will now turn to the last chapter in which I take up the topic of ecology. Needless to say, with Latour we find ourselves in a critical position toward any of the sciences. However, Latour also pointed out the way in which the scientist can be a spokesperson for nature. As such we can also learn from the engagements of the sciences with nature, in order to come to a new understanding of the places that determine us. Latour seeks to step beyond an opposition of ecology as a science of objects and politics as a science of subjects: "Instead of a science of objects and a politics of subjects, by the end of the chapter we should have at our disposal a political ecology of collectives consisting of humans and non-humans" (Latour 2004, 61). It seems fair to assess this objective as a rather optimistic, yet interesting goal. Moreover, it might be the only viable option: we are not going to change human thinking and acting from behind our laptops, smart phones, or with protesting. The only way to radically change our behavior, as I argue in the following chapter, is to radically change ourselves. This much-needed change can only occur through a radical change in our relationship with the rest of the world. Part of the aim of the final chapter of this book is to think through this idea of a political ecology, an idea we find in a different version in Leopold, Dōgen, Watsuji, and aboriginal thinking.

Notes

1 Stephen Kellert describes the inconsistency between the appreciation of nature in Japan and destructive practices (Kellert 1991).
2 In an encounter with a wolf, Nick Jans observes how it is not the teeth of the wolf that we fear, but its wisdom, which we can see in its eyes (Jans 1993, 161–2).
3 Interestingly, if we would have to choose a point in time when things were most stable, we would probably end up with the time before life appeared.
4 I would like to thank Brian Schroeder for helping me reach this insight.
5 Another fabulous work on walking is Solnit (2000).
6 As Ed Casey expressed this in his keynote address to the annual meeting of the Comperative and Continental Philosophy Circle in March 2014 in Santa Barbara.
7 See also Mayeda (2006, 40).
8 In comparison to Native American cultures that are tied to regions and places, the so-called world religions are always on the move and spreading across the globe. These are not place-bound religions, but universal religions that can be practiced everywhere. This does not always mean that, for example, Christianity is the same all over the globe and is not always simply spread by converting people to the same religion. For instance, it is well known that when the Jesuit Ricci traveled to China in 1582 he spent years learning the Chinese language and customs. His mission is in stark contrast to that of Columbus, who wanted to enslave (or kill) natives and turn them into Christians.
9 On the packaging of our food we find names of countries or states: "Produce of California", "Product of Bolivia", etc. I have never been to Bolivia, while I eat a product called quinoa from that country. I happen to live in California, but where the butternut squash that I am eating is grown, I honestly have no idea. I have no knowledge of the source of the wood used in building the house I live in. The cell phone I am carrying with me contains resources and labor from all over the world. And so on, and so on. Although we are connected to many different places we are at the same time completely disconnected from these places. And yet, we can also hear stories that provide the kind of knowledge that is not essentially different from the Tlingit knowledge of their places.
10 The closest we can get to such an experience would be through technology such as drones. Even the most advanced drones and satellites can gather a ton of information, but all the data these instruments, even collectively, put together are ultimately poor in comparison to the wealth of an actual experience of a place. We, thus, can never experience the world like a bird such as the raven or, more famously, as a bat (Nagel 1974).
11 In regard to the following analysis, I am indebted to Jason Wirth and Michael Eng, with whom I was on a panel discussing "The Woman Who Married a Bear"

at the Pacific meeting of the American Philosophical Association in April 2015, Vancouver, BC.

12 I am using Gary Snyder's version based on the story as told by Maria Johns, as documented in McClellan (1970).

13 See for a detailed discussion of the relationship between women and bears: Nelson (1983, 178–89).

14 In a contemporary version found in the mystery novel entitled *The Woman Who Marries a Bear*, John Straley uses the story in a slightly different way. This time it is the daughter who kills her father, the bear. His bear-like qualities consist of being a Tlingit hunter, who warns her about not stepping in bear droppings. He is embarrassing to the adolescent girl, since other girls make fun of her when she talks about bear excrements. When the opportunity arises and she sees her dad, the bear, in the direction where she is pointing her rifle, she pulls the trigger. This somewhat Freudian twist to the story provides such a powerful metaphor to the way in which we have killed any place-based thinking (Straley 1992).

15 For a definition of "actant" see (Latour 2004, 75, 237). He uses both the words "actor" and "actant," the latter particularly to address the fact that an actor can be non-human.

References

Benjamin, Walter. 1999. *The Arcades Project*. Cambridge, MA: Belknap Press.

Dōgen. 1985. *Moon in a Dewdrop*. San Francisco: North Point Press.

Dukeminier and Krier. 1993. *Property*. Boston: Little, Brown, and Co.

Ingold, Tim. 2000. *The Perception of the Environment: Essays on Livelihood, Dwelling & Skill*. New York: Routledge.

Jans, Nick. 1993. *The Last Light Breaking: Living among Alaska Inupiat Eskimos*. Anchorage: Alaska Northwest Books.

Kellert, S.R.. 1991. "Japanese perceptions of wildlife." *Conservation Biology*, 5, 297–308.

Latour, Bruno. 2004. *Politics of Nature: How to Bring the Sciences into Democracy*. Cambridge, MA: Harvard University Press.

——— . 2010. "May nature be recomposed? A few questions of cosmopolitics." *The Neale Wheeler Watson Lecture 2010*. Nobel Museum: Svenska Akademiens Börssal. May 11.

Leopold, Aldo. 1968. *A Sand County Almanac and Sketches Here and There*. New York: Oxford University Press.

Lyman, Howard F. and Merzer, Glen. 1998. *Mad Cowboy: Plain Truth from the Cattle Rancher Who Won't Eat Meat*. New York: Scribner.

McClellan, Catherine. 1970. *The Woman Who Marries a Bear: A Masterpiece of Indian Oral Tradition*. Ottawa: National Museums of Canada.

McRae, James. 2014. "Triple negation: Watsuji Tetsurō on the sustainability of ecosystems, economies, and international peace." In J. Baird Callicott and James McRae (eds.) *Environmental Philosophy in Asian Traditions of Thought*. New York: SUNY.

Mayeda, Graham. 2006. *Time, Space and Ethics in the Philosophy of Watsuji Tetsurō, Kuki Shūzō, and Martin Heidegger*. New York: Routledge.

Nagel, Thomas. 1974. "What is it like to be a bat?" *The Philosophical Review*, 83 (4), 435–50.

Nelson, Richard. 1983. *Make Prayers to the Raven*. Chicago: University of Chicago Press.

Snyder, Gary. 1990. *The Practice of the Wild*. San Francisco: North Point Press.
Solnit, Rebecca. 2000. *Wanderlust: A History of Walking*. New York: Viking.
Straley, John. 1992. *The Woman Who Married a Bear*. New York: Soho Press.
Thornton, Thomas. 2008. *Being and Place among the Tlingit*. Seattle: University of Washington Press.
Watsuji, Tetsurō. 1988. *Climate and Culture: A Philosophical Study*. New York: Greenwood Press.

5 Conclusion

Toward an ecopolitical homelessness

We started our journey with the image of Odysseus, who returned home suspicious and in disguise. His act of violence was a re-appropriating of his home as his place. In the previous chapters I have discussed other violent appropriations of places, creating identical places and suggesting a lack of relation to particular places. I have suggested that we have been displaced so much that home is potentially anywhere, and as a result we lose the notion of home as a place that provides authentic identity. Nietzsche, the guiding thinker in this book, questions our home in the human, the place we think we occupy by not being animal, by being rational, by speaking, and so forth. To question the human being as a home is a radical move. It means that we are not tied to an essential category and thus it creates an existential homelessness. In order to avoid this anxiety of being lost, we forcefully and violently hold on to the categories and boundaries that create order, and with that the sense of being at home.

Throughout the book I have moved in a direction in which we think beyond the human realm and beyond the opposition between (human) culture and nature in our relationship to place. We find our place within a greater context of "climate" or environment, not simply as something that surrounds us, but of which we are a part which is part of us. Our surroundings thus provide us identity or determine who we are. In the preceding chapter, I have argued along with Dōgen, Native American thought, Watsuji, Snyder, Leopold, and Latour for a non-anthropocentric and non-anthropomorphic relationship to the places that we occupy, and that shape us. The nature of this relationship is a political one, in which we become members of a larger political community. The idea of a political community itself might be considered anthropomorphic in nature. Yet, with the aid of thinkers such as Nietzsche and Dōgen we have developed strategies to step outside of our perspective and study mountains and the kind of community we find in it.

Throughout this chapter I will use the notion of "the other," which indicates any form of otherness that is opposed to a self or community. It can be nature or the animal (as the other to the human), it can be a foreigner (as opposed to a native), it can be a person of color, as opposed to the white person, it can be the exotic or non-native species as opposed to the native.

It can be any otherness as opposed to the self. In all instances we find a boundary that identifies a self or community through identifying (and excluding) what it is not. We have seen through Nietzsche, Heidegger, and Deleuze that the self is inauthentic, not what it is, and is lacking a philosophical, or existential homelessness. The self is not becoming, and is not itself. Likewise, the ideas of the other discussed in this chapter lead to inauthentic determinations of the self, and solidify one's position at the expense of creating a negative homelessness for others, who are excluded from our community. It is this exclusion that this last chapter seeks to reverse.

In order to now take a step in the direction of what Latour describes as a democratization of nature, I will turn beyond the human realm, to plants and animals. This last chapter will partly turn to ecology, but within the framework of homelessness and nomadology that I have developed. While we turn to animals and plants, and explicitly leave the political realm of the human, I will use a recent trend in biopolitical thinking: immunity. Roberto Esposito has used this term to think through human politics, but because of the term's medical and biological connotations, it provides a helpful bridge with non-human species or organisms. Immunity will, thus, be an important tool in overcoming our current political status, that in a sense "immunizes" nature, by keeping us distinct from it. The goal is to establish a politics of nature, not by keeping us out of it, but by becoming integral to it. Within this new politics, everything will change. First of all, we ourselves will change. I call this new politics of change an ecopolitical homelessness. "Being with" the other than human will, I argue, retrieve a sense of place and with that create, or recreate, an identity. Yet, we will not simply find a home in nature; we will rather regain a sense of our homelessness. The chapter, thus, develops important insights in how we conceive of our relationship to nature, and how we can change it. In this rethinking, nature also becomes homeless.

I assume that the average reader recognizes the need to change our relationship to nature. Using natural resources at the rate we do, by way of destructive practices and with an increasing world population, is unsustainable. It is my contention that the lack of intimate and political relationships with the places around us is an immediate factor that determines to a large degree how we behave toward nature. While placing ourselves in a collective with other beings, such as plants, animals, mountains, and rivers, is potentially a dangerous proposal (for have we not already destroyed enough of it?), I argue that a political unity, an ecopolitics, is the only way in which we can develop a healthy relationship with nature.

The existing literature on ecopolitics typically focuses on the human political realm and attempts to speak for nature within the context of the existing political system. Some might ask for a radical change of the existing discourse, but nevertheless the context remains human.[1] With Latour, Dōgen, and Leopold in particular, we find a much more radical suggestion by considering the human being as one among many in a larger realm. It is then the realm of the natural world in which *we* now have to find a place, rather than finding a place for the natural world in our democracy. This is a radical approach that might be deemed unrealistic or merely a philosophical thought experiment. However, we have seen that within aboriginal cultures, communities in which one practiced and thought in terms of being part of the natural world, have long been established. It is the quest of the Western world to kill such thinking and practicing, and within that context it is logical to deem the democratizing of nature unrealistic. The reality of today is that society and its political discourse are dominated by corporations, industries, and the stock market, rather than by human beings and reason. If we can accept living in a unity that is ultimately destroying the possibility to exist, could we not live in a unity that is ultimately supporting the possibility to exist?

Yet, how do we create a new democracy? Where to begin with such a daunting task? One of the lessons we learned from Nietzsche and Heidegger is that language is not a neutral instrument, but is actively creating reality. By changing the way we speak about nature and our relation to it, we can change the way we think about that relationship. For that reason I approach this last chapter through the *logos* of the field of ecology, the scientific field that studies the *oikos* or the household that is called an ecosystem. In particular, I discuss how ecosystems are working together as a unity and how ecology envisions our role, both in terms of disturber as well as restorer. In both cases the human being is seen as external, as a temporary intruder. While ecology uses a strong sense of belonging and not belonging (whereas I suggest thinking more nomadically and rethinking our relationship to place) the discipline provides important insights into ideas of place and identity. By the end of the chapter, I propose to fuse the human into the ecosystem, in a nomadic way, constituting an ecopolitics.

Immunity

In Chapter 3 I discussed Foucault's biopolitics and the way it manipulates our entire lives. My analysis focused particularly on our sense of place that has been radically altered by having the same places all around the country, and increasingly around the world. In order to relate biopolitics to the proposed ecopolitics, in which not only human but also non-human actors play a role, I use the recently developed idea of immunity. Introduced by Esposito, the concept is closely related to biopolitics and offers an additional way to critique our current political system. Beyond Esposito's intentions (although his most recent work expresses an interest in the politics of nature) it also provides a way to rethink ecological discourses, on our place in the natural world, beyond the human political realm. While, for Esposito, immunity is a concept applied to humans, in the sense of protection, either medically or politically, it is first of all a biological term. As such, it is a helpful approach to think beyond human relationships.

Starting with the human realm, Esposito uses the term immunity as "a protective response in the face of a risk" (Esposito 2011, 1). Strategies against computer viruses, battles against epidemics, and fights against illegal immigrants are some examples used by Esposito to explain the diversity of threats and our reactions in order to secure us against such threats. In each case, something frightens us that seems uncontrollable and unstoppable. The threat is a force that can alter, corrupt, or contaminate our body, our computer, or our society. In the case of illegal immigrants we are worried about the corruption of both society and our bodies: undocumented foreigners are illegal and thus already criminals. They are also seen as potentially harboring illnesses that might threaten our own health. Our societies, thus, seek to defend themselves against such threats, in order to become immune. In the human (and animal) body, the immune system attacks foreign, unwelcome cells. Immunization prepares the body to recognize such foreign cells by injecting a small amount of the foreign into the body. The body is, thus, being taught or has been prepared to recognize and fight this dangerous other, which otherwise might have been regarded as an opportunity, rather than a threat. Drawing a parallel with the medical world and immunization, Esposito argues that in a given society's quest for immunity, the paradigm "does not present itself in terms of action, but rather in terms of *reaction* – instead of a force, it is a repercussion, a counterforce, which hinders another force from coming into being. This means the immunitary mechanism presupposes the existence of the ills it is meant to counter" (Esposito 2011, 7). Thus, it always already assumes that it itself is good as opposed to the bad (or evil) counterforce that will attack it.

In the case of illegal immigrants we have assumed that this land is our land, that we own it, and that some others will try to invade it in order to own it themselves. These assumptions are constantly affirmed when others try to penetrate the borders that we keep strengthening in order to immunize ourselves. The USA keeps building higher fences and more sophisticated structures around its borders, in order to keep those who do not belong out. Immigration reform is an important election agenda item. Likewise, some European politicians promote an agenda that focuses entirely on immigrants, as foreign forces that should be kept out. This is one way in which "the other" evil force is included in order to protect us against this force – similar to the way medical inoculation works, a "homeopathic protection practice" (Esposito 2011, 8). Esposito's theory, then, does not so much focus on the forces we keep out, such as in the immigration crisis outside or at our borders (for example at sea, or at the southern US border). Rather, his theory focuses on the other forces that are included in order to thwart them on a larger scale. One could exemplify this with undocumented workers who strengthen the US economy. Our foods, childcare, cleaning services, carpentry, and garden maintenance would be unaffordable without these workers. Some border patrol agents are legalized citizens, "others" who have become truly incorporated, and now stop others from pursuing the same path.

In terms of home and homelessness this means that we are creating our home by excluding others, who are now homeless while explicitly wanting to be part of our home. We create our home, in fact, by immunizing it against other forces. This immunity creates a false sense of home, or what Esposito calls the opposite of community. The excluded other is a part of our community in a positive and negative way. The other is part of community positively in the sense that a community diverts, or becomes resistant to, a lethal force or principle. Negatively, in constituting community through exclusion immunity is its opposing force: "immunity constitutes or reconstitutes community precisely by negating it" (Esposito 2011, 9). While the resistance to lethal forces is important in order to protect a community, the exclusion of others is a negative and destructive force. Likewise, the exclusion of community from our own lives (another form of immunity) negates community. This latter form of immunity came up in Chapter 3, when I discussed different technologies, such as the radio, television, and car, that each create community, but in doing so actually isolate and immunize one's existence. Today a movie theater is a place to encounter germs (or bullets). A car is a personal sanctuary, not to be shared with others. Both these negative forms of immunity and also the more positive immunizations against lethal forces aim at security. For Esposito immunity leads to the opposite of community, to its negation, when we exclude the other altogether from our lives, either by isolating ourselves from our community or by excluding particular others from it. The security provided by immunity, in the sense of the protection against foreign "other" forces, can, according to Esposito, become dangerous and on many levels already has become dangerous. Autoimmune diseases turn the body against the immune system it is supposed to protect. Likewise, the immunity we find in our society has reached a level at which it can turn against those it is supposed to protect, Esposito argues. He uses Luhman's insight that the "immune mechanism is no longer a function of law, but rather, law is a function of the immune mechanism" (Esposito 2011, 9). The drive for security is setting the agenda, is inscribing the law; instead of protecting, it actually destroys community.

This model of immunity with the aim of security can be found in the plastic places described in Chapter 3. These places allow for some, while leaving others out, providing a sense of community that is based on exclusion, and that provides a sense of security that is implicitly hostile against true living and, as we have seen in Chapter 3, against nomad thought. In terms of our relation to nature we seem to immunize ourselves from anything associated with nature. We can build our houses in a natural setting, using natural materials, but insects, dirt, animals and even the climate are to be kept out. This kind of immunity, driven by a sense of security and fear of the other, provides an interesting parallel to the fear of the foreigner, to be kept outside of the border. Both others – the foreigner and nature – are seen as threats that might contaminate our bodies and our society. Thus, we find (again) the separation of the realms of nature and society. The model of immunity shows that these are not entirely mutually exclusive places: Society, or culture, has some place for nature, but the amount is miniscule, and human beings control it in order to avoid contamination. Thus, we have a garden, a lawn, and flowers on the kitchen table. Likewise we eat vegetables that have been purchased at the grocery store, contained and regulated by several companies and government agencies, providing the illusion that nature has been made safe enough to interact with the human world. The small amount of nature allowed in and around our homes and bodies allows us to control it, so that it does not control us.

In terms of immunity and otherness, we return here to the author of *The Island of Dr. Moreau*, discussed in Chapter 1. H.G. Wells wrote the three-volume book *The Science of Life*, with his son G.P. Wells, and Julian Huxley (Wells *et al.* 1931). The 1,500-page book on evolution discusses, among others, epidemics and illnesses, and influenced Burnet's Nobel Prize–winning work on immunology (Tauber 1994, 94). Immunology is one of the theories that (along with ecology and others) was a direct result of Darwin's theory of evolution. It develops a strategy against evolving germs and seeks to adapt the body (by becoming resistant) to certain environmental threats. Wells's Dr. Moreau has immunized himself from society by retreating to an island where he attempts to cheat evolution by changing individual bodies, as opposed to the slow evolution that occurs over thousands or millions of years to larger populations. Immunology, with different strategies, also tries to change the individual body.

While Dr. Moreau's techniques, if they were possible, present some obvious problems, keeping out or destroying organisms that might make us sick is not a problem in itself. However, ethical questions arise, or should arise, when the organism in question is a foreign person. Furthermore, the idea that this other might make us sick or harm us is based on false presuppositions. It is typically us who make the new immigrants sick, exposing them to germs they have never encountered before. Lastly, the whole idea of immunity as a drive for security excludes the other, the foreigner as well as nature, from participating in our society, in our culture, in our economy, and in our political system. It turns the other into a homeless being, who does not have a place in our world. While we encountered homeless or nomadic thinking in an existential way as a prerequisite for thinking, the exclusion of the other is not an existential condition, but rather a destructive moment. When one is displaced by political, environmental, or economic circumstances and one only meets hostility, exploitation, and abuse, one is merely struggling for survival, hoping for a lucky break. One is far from any philosophical thinking. The exclusion one faces in this kind of displacement is, partly, Esposito's point when he argues that immunity is the opposite of community. It creates a double problem: not only does immunity create homelessness, but it also targets it. Immunity then suggests that we are tied to places (our body, our home, our country), or that those who are not tied to places are bad, corrupt, or not to be trusted. Being tied to a particular place is possible through exclusion of the other. Anything and anyone that does not fit will be kept out with just a few exceptions, which mostly serve our own interests. Homelessness and homeless thinking are the target of immunity. The foreign, or other, including foreign ideas or ideas of otherness that question boundaries of self and other, are securely left out.

Esposito argues that excluding foreign elements altogether is the opposite of community. Immunology in the medical field recognizes individuality within a context, within a community. As a (bio)political strategy, immunity "unburdens from this burden" (Esposito 2011, 84). His concern is that

> [a]lthough immunity is necessary to the preservation of our life, when driven beyond a certain threshold it forces life into a sort of cage where not only our freedom gets lost but also the very meaning of our existence – that opening of existence outside itself that takes the name *communitas*.
> (Esposito 2013, 85)

We could say that the reaction we currently have to otherness is to fight the foreign element. We fail to recognize the other as a force that could enrich our community. We fail to recognize that the other can also bring new possibilities to our lives. In the analysis of plastic places in Chapter 3, we found this kind of immunity in the creation of identical places, which provide an identity to those who move around: the settled nomads. This immunity consists in not letting any other places exist, i.e., in not being exposed to any places that might challenge us. This lack of exposure to any other places constitutes a lack of freedom. Freedom itself becomes defined through a series of choices between nearly identical products that can be bought in nearly identical places. To be free means to choose which brand of cola one drinks, what kind of shoes one wears, and what kind of phone one owns. Individuality as an expression of our freedom occurs within a structure of oneness, of the same repeated in slightly different expressions, but always excluding otherness. Community turns into immunity in which one finds satisfaction as an individual in shopping, or in using the immunizing, i.e., isolating, technologies purchased: smartphones, tablets, computers, cars, and so forth. These items all provide security: one knows who one is, what one should do, and what one should not do. Within Foucault's panoptic structure, one also self-regulates one's behavior since one is always afraid to deviate from the norms that society has prescribed. Nomadism, or homeless thinking, does not need to be forbidden; society has already secured our thinking and acting.

In opposition to this overly secure sense of immunity, we need to rethink community, in which we can experience existence as co-existence, i.e., to be in community with others. Latour, as we have seen at the end of Chapter 4, argues that such a community should include non-human actors, placing us in relation with the members of ecosystems, or rather placing us within ecosystems. Today, we tend to immunize nature: ecosystems are protected (often rightfully so) against humans, and with that we immunize ourselves. In providing security for other species we, in fact, also ensure our own immunity from other species. It is not just in protecting other species that we find such closed off, separated worlds. In our political, social, and cultural endeavors, nature does not have a place. Nevertheless, we constantly use nature as a resource. Because of this separation between nature and culture, it might appear that nature is infinite; we are doing fine, and since we lack real knowledge of the places around us, nature seems to be doing fine as well. This is a very dangerous kind of immunity that creates delusion.

Changing environments

In order to overcome this immunity and to (re-)place ourselves in a larger community, I will now discuss our interactions with nature, first through urban ecology. Here I want to unpack the way nature has a place in our cities. I will do this not simply in terms of natural beings that somehow can coexist with human beings in an urban setting. Rather, I consider how nature itself is shaping, and has to shape, our environments. As such we are in a reactive and political network engaged with actants, which include animals and plants, as well as environmental factors, such as heat and cold.

Our starting point is urban ecology, as discussed by Mugerauer. In the helpful essay "The city: a legacy of organism–environment interaction at every scale," he rethinks the way in which nature exists in the city: not as a tree or a squirrel that can live in an urban or suburban environment, but rather on the organic level in which all organisms do not merely "fit in" as they are selected by their environment, but actively change their surroundings (Mugerauer 2011). Mugerauer uses the concept of the niche construction. Whereas in traditional evolutionary theory "inherited genes are selected by environmental factors," the niche construction suggests that the organism actively participates in altering its environment:

> an organism comes to life in an environment, partly constructed by other organisms of the same and different types; the environment modifies the organism as an existing individual and genetically, so that offspring are affected; the genetic changes make a difference to the organisms in action; the organisms interact with the transformed environment as other organisms select those dimensions that might count as a niche and further modify that environment, and so on.
>
> (Mugerauer 2011, 266–7)

Organisms not only interact with, but also are actively engaged in the construction of their environment. Mugerauer provides examples of trees and insects like ants that change the environment of which future generations benefit. For example, pines change the soil in such a way that subsequent seedlings may grow up to twice as fast.

Mugerauer is particularly interested in cities. Drawing a parallel with the way in which organisms actively participate in re-creating their environment, cities also do more than merely erect buildings and infrastructures that suit the particular climate. Cities and even particular buildings can change the climate. Cities raise the temperature, and skyscrapers increase wind and alter weather patterns. Moreover, he points out how generations of architects have learned how to interact and integrate buildings in particular environments. "Sick buildings" provide important lessons in how not to build. Integrating heating and cooling systems (within structures and within the larger context of a whole city) reduces energy use and also creates a healthier living and working environment. Following Mugerauer, integrating nature in building principles, or integrating nature in urban planning, are some possible directions to take.

In another work, Mugerauer suggests using Latour's actor–network theory as a device to understand the interaction of human and non-human organisms (Mugerauer 2010). It seems, indeed, that when we build we need not only alter the place in which we build, but also anticipate how the changed environment will react to supporting a structure in this place. As Watsuji points out, many aspects of our culture, including architecture, are dictated by engagement with the environment, or climate. A cold or rainy climate will require a particular way of building. Latour places such engagement with our environment within a political structure, in which we do not only listen to our own interests, but also to those of the non-human actant. For example, building in an area with wildlife will require some negotiations and thought, so that we do not get upset when our cat is eaten by a coyote, when our commute is doubled in time because of a flood, when our cabin is destroyed by a bear that developed a taste for chocolate, or when at dusk our car is destroyed after an encounter with a deer.

The idea that our lives are entirely separate from nature, even when we live in remote areas with other species, again suggests immunity, a cognitive and physical attempt to separate nature and the human. The urban relationships Mugerauer describes can be understood in terms of the actor–network theory. I take this now a step further: not only within urban environments, but the homes of other species can also be reinterpreted as places in which we have a shared political interest.

Field trip: a short excursion to the Sutro Forest

Let us take a quick excursion exploring nature in the city, in this case the Sutro Forest in San Francisco. It consists of about 30,000 eucalyptus trees spread out over 80 acres. The trees were planted between 1830 and 1898 and today form a popular forest in the heart of San Francisco. Besides the eucalyptus and the always-present poison oak, the forest is home to over 90 different species of plants (including acacia and blackberries). The wildlife consists of raccoons, opossums, skunks, great-horned owls, foxes, coyotes, pygmy nuthatches, and many songbirds, among others.

The history of the forest is significant in a few ways: to start, human beings brought the eucalyptus trees to California during the Gold Rush. As such, they are considered non-natives. The trees do extremely well in the area, following exactly the new evolutionary path described in the previous paragraphs – the trees do not merely adjust to the new environment, but actively change their environment. Located on a hill often covered in fog, the forest receives several inches of precipitation during the dry season as water collects and drips from the long eucalyptus leaves. Even after months without any actual rain, one often encounters deep puddles of water on the trails that wind through the forest. We see here immediate evidence of how an organism can change its surroundings. Besides precipitation, the trees also change the soil structure and outcompete other trees, while allowing other bushes to thrive. The forest is also a pleasant place for human beings to walk. Lastly, the forest provides an important aesthetic component to the city. Since the forest is located on a hill, it can be seen from many parts of the city and from across the bay. It is, in fact, amazing to find this forest in the center of a big city such as San Francisco, where space is limited and expensive.

Considering all this, it is not surprising that when the University of California at San Francisco (UCSF), which owns the land, announced they would take down the eucalyptus trees as well as the underbrush, protests quickly emerged. The argument made by UCSF (through the logos of the ecologists) is that the forest consists of 80 acres of weeds. San Franciscans, on the other hand, do not want to lose a seemingly healthy forest that provides a habitat for wildlife and a perfect place to hike after a day at the office. The debate was even covered in an opinion piece in the *New York Times*, entitled "Hey, you calling me an invasive species" (Klinkenborg 2013).

Perhaps it is surprising that ecologists would be this aggressive toward trees growing in a city. It might again be the power of language as world-forming at play here. The proposal to cut down the trees would probably never have occurred if "Sutro Forest" had been named the "Sutro Park," suggesting that it was man-made instead of a natural forest. "Forest" is derived from the Latin "foris," meaning "outside," suggesting uncultivated land. Man-made parks, on the other hand, are widely accepted even while those often predominantly house non-native plants. Parks do have important functions for human beings. It seems that in the mind of ecology, forests (or nature in general) does not function as a place where people go for a hike after work, walk their dogs, enjoy the views over the city, and where some unnamed philosophy professor even brings his students to engage in the impossible task of studying how a forest thinks. Acting as such affirms the forest as an actual place, rather than a site or heterotopia. For ecology the forest is a place that should not be, or that should not be a place. We seem to work here again with the (false) notion that nature is not an actual place for us humans. The human and natural realms remain fundamentally separated. This distinction in turn plays a significant role in the way the Sutro Forest is judged, since in the logos of ecology it is explicitly not a Californian forest.

For my purposes here, the Sutro Forest provides a perfect example of how nature, in fact, has become part of our political actions. To cut or not to cut down the trees is not merely an ecological question (I will leave aside the question of whether pure ecological questions even exist). It is a political question. In the debates, residents will speak up for their own interests, but also for those of the animals who live in the forest. In this respect, nature is not something outside of the human realm, but is integrated in urban life. Within that context it partly does its own thing, but not without changing its environment, including the human beings who enjoy the forest, either by looking at it from a distance or by actively walking through it. This is important to understand: we are not immune to the forest; we are part of the environment of the trees, are transformed by it.

The idea that our environment transforms us, indicates that we are, indeed, in a reactive relationship with it. One recent study discusses how safe routes to school not only enhance children's positive experience of their neighborhood, but also contribute to learning. The study concludes that "as exposure to auto traffic volumes and speed decreases, a child's sense of threat goes down, and his/her ability to establish a higher degree of spatial knowledge as a richer cognitive connection with their community rise" (Appleyard 2015, 35–6). This is another example of how we change depending upon our relationship to the places in which we live. Perhaps this is a form of adaption, but it seems more than that since the study indicates that we do not adapt as easily to an environment in which we experience danger and feel threatened. Dealing with fast traffic will be our priority and this priority will, in fact, be detrimental to our learning.

Thus, we do not merely change our environment, our environments change us and likewise we are with other organisms in a symbiotic or reactive relationship in shared environments. All living beings are changed and change their environment. In this way we are already in a political community with nature. For even while the Sutro Forest is a fairly particular example, all cities, even the most industrial ones, fail to exclude nature altogether. Non-human organisms always find new ways to inhabit challenging environments. Like human beings, they will not simply find a place that fits them, but every living being changes to adapt to its surroundings, and changes its surroundings to adapt to it. When the root of a tree finds an obstruction, it will push it aside. Smart city planners consider such behavior since trees with shallow root systems will push asphalt and concrete up, resulting in expensive repairs of roads and sidewalks. Thus, we find a community in which tree and human are reacting toward one another, as actants within an ecopolitical unity. That this unity is found in the city does not make it any less natural. As Snyder indicates, the wild can be practiced anywhere. The tree, at least in this way, is already part of the political discourse.

Obviously, non-living things also have to be negotiated. The potential for earthquakes, floods, rock- or mudslides all have to be part of the political discourse. Preventing floods and slides involves planning and carefully engaging with nature. Poor building practices or lack of vegetation can lead to erosion. We humans are often poor politicians, both in the traditional political realm and in the realm of nature. Anytime a road is built, we severely disrupt the lives of all kinds of constituents: organisms, such as plants, animals, and human beings. We also move earth, destroy rocks, and redesign the way water systems flow. When such construction and engineering is done poorly by not "listening" to the interests of these parties, a new road can be destructive. The least powerful become the victims: among humans the poor and among the rest of the natural world it is those whose interests are somehow underrepresented. Sometimes elaborate systems are constructed to limit the interruption. As discussed in the previous chapter, Latour provides the example of a tunnel under a highway made for toads. The new highway would otherwise cut off their path to the place they were born, where they would (following their natural instinct) lay their eggs. Yet, despite their instincts, the toads refused to use the tunnel and laid their eggs elsewhere. Such behavior confirms the possibility of actants to readjust or adapt, and to create a new place as their "home." The toads rejected the compromise that was offered. What we need to do is listen to their rejections, so we can propose better compromises in the future.

Roads are surely a threat to all kinds of beings. Roads either limit many animals' ability to find food, or kill them when they try to cross. Roads through mountainous areas require severe violence. Many urban roads and overpasses run through poor areas, causing noise, air, and aesthetic pollution. Planners have also run roads through ancient burial grounds, disrupting indigenous relationships to the place. All of these should be important considerations when building roads, as well as considerations in deciding whether to build a road in the first place. All voices should be heard.

An ecopolitics requires a new discourse. The *logoi* of politics and ecology do not merely need to be supplemented, but rather radically altered. One thinker who points out the power and possible evil of discourse is Lyotard, who uses the concept of the *differend*, the situation in which rights are violated by excluding or targeting a particular group. More particularly, the *differend* is "the case where the plaintiff is divested of the means to argue and becomes for that reason a victim" (Lyotard 1988, 9). Even while one is poorly treated, one cannot testify to this treatment, since one, for example, does not have a voice in the legal system. One is denied a voice. Pre-abolition American laws or Nazi laws are some extreme examples of how discourses that exclude and oppress can have serious ethical consequences. The principle of the *differend* is that one discourse dominates other discourses. For example, the discourse of economy can dominate ethical discourses. In today's discussions of immigration, economic goals including job creation dominate the politics of immigration. Ethical discussions are often ridiculed, or ignored entirely. Within this discourse, illegal immigrants, or those who would like to immigrate, have absolutely no right to participate. Voting, for one, is a mechanism through which the majority rules, which – as Kant pointed out – can be a tyranny against the minority. Moreover, many have no voting rights whatsoever (while others are actively kept from exercising their right to vote). As such, the legal system discriminates against those who, for one reason or another, are not citizens. The fact that thousands of people die trying to cross borders every year, struggle with work-related injuries, and are not equally treated in terms of pay, housing, or law enforcement, could be blamed on those individuals who treat them poorly. Those individuals, however, are not the only ones to blame: overall the Western world creates an environment in which such maltreatment is inevitable. Our drive to make profits can push people toward extreme and unethical actions. When a person is illegal they become the natural target of such actions, since they have no rights, and often lack the language, skills, and education within a system that is utterly foreign to them.

Of course, we all read the *New York Times* articles on immigration issues with horror. Still, we continue to participate in an economy that drives on keeping certain people out. Likewise we support practices against nature, against the earth that supports us, for Nietzsche the greatest sin of all, since it is a sin against life itself, and with that against ourselves. In today's society everything – including how we treat one another, who is allowed in our country (and who is not), how we plan our future, whether we should stop global warming (in fact whether we should save the planet), in general what we should do or not do – is framed within the discourse of economy. We have learned and are constantly told that every time we buy something we support the economy and do something good. As Lyotard points out, one discourse that dominates other discourses constitutes an ethical problem. When all our actions are judged and all our questions are answered in terms of whether something has economic value are not, we are ignoring other important discourses.

Illegal immigrants are excluded from, and yet participate in our society. For example, undocumented workers provide a key contribution to our economy. Incarceration is another way in which minorities are included in our society – an inclusion that consists in an excluding containment. In that regard we follow the paradigm of immunity that allows the other in our political body, in order to contain it, to use it to our benefit, without letting it thrive. We do leave many communities without any real opportunities. Every major urban area in the USA has at least one, usually several, areas that are defined by gang violence, drugs, no job prospects, no healthy foods, no healthcare, and poor education. Our government gives tax breaks to large corporations, not to communities that are slowly but surely sinking away. We live in a society in which our actions are, to a large extent involuntarily, decided by the economic system that prioritizes profits over moral values. Thus, our governments subsidize companies that will bring jobs and revenue over communities and people.

The way we treat these others is related to how we treat natural places and the environmental crisis. First, the way in which we treat animals, trees, rivers, etc. often correlates with the way we treat other human beings. It indicates a lack of respect for what is other than us, other in terms of race, gender, species, and so forth. As Lyotard has pointed out, we can make a human being into a victim, while the animal is the "paradigm of a victim": if damages cannot be established "according to the human rules [. . .] then there are not even damages" (Lyotard 1988, 28). The illegal immigrant is always already in this position of the less than human, and this is by definition the case for an ecosystem or the beings that live in such an ecosystem. Thus, we find a society in which we dispose of certain humans, our natural resources as well as certain communities. Second, in both cases (the environmental crisis, and the social economic crisis in poor communities), the decision-making process is driven by economic values. Third, as many others have pointed out, the people mostly affected by environmental problems such as pollution and hazardous waste, as well as the health problems that arise from exposure, are not the people who are causing the problems. It is mostly those who are poor and the least powerful who face the brunt of these problems.

Thus, we maltreat human others, animals, living things in general, and inanimate objects on the basis of this problematic relationship to otherness. Economic values dictate what we should do in relationship to one another, and to the places that we live in. This is, for Lyotard, the *differend*, the conflict between the goals of different genres of discourse, goals that we should seek to separate. For, if we let one discourse (such as the economic) drive the agenda, we will ignore other discourses, such as education, health, humane treatment, and so forth. Within the context of this book, I push this idea further, by arguing for not merely a humane treatment, but also for a fair treatment of animals, of forests and rivers, of wetlands and swamps, of oceans and mountains.

Beyond the city

Let us now move outside of the city in order to think through the involvement of human beings in ecosystems. We are, mostly, disturbers or destroyers of ecosystems, but we also participate in other practices such as restoration of disturbed environments. How is this latter practice understood by ecology – how does the field of ecology judge our relationship to ecosystems?

Within the discourse of ecology an ecosystem is a balanced unity of different players, a household, derived from the Greek word *oikos* (also used for economy). Ecology is the *logos* of *oikos*, the discourse of the house(hold) or economy of nature. At least this seems to be the original intention when Ernst Haeckel first used the word *oekology* in 1866. It is the study of parts and wholes: how an organism relates to the environment in terms of mechanical housekeeping relations (Stauffer and De Beer 1957).[2] Haeckel uses the term "mechanistically," which seems to lack the more organic, or synergistic model of reactivity that I propose, but the more interesting aspect in his definition is the use of the household. A household is the smallest political unit, in the sense that it has a head, as well as that it is placed in a larger political unit. Ecology, thus, is the *logos*, reason, rationality, language, discourse, or story of this household. Humans are typically placed outside of this household. They can be disturbers in the sense that they, for example, log trees, threaten the existence of a particular species, or introduce new species into an existing ecosystem. The other role they can take is as a restorer, i.e., as a person who attempts to reverse previous disturbances. Interestingly, this restoration is portrayed as a temporary involvement, after which an ecosystem returns to its autonomy and the balanced state of integrity. The reality, however, is quite different; most restoration projects are ongoing and often only finish when funding runs out.

Ecology traditionally regards the human being as something that is supposed to be external to it. We find a clear separation between the human realm and the natural realm. Throughout much of this book I have questioned this opposition. Ecology, mostly, holds on to this opposition. Some have described restoration ecology by using Aristotle's distinction between nature (*phusis*) and those things produced by human beings (*techne*) (Glazebrook 2000). For Aristotle (and the Greeks), *phusis* is understood as self-production, entailing in itself its own cause, matter, form, and goal. *Techne*, on the other hand, is the human manipulation, source, or motive in which an end is externally derived. In restoration ecology we find a strange and complex mix of *techne* and *phusis*, in which humans try to restore the autonomy of natural production. What the auto-production exactly should produce is then an end determined by an external force and manipulated through human *technai*. While the external influence in restoration is undeniable, restoring implies a return to nature, to auto-production. We namely seek to reverse our disturbances, while taking into account certain natural evolutions in order to eventually have nature take its course again, without us and without our *techne*.

In ecological restoration we find the human being as Latour's spokesperson who provides a voice for the non-human. Different than what Latour (and this book) envisions, ecology works with the conception of a system that is non-human: an ecosystem that runs autonomously, without human intervention. The only human intervention is that of the ecologists who speak up for the non-human against the violence the human has inflicted. If we compare this picture to that of nature in the city, we find a striking imbalance; whereas nature in the city learns to live with and within the human realm, we conceive of this external nature as entirely outside of the human realm. If we want an earnest politics of nature, we should not only avoid excluding or silencing the non-human, we should also make sure that we (humans) are represented in the collective, both inside and outside of our realm. Only by placing ourselves within nature can we become responsible members. As long as we remain external to it, we will never recognize our responsibility to act in a non-destructive way. In an external understanding of nature we lack the insight that our destruction of nature is also a self-destruction. Furthermore, by being outside of a system, any involvement will always be violent and disruptive, which will make it difficult to distinguish between harmonious and destructive practices since our very presence is already too much.

One of the countless examples of destructive practices can be found in Staragaven, today a young-growth forest on Baranof Island in Southeast Alaska. The Staragaven area consists of a valley that was logged in the 1960s in order to produce paper. The pulp mill and the workers (and the minimal profits) are long gone, but the effects of this industry are long-lasting. The workers left their trailer-homes on the shore (today the cheapest living quarters on some of the most expensive land on the island) and left a valley without trees. The trees grew back, but are all approximately 40 years old, which means there is little variety in height and the forest lacks any clearings that would naturally occur over time. The lack of clearings means that little light reaches the ground, resulting in minimal undergrowth, and a dense forest floor that is hard for deer and other animals to negotiate. While I personally do find this forest aesthetically pleasing, it creates a very poor habitat for animals that used to live there. For an ecologist, it is not a normal landscape. Restoration involves finding methods that speed up the recovery of the landscape back to its "original," "normal" state. Such recovery often involves destruction, mimicking natural disturbances such as the effects of a storm, resulting in clearings that allow undergrowth to develop.

While untrained eyes like mine need some assistance to notice it today, the damage done to the area is tremendous; not only was a whole valley clear cut, the creeks were used as a logging road, destroying the spawning grounds for salmon. The area actually appears somewhat tame and organized, thus lacking the wild aspects of the landscape one typically encounters in this part of the world. The destruction, while barely visible on the surface, exemplifies how the destruction of an ecosystem has wide-ranging effects. While the logging brought a short-term boost to the local economy, the destruction of the spawning grounds had a negative effect on the salmon population. Salmon no longer return to this area, depriving it of the rich nutrients that used to feed the forest. In addition, the decline in the salmon population hurts the fishing industry. Restoring the forest and creeks in this area is, thus, a project that does more than benefit the salmon, the trees, and the wildlife – it rehabilitates the salmon population and with that the fishing industry.

The case of Staragaven reveals how the interest in restoring (and not destroying) this area is not merely that of the white middle class with little else to worry about. A healthy environment is important to the fishermen, those who are supported by the fishing industry, those who do subsistence fishing in order to feed their family and community members, those who buy fish in a store or restaurant, and even our pets who might eat ground-up fish in their canned or dry food. If fish like salmon become scarce, we will be forced to look for other food sources, resulting in more disturbances and overall higher food prices. Staragaven shows why we need sustainable "harvesting." In the end, the depletion of natural resources has an effect on us all

The troubling factor about the destruction in this Alaskan forest is that most parts of the world are in a far worse condition. A valley in Alaska will eventually rebound because the surrounding area thrives, and provides a habitat for the abundant wildlife that is slowly returning. The species that used to live in the valley did not go extinct and will return. This situation is incomparable to what happens when we, for example, blow-up mountains or even big parts of mountain ranges, when we pollute water streams and the air, or when we cut down over 95 percent of our forests. These actions have become the norm in a world in which we fail to include the other-than-human in our political unity. Even within human economics the cost is, in the end, higher than the profits. Attempts to restore natural habitats, clean up oil spills and other environmental disasters, the social toll of illnesses and associated health care, and rising food costs are some of the expenses that we typically fail to calculate. One can only guess at what the potential costs of rising sea levels and global warming will be. Company profits are prioritized over such environmental costs. As David Orr points out, we need to start including environmental costs such as soil depletion into our calculations (Orr 1994). This economic inclusion is another way in which we can think about the political collective; however, what I am proposing here is something entirely different in which economy itself, if it still can exist, will be radically restructured so that money becomes just one aspect. Until grizzlies can open a bank account, their interest is not going to be served by the financial world.

What we can learn from a disaster such as the clear cutting in Staragaven is that we are not immune to the violence we exercise over nature. Turning trees into paper was a mistake that cost significantly more than what was gained. We must learn first of all to leave a habitat for the other members of the collective, in this case brown bears, deer, salmon, spruce, hemlock, and so on. Second, we should understand the ecosystem in relation to the human realm. When hatching grounds for salmon are destroyed, the fishing industry and the communities that support the industry are damaged as well. This does not mean that we cannot harvest some trees; we need to learn to do it right, in moderation, at the right time, and without destroying the surrounding area, such as a creek bed. By learning from these destructive practices and by not repeating them, we in fact affirm our place in nature. It avoids the situation in which we have, on the one hand, dedicated wilderness areas that we can only visit, while we completely destroy other areas. We need to learn how to be in a community with nature and think deeply about ways we can sustainably harvest different natural resources for an ever-growing world population. Once we truly start to understand the perspectives of the proposed collective of natural beings, we will also understand that a sustainable future is the only future in which the human still has a place.

Bringing the human into nature is not some kind of romantic return. It does not mean that we return to a previous state of being. We move forward, but in a different way and a different direction, in one sense by bringing technology into nature, recognizing the use of human technology as natural and a way to enhance natural processes. The new collective then not only makes the human more natural, but can also make nature more industrial.

We certainly need to restore nature and move toward more sustainable ways of engaging with nature, but we can also try to enhance nature, to unite nature and the human.

Here, I am treading into controversial territory. Putting the human into nature has, so far, had mainly disastrous effects. We have already destroyed so much, and we think that we know while in fact we know so little. Using our knowledge is putting nature at risk. I agree that caution is important. We do not know what the long-term effects will be of the experiments with genes of food crops. Since research is controlled and done by large corporations that seek profits (and not an ecopolitical unity) we should be particularly suspicious. We also, for other reasons, should be careful with the science-fiction models of a climate that is entirely controlled by humans. I am convinced that we will learn more over time, but to rely on human inventions as the ultimate solution to climate change and other looming environmental disasters seems to put trust in the modern mindset that created all these problems in the first place. Going back to Latour's analysis of the cave, it is the false perception that science has obtained the truth and, in this case, has not only left the cave, but will be able to control it. To put us into nature, however, does not simply mean to place us there; it also means to change ourselves, to re-place ourselves. Yet, we will remain technological – it is part of our nature. Technology and industry (in the sense of its Latin meaning, diligence) will not be simply placed in nature, but will be changed by nature, through the collective of beings with which we surround ourselves.

Instead of thinking that we can control nature, we can, for example, find ways to mimic natural processes. We have done this for millennia by producing food crops, and for over a century we have also mimicked natural lifecycles of fish through hatcheries. I will use the salmon hatchery as an example of how we can put technology into nature.

The industrial facilities of the salmon hatcheries are a significant mechanism in restoring fish populations. Other than salmon farms, in which the fish are held captive their entire lives, salmon born in a hatchery are released as soon as they are ready for the ocean (when they are about six months old). Since salmon always return to their origin, they eventually swim back to the hatchery, where their eggs and sperm are extracted and mixed. The fertilized eggs will be kept in fresh running water (mimicking a river) until the fish are born. The fish are initially moved to tanks with running water until they are ready to swim freely into the ocean, completing the cycle for another generation.

Since the fish are semi-wild, the practice has been criticized. Even while the hatcheries have to follow strict state rules that keep the salmon as wild as possible, some worry that over time they become a different semi-wild species. Similar to the better-known GMO debates, we simply do not know the long-term effects and possible negative consequences of this practice. Yet, since most of their lifespan is spent in the wild and the fish are not in any way genetically manipulated, it seems that the hatchery is not a real threat to the salmon, but instead enhances the population. In places such as Alaska, where the majority of the economy relies on the fishing industry, hatcheries are very important to and financed by the fishing industry.

At this point, we should ask some ethical questions. In their natural cycle, salmon swim up a river and find a spot to lay their eggs, where the male then disperses his sperm, fertilizing the eggs. The whole endeavor of swimming up the river (without eating) and laying or fertilizing the eggs is exhausting and marks the end of their lives. In a hatchery the fish are killed before they lay their eggs or fertilize them, thus never reaching their "goal." Since their final destination is a basin in the hatchery, they do not lay their eggs and fertilize them (the fish are killed, after which their eggs and sperm are manually extracted and mixed in order to fertilize the eggs). The killing is done quickly and painlessly and, considering that the wild fish die of pure exhaustion, it could be argued that the hatchery actually saves them from this torturous journey. Nevertheless, taking away the destination toward which these animals are so naturally driven is not free of ethical complications. The fish are unable to return to their natural state of being: in the cycle of their life they are entirely dependent on the hatchery, both in terms of their birth and in reproducing.

While I do not seek to brush these possible ethical objections aside, the hatchery provides positive consequences for the overall salmon population. The primary goal of the hatchery is to enhance the salmon population. The focus is the enhancement of an industry, not the restoration of an ecosystem. Nonetheless, it has positive effects on wild salmon populations. Interestingly, since fish populations are improving because of the hatcheries, natural salmon runs are also improving. The production of fish in the hatcheries means that the overall salmon population continues to grow. With the same amount of fish caught yearly, fewer purely wild salmon are caught. Thus, one of the results of the hatcheries is that it actually helps restore the wild salmon population.

Enhancement could in some instances be part of restoration, or provide an alternative. Instead of restoring ecosystems to a historical situation, ecologists can then understand and promote their work as one of enhancing the disturbed ecosystem, instead. Enhancement then promotes biodiversity, ecosystem functions, as well as balance and health. We are then certainly using economic criteria and standards, which might not necessarily represent how an ecosystem works or even thinks. Yet, what the salmon hatchery does is to use certain economic principles (and incentives) to improve the population of wild salmon.

Economic criteria, when calculations include environmental factors, could thus potentially be part of an ecopolitics. Still, the greater goal is to step beyond the human economy of money and profits, in order to establish an economy in which all members, including the non-human actants, have a say. It seems fair to suggest that wild salmon fish populations would agree that their circumstances have improved because of the hatcheries.

Nomadic others?

Besides placing ourselves within the context of nature, I turn again to the placement and displacements within the proposed new political system. In the other chapters I have discussed our own homelessness, in both positive and negative ways. Chapter 3 focused in particular on how humans are increasingly nomadic. This has led us to a view of nature in which we are less attached to certain landscapes, geographical features, and other natural identities. Since we do not know ourselves through the place in which we live, we have also lost the places themselves.

Interestingly, ecology provides a very strong sense of placement and belonging when discussing non-human organisms. We find a rather strong sense of identity of places in concepts like "California forest," "Midwest prairie," "Australian eucalyptus," or "Asian carp." These names suggest that certain species originate and belong in certain areas, while they do not belong in other places. Yet, any natural being is on the move, either individually or generationally. When we restore ecosystems, we should be careful to avoid constructing prisons that limit the freedom of species to adapt and change their surroundings. In a new politics of nature, we have to engage with these other beings that are not always neatly tied to the places they receive their names from. As we need to place ourselves in nature we need to recognize natural beings as nomadic others, organisms that, just like us, are on the move.

We can return to Nietzsche and Heidegger, who pointed out that we seek to know everything. Ecology is a *logos*, and thus seeks to know how ecosystems function, how they are balanced and healthy, and so forth. Furthermore, ecology actually describes what it means to be healthy or balanced, and how nature should function is predetermined. Restoration ecology applies this knowledge using notions of balance and health, rooted in the idea of *oikos* as a household in which only certain members belong. The knowledge and application of ecology can be seen as an attempt to solidify at least one aspect in a world in which everything is in flux. While we ourselves do not belong to particular places, we create an image in which other species belong and do not belong in the places around us. Even while we seek to reverse our disturbances of nature, this reversal only occurs through manipulation, through control and further disturbances. The knowledge of these ecosystems can be interpreted as yet another attempt to control: we know better than nature, or rather we know and we assume that nature does not know at all. But in studying any ecosystem, we assume a certain rationality and order is at work. Is ecology trying to understand the rationality of ecosystems, or is it trying to control these natural places?

Within scientific discourses, for example biology, other species cannot be nomadic unless they are specifically labeled as such (as is the case with migrating birds). Here we witness Heidegger's notion of world-formation at work. Language is not a neutral tool that describes the world, but is itself part of reality, creating boundaries and labeling the natural world. We see ourselves as subjects observing the objective world, while, for Heidegger, language opens up the world to us as an event that we experience. Who or what is subject and object is obscured in this event, since we find an interaction, action, and reaction on both the side of the experiencing subject and of what is experienced. Yet, when we find that species belong here or there, as indicated by adjectives designating them to a particular region, we consider ourselves simple observers of an objective fact, failing to recognize that we are interacting with those objects through language. This is not to say that we should not attempt to keep non-native invading species from radically altering ecosystems. Nonetheless, if we are to truly engage with the members of an ecosystem, we would need to first of all acknowledge that we do not yet speak its language, but only ours, which at best is a poor translation of what the members of the ecosystem have to tell us.

Ecology makes an important argument in showing the negative effects of disturbances, as we have seen in the example of Staragaven. Disturbances in the form of non-native species can be similarly destructive, since they often actually diminish diversity. A typical invading non-native species does not blend in, but takes over. Perhaps the real threat is that non-natives then take our role: they gain control, we scramble to take them out, and each time we turn around they creep back in. As a consequence, the world as we ideally envision it (with a clear distinction between native and non-native species) falls apart. Thus in ecology, natural places have a particular identity in terms of what should be there and what should not be. This stability, the stability of language and technology, all provide a home for us in the world.

While natural places have designated inhabitants, we, on the other hand, can travel and move anywhere. Even in doing so we remain, apparently, who we are: Europeans can move to California, without becoming Californians. Midwesterners can move anywhere without ever becoming something other than a Midwesterner. Latin Americans will not lose their "Latin" identity. When species move, their names play a similar role. Yet, movement of both humans and other organisms does not remain without consequences. I am not a European or Dutchman who is unchanged by American politics, manners, foods, or climates. To the best of my abilities, I have adapted (and will keep adapting) to this new climate. This is true for all of us: unless we move between the identical points described in Chapter 3, we cannot be immune to a new place and its climate. Other organisms – ones that are actually much better at adapting than we are – are also changed by a new environment. Even while their names are fixed and their names try to fix them, their identities are always moldable. Ecologists are not so much concerned with the way in which a species changes due to its new environment, but how a species is changing the environment it is invading. We found the dynamic of how organisms change their environment in a positive way in an urban setting, but what happens outside of the city?

The distinction that we find in ecology between native and non-native species, and the static image of ecosystems, is a reversal of our own lack of place. Plants and trees belong to certain households, and the same is true for animals (or if they are nomadic they may migrate between particular households). When ecologists do restore a historical ecosystem, they apply all their knowledge in an attempt to recreate "health" and balance. Models of natural trajectories without human disturbances are applied. We then believe we know what the ecosystem should be like today, had those disturbances not occurred. The ideal of restoration is to aim for the historical system that has reversed human disturbances, while taking into account natural trajectories. In this ideal, the role of the human being is entirely negated. Any historian (and common sense) tells us that the past cannot be changed. It is what always haunts us. Reversing the past can never be completed, but that does not mean that we cannot move forward.

Moving and thinking forward does happen in some cases when, for example, the restoration of ecosystems turns out to be impossible or impractical. Invasive species can be tremendously challenging. Funds and labor are often limited and choices have to be made. One new and controversial approach is to accept that some ecosystems have been changed forever and that these are now novel ecosystems. This approach indicates a new politics of ecology. It reminds us of the political aspects of the ecological field – as Latour argues, all science is involved in the political. To accept or not to accept certain novel ecosystems is a politically driven process that involves, among others, worries about funding. If ecology is going to accept that certain ecosystems are novel ecosystems, questions about the validity of restorations are inevitable: should we not just accept all changed ecosystems as novel, and spend our tax dollars on something more valuable? Still, other considerations argue for an acceptance of novel ecosystems, like the fact that the earth's climate is changing. What if some of these novel ecosystems are actually ready for a new climate and turn out to be more sustainable?

The latter question is a convincing argument to many for the allowance of some novel ecosystems. Let us think here, though, about the assumed role for the human being. To allow a novel ecosystem for particular reasons indicates that we (or the ecologists) are in control, and that our reason can make the right judgments. To think forward and plan for a changed climate involves a trust in human reason: we are smarter than the plants, the forest, the river, or wetland. Even while ecosystems adjust to changes constantly, our models can predict and plan. Knowledge, the same instrument that is responsible for climate change, is then assumed to be able to assist in creating ecosystems that are ready for the future climate. Of course, reason has been and can be used for both negative and positive purposes, but we need to know what we are doing in order to avoid more negative outcomes that can occur even with the best of intentions. Since no one knows how and where the climate is going to change (is it going to be wetter or dryer, warmer or colder and where will it be wetter, dryer, warmer or colder?) it is really questionable whether we are smarter than ecosystems and can plan for an uncertain future. One strategy is to plan for multiple scenarios, so that at least part of the ecosystem will do well in the future. Again, it seems questionable how effective our involvement will be. Plants, trees, and animals have done very well, or in fact much better, without us. We now need to figure out how nature can do better with us, or rather, how we can be part of nature in a positive way.

While it seems wise to be ready for the future and that this paradigm shift should be welcomed, it continues to express an idea of human superiority over nature. Instead, we should consider a more radical paradigm shift in which novel ecosystems incorporate human industry, human pollution, and human culture and society in its very core. By doing that we are integrated in a political system in which we recognize our destructive practices by listening directly to those affected. Instead of listening to a scientist explain that 350 parts per million is the safe level of carbon dioxide, we need to hear how other members of the community are suffering, directly from those members. We are poor at this in both human and non-human contexts. Small communities that suffer a high rate of cases of cancer often face a scientific problem since the population is too low to generate supposedly significant data. Here we have to recognize science as a story among others, rather than *the* science. Other narratives need to be recognized. Likewise, we need to extend our narratives on an ecopolitical level. The scientific discourse will not disappear, but its status changes to that of one story among many others, so that it also can step into this ecopolitical collective.

The philosophers discussed in this book are fairly critical of science, as well as of philosophy itself. Husserl suggests that by merely attributing itself to facts, human thinking impoverishes itself. Nietzsche calls all philosophy an expression of the sickness of the philosophers. Heidegger focuses on the issue of the oblivion of being, a notion he seeks to re-investigate. Both Heidegger and Nietzsche are also highly critical of the natural sciences.[3] Nietzsche describes the scientist as someone seeking shelter under the structure of language that creates a truth. The scientist is worried he will be lost if the structure collapses: "the scientific investigator builds his hut right next to the tower of science so that he will be able to work on it and to find shelter for himself beneath those bulwarks which presently exist" (Nietzsche 2006, 121). Scientific language not only creates access to the world, but also inhibits our developing new ways of thinking, new ways of investigating. Heidegger accuses science of turning nature – as the object of its research – into a standing reserve. Thus, we find the idea that science treats nature in a similar fashion as the technologically driven corporation that turns a landscape into a coal-mining or fracking district. The human being "has already been claimed by a way of revealing that challenges him to approach nature as an object of research, until even the object disappears into the objectlessness of standing-reserve" (Heidegger 1977b, 19). Heidegger's claims might seem quite outrageous: Why should we not research nature? While large corporations that seek to exploit and challenge the earth pay for the research of many scientists, many others, ecologists in particular, have entered their field out of a deep concern for nature and the earth. How could scientists make nature into an object and a standing reserve?

The very idea that we research nature implies a certain distance between the two: We objectify by measuring, collecting data, and so forth. Yet, we always fail to grasp the essence of anything when we simply follow the order of a system. Heidegger provides the example of physics, a discipline that regards nature as "a coherence of forces calculable in advance, it therefore orders its experiments precisely for the purpose of asking whether and how nature reports itself when set up in this way" (Heidegger 1977b, 21). We objectify nature and reduce it to this simplicity so that we can measure it and affirm the theories we had before we even set up the experiments. As Kuhn and others have pointed out, theories are largely taken for granted and the main question of a given experiment is how we can affirm the theory. For Husserl and Merleau-Ponty, science reduces nature to what can be measured, to facts. The theories we seek to confirm and the instruments with which we measure already predetermine what those facts are.

The point here, in terms of the ecopolitics that I propose, is that in the natural sciences – in philosophy, in economy, in our general practice and thinking – we seek to dominate and subordinate nature. Nature is always oppressed and exploited and never considered as a member of the collective. We fail to inquire honestly into its well-being and what it wants.

When we consider the restoration or conservation of ecosystems, it might seem that we are leaving the technological mindset that determines everything as a standing reserve, something to be used. The criticism of the technological mindset clearly suggests that we should care about the health of ecosystems that will be destroyed if we, for example, build a dam. However, the criticism of the engineer who wants to build a dam because the technology is available also pertains to the ecologist who wants to restore a native forest (or river). Both the ecologist and the engineer work within a particular ideology. Their ideologies are opposing – exploitation versus preservation or restoration – and so are the outcomes. Still, the relationship to nature is in both cases similar: nature is something that can be manipulated, changed, and corrected. Thus, the ecologist enframes as the engineer enframes. The engineer envisions what the river can become. The available technology for building dams and turbines, in a sense, *must* be used. It would be a waste to not do so. The engineer's ideas are given shape through the ideals of technology. In her/his mind it would be a shame to not exploit the river. The ecologist uses the advanced knowledge of how an ecosystem is supposed to function. With that theoretical knowledge, ecologists envision what an ecosystem can become (again). For the ecologist who wishes to restore, her ideas are given shape through the ideal of a healthy and balanced ecosystem.

In terms of immunity we find here two different ideas at work. For the engineer who builds a dam, nature is incorporated in the human realm by, if not destroying, taming it. Nature is no longer what it was, but literally contained by a dam. The reaction of the ecologist, a fair one within the given context, is to immunize nature from us. Humans are considered the "other" than nature, the foreign body that is threatening its very existence. The only humans allowed in nature are those who restore it, or those who respectfully leave the place again as they found it. Both the mindset of the engineer and that of the ecologist are thus driven by certain ideas about what should be, and what should not be. They might be on the opposite sides of the scale (exploitation and restoration or conservation) but both seek to accomplish their goals by manipulation. How can we now join these different forces as complementary ones within the greater context of an ecopolitics? I explore some further ideas by returning to biopolitics and immunity.

Biopolitics and immunity

One of Foucault's main insights into the construction of knowledge is that knowledge does not only create power, but that a power must already be in place that determines knowledge. Latour, we have seen, uses that insight to criticize the position science has taken: outside of the cave, studying facts, rather than constructed ideas. With this in mind, we can first of all classify the very idea of an ecosystem, a unity of different household members, as a construct or story. With that insight we do not bring ecology down, but we open up the possibility for philosophical reflection, not from the outside by an ignorant philosopher failing to understand the dangers of non-native invasive species, but from within.

The first insight is that ecology attempts to control the place of non-human beings. Using concepts such as health and stability, it seems that its goals are similar to human biopolitics. Analyzing the two aspects of biopolitics, we can first of all say that ecology deals with *bios*. Second, ecology as a discipline is political, in the sense that all science is political, involving different interest groups and hierarchies. Even more, ecosystems, the subject of ecology, are conceived of as a small political unit, the *oikos*, the family or household. Perhaps everything is political, and certainly running a household, the *oikos*, including the household of ecology, is a political task. Its subjects are not necessarily obedient, not uncommon for human subjects either, but ecologists seek to manipulate their behavior and every aspect of their life.

In Chapter 3, I discussed what biopolitics on the human level attempts to control: the entirety of the human species. The construction (or reconstruction) of similar places is one of the control mechanisms of populations, determining where people will live. Foucault's theory allows us to think about architectural features that attempt to control, like those found in the famous panopticon. The construction of the same architecture does not merely control what we do and think, but also controls where we are or can possibly be. It creates a false sense of freedom, first of all because it determines where we will go, and second because it determines who can go where. Ecology engages in similar strategies with similar goals. While human biopolitics seeks to create flexibility so that labor will move to places where it is needed most, ecology typically seeks the opposite: species should stay where they belong. Thus, while in the human realm an inauthentic homelessness of settled nomadism is created, ecology restricts the movement of species and its members.

Ecologists seek to gain knowledge of an ecosystem's population (consisting of plants and animals). With that knowledge (a constructed knowledge) they create a certain image of health. That image is then pursued by way of manipulating death and birth. Certain species are not supposed to be present and are killed; others need to be reintroduced and everything possible is done to multiply their numbers; other species are too abundant and their numbers are controlled as well.

In one sense, biopolitics works better in nature than it works in human populations. Humans have to be respected as individuals, for whatever ethical arguments or ideological principles one follows, creating an obstacle for effective biopolitics. For example, in most political systems people, for the most part, cannot be forced to reproduce, although one can encourage them through different mechanisms. When one deals with plants, such ethical objections do not exist. Animals can be sacrificed as well. Unless an animal is on the endangered species list or otherwise protected (in which case an ecologist would not want to get rid of them in the first place), restorations are not bound by ethical boundaries. Sometimes people do speak up and protest when animals are killed in the name of restoration. Nevertheless, the law and our norms do not protect most animals.

Even while biopolitics in ecology is, in principle, easier to apply since it does not face the same ethical restrictions, the subjects of ecological biopolitics are difficult to manipulate. Not-so-subtle forms of violence and force have to be used on large scales. While human biopolitics is not immediately visible, the opposite is true for ecology. In the chapter on biopolitics I argued that the creation of similar places all over the Western and Westernized world creates the possibility for a flexible workforce. While the creation of these places involves force and violence, the manipulation of human subjects is far from obvious. As already mentioned, the two forms of biopolitics also have opposite goals in mind: ecology seeks to return to a supposedly normal ecosystem by returning species to their proper place. Human biopolitics does the opposite by creating flexible human subjects who can feel at home anywhere. We need humans in any place where money can be made.[4]

Comparing human and ecological biopolitics, we can make a few additional observations. First, by drawing the parallel between biopolitics exercised in nature and human population, we can recognize the radical nature of restoration. It engages in a radical attempt to control a population of plants and animals that involves birth and death in all its aspects. Furthermore, by thinking about the magnitude of our influence on the earth, on virtually all ecosystems, we can recognize (as well as pose some questions about) the significance of restoration. Restoring some of nature to its historical state can be regarded as highly valuable. Economy dictates that anything that is scarce is valuable. Finally, ecosystems have important functions, some of them crucial to human beings, either directly or indirectly. For example, trees provide oxygen, without which we could not live. Yet, does it matter which trees provide our oxygen?[5]

The overarching point is that things change, that over time we move from one species to the next, and that different environmental factors determine such changes while we, with our technology, poison, and relentless energy of volunteers, sometimes have to accept that we fail to make any impact. It is difficult to accept that natural norms are changing naturally, without us. Ecosystems never consult us, but might be reacting to whatever we are doing to it, directly or indirectly. Perhaps this can be described as yet another homelessness: we want to find a home in the task of restoring nature, while it seems to reject us.

Another interesting abnormality that suggests homelessness, and that we have no control over, is the interbreeding of different plant and animal species. I mentioned above how polar bears and grizzlies have successfully reproduced hybrid offspring both in captivity and in the wild. For scientists, this behavior is truly abnormal since it brings the very notion of species into question. The boundaries of species are defined by the (im)possibility to successfully reproduce. A polar bear and a grizzly bear should not interbreed, since it will create some kind of intermediate species, a pollution of the genes, and a messy picture of nature, against science's goals to identify and maintain order. However, with melting ice and thus a disappearing habitat for polar bears, interbreeding (resulting in the "grolar" or "prizzly bear") might be a good strategy and their only chance of survival. Furthermore, while polar bears are probably not thinking too much about the survival of their species, a changing climate results in a common environment for grizzlies and polar bears. While previously these different bears would never or only rarely encounter one another, they now share a habitat, making romantic encounters a real possibility.[6] In other words, the two species do react to their new circumstances and adapt to it.

In recognizing the process through which species arise (a process of which we are a result), we can also acknowledge that hybrid species must necessarily exist. Different hybrid links between chimp and human must have existed at some point. We cannot interbreed with chimps, but some "intermediate species" must have been able to. The fact that today we have two different species that can no longer interbreed does not mean that this was not possible in the past. Likewise, polar bears and brown bears, recognized as two different species of bears today, were at some point related. The hybrid polar/brown bear is, in that regard, not a new freak creation, but rather a reinstitution of a being that previously existed, perhaps resembling the origin out of which both species of bear developed. Evolutionarily, it might turn out that in a changing climate the evolution of the polar bear is unsustainable and that a return to a previous state, by interbreeding with a grizzly bear, is its only realistic option to survive as a species.

When we think about hybrid beings, we notice a deviation from a norm. For Nietzsche, concepts create artificial boundaries and norms by arbitrarily grouping together different things as one concept, making equal what is unequal. The idea of species does indeed group beings together, but instead of creating equality among inequality, it seems to do the opposite: it excludes and tells us what should not happen, namely the interbreeding between different species. Since the definition of species relies on the possibility to successfully reproduce, it seems that when two different species are able to reproduce fertile offspring we should either redefine these two species as being one species, or we should question our definition (or, more radically, the whole idea) of species. The easy solution, the option we mostly choose, is to maintain our theories and distinctions. We either declare such reproductions abnormalities, or we destroy the offspring, the hybrid being that does not fit our categories, our theories, and our norms or values. The existence of hybrid species is, ultimately, a threat to our home, the human: By questioning the boundaries between species, it also questions the boundary between human and animal. Hybridity points out that the very notion of species is a construction, nothing more than a story or myth, kept in place by language.

In ecological management our role as restorers is simply accepted. We believe that nothing will be restored without our involvement. We also operate under the idea that the ultimately healthy ecosystem is one that does not need our support any longer. This is not a contradiction: The ecosystem is abnormal and unhealthy now, but we work toward normality and health. Such normality and health includes the very independence of the ecosystem in which the different elements are again in balance. Here, I propose a different trajectory in which we do not restore as external agents, but become part of the ecosystem. Instead of immunity, in which the other (the human element) is kept out in order to protect ecosystems, I suggest that we integrate ourselves in the larger system. In the spirit of Esposito's insight that too much immunity can be life denying, I suggest that the human can be something other than a threat: it can also be an opportunity, a bridge to something else. We know that in the social world norms and normality change over time. In the same way that laws, the legal tools that indicate what is accepted and what is not, change over time, ecosystems change. It is another social order that will change when it faces different surrounding realities. My suggestion is to become more flexible when we think about ecosystems. Our planet is more polluted than ever. It is warmer than before in some areas, colder in others, warmer *and* colder in others, wetter and dryer, more extreme, and so forth. The planet needs different ecosystems and a different relationship between humans and nature. We need systems that provide perhaps more shade in warmer areas, systems that are more tolerant to drought, or that deal better with more extreme weather. We need plants and trees and animal life to increase, and evolve accordingly.

This is not a proposal for a biopolitics that attempts to completely control all life on the planet. Even while it involves interferences in life and death, it will be a more "ecological" politics, i.e., a politics understood from out of the oikos itself, and of which we are now an integral part, as a reactive actant among other reactive actants.

Let me repeat here the idea of the earth ethics developed out of Nietzsche's proclamation to remain true to the earth, discussed in Chapter 1. I argued that an ethics of the earth is one of hybridization and nomadism of all beings. We change and we change the world around us. The earth ethics is not bound by any classifications or values, so that we, other species as well as the very idea of species, become homeless or nomadic. We let go of categories such as self and other. We step beyond ideas of belonging of native and non-native. Nietzsche's earth ethics, thus, entails a being open to the other, or otherness. It is this otherness that we will become. We thus find the other in ourselves, and we find ourselves in the world that we inhabit. It is in that regard that we find that man is "a bridge and not an end" (Nietzsche 1995, 15). The ecopolitics proposed here is along these lines developing a unity of the human within nature, in which we dwell homelessly, i.e., we wander around in order to become a new self.

Conclusion

One thing we keep discovering, and that we should not forget, is that we know so little about the natural world and that, in fact, we are not only making very slow progress, but that we are also losing knowledge. The knowledge Native Americans had of their natural environments is virtually all lost. After most of the native population was either killed or displaced, today for many tribes the main line of business involves gambling. As a result, most of their intimate knowledge of the land is lost. Many of us might discard that wisdom as spiritual nonsense, in which, for example, animals are given powers that cannot be measured with any scientific instrument. Although I, too, doubt the existence of such powers, it is important to notice that the scientific instruments and the data that we can generate with those instruments have themselves become a spiritual power. The call for data – "we need more data," "the data are non-conclusive" (and thus we need more) – has become a faith that proclaims a command. This command and the underlying faith drives most scientific research (and administrations). Marx wrote that money has become a demi-god. While this might still be true today, we can add that data have become a demi-god as well: We can never have enough of it, it can solve all the mysteries and secrets of the world, it is the truth, and in many research methods (and many faculty meetings) it is revered. This drive is a result of what Latour pointed out as the myth that the facts speak for themselves.

The above is not meant to ridicule the natural sciences, but rather to acknowledge that even the most rigorous quantitative scientific research includes an element of faith, namely that the numbers are somehow going to reveal the truth. As Latour points out, the natural sciences do fabricate stories, which is exactly their task. As such, science and Native American philosophies, largely expressed through narratives, might be closer to one another than generally assumed. Native American wisdom is derived directly from living in and with their environment. Besides the occasional collection of data from the field, the sciences engage most of all in data collection and running models in labs. Both data and spirituality construct narratives. I suggest that we not place science and myth in opposition, but instead have them complement one another, since they are in the end the same. Myth is *a* science; science is *a* myth. Data will not have priority over spiritual practices. Rather, what is prioritized is the ecopolitical unity that respects all living and non-living beings. This does not mean that we start to trust shamans over medical doctors; it merely recognizes that both shamanism and treatments in the modern medical world require elements of faith, constructions, and narratives.

If we do allow the biggest threat to all ecosystems, the human being, to become part of an ecosystem, we face the obvious question – how can this threat literally become a part of an ecosystem, without destroying it? How can this foreigner be incorporated? Let me, first of all, return to immunity.

Immunology in ecology has mostly focused on individuals, but with some recent interest in a system-based approach in which an ecosystem in its entirety is discussed in terms of immunity. In fact, Alfred Tauber points out that in the last couple of decades in the field of immunology the very idea of individuality and self, as opposed to the "other," has become increasingly problematic. Traditional immunology (developed in the second half of the nineteenth century) considered the self as an organism that defends itself against the "other" or "non-self." In this conception, the self recognizes certain bodies or cells as not-self, which are then attacked and excluded. Today's immunology has moved to an idea of "immune reactivity." This reactivity is not merely a self in opposition to others, but is rather a network. In order to move from a model of the immune self to this network theory, Tauber considers immunology within the greater context of ecology, or an ecological orientation, in which the individual is subordinated "to a collective picture of biological function, and in place if differentiation, [between self and other] integration and coordination serve as organizing principles" (Tauber 2008, 228).

Tauber argues that with the notion of ecosystems (introduced in the 1920s), animals were placed within a greater environment, and he uses this insight to reassess the notion of reactivity in immune systems. Animals are not living in an environment of constant strife, as Darwin's theory suggests. Rather, any animal (and plant, we could add) will encounter both threats and opportunities in its environment. Immune systems had previously been regarded as systems that turn on and off. By placing immunity within the context of a greater network, such as the ecosystem, Tauber argues that immune systems are always on, but react in different ways, depending on the kind of "other" it encounters. Some need to be kept out, while others are beneficial. He argues, thus, that "the immune system functions as the interface of host organism and its environment both defensibly and cooperatively" (Tauber 2008, 232). This idea of the interface can be the model for a new ecopolitics in which human and non-human actants alike co-exist by acting and re-acting. It is within that interface we can find or recover a sense of home rooted in homelessness. We can be nomadic, move to different ecosystems, and learn to evaluate and react to each unique place.

Tauber uses the idea of the ecosystem to rethink the immune self and how immune systems work. We can also use the immune system to rethink an ecosystem. One could argue that ecosystems have dysfunctional immune systems: if others are not kept out, their immune system – if there is such a thing as an immune system for an organized natural whole – is, in a sense, failing. Restoration ecologists try to heal the consequences of this failure, but do not address the immune system itself. One of the interesting aspects of Tauber's approach is that he speaks of immune cognition, by which an organism knows its environment. Applied to ecology, or rather to ecosystems, one could argue that organisms need to know their environment. They do not only keep dangers out; they react to threats and dangers. What that means within the immune system is that not every foreign body is regarded as an enemy; some provide an opportunity. In this regard, we can learn from immunology: some non-native species and some threats can actually strengthen rather than weaken an ecosystem. We need, then, to find ways of being in an ecosystem that strengthen rather than weaken it.

An additional suggestion could be that human beings, ecologists or not, could function as this immune system, preventing foreign elements from establishing in the first place. However, as we have seen, ecologists are not in the field of preventative medicine, but instead try to remove well-established diseases. In the medical field, new developments in cancer research show that bodies seem unable to recognize cancer cells as cells that do not belong and that should be attacked. It seems that something similar happens in the process of introducing new species into ecosystems. The system does not recognize this new species as an intruder, but in fact welcomes it. The ecosystem provides everything it needs and the typical non-native intruder lacks natural enemies.

In closing, I will discuss some of the directions that we can take this eco-political discussion. The problem with the idea of the *oikos*, and that certain things are proper to the household of the ecosystem, is that it creates a picture of an ideal and original ecosystem. Non-native invaders are then regarded as uninvited guests. The biopolitics of ecology tries to reverse disturbances by removing invaders and returning the members of the family. The most extreme reversal of this attitude would be a nomadic ecology, which considers that all living things and their home, the *oikos*, or ecosystem, are always changing. Nature, life, or an ecosystem does not have an original state. Since everything is in flux, we stop making distinctions between native and non-native.

I do not seek such a radical conclusion, but rather a more moderate ecopolitical homelessness that allows for change and that places us, humans, in nature. Our new position will not be a settled one, as we, as all other animals, need to move in order to survive. Our environment will keep changing and so we need to change along with it. Moreover, we will also change our environment. Humans have always done so; animals change their environments; in fact, all organisms do have some kind of impact on their environment. In other words, it is entirely natural as well as necessary to change one's immediate surroundings. We still need to learn how to do that with moderation in order to avoid disaster.

It is important to remind ourselves that we keep losing ecosystems at an ever-increasing rate, and I agree with ecologists that we have to limit and reverse environmental destruction due to human impacts. We also have to keep reminding ourselves that we know nearly nothing and that, in Leopold's words, we do not know what makes the clock tick. Within that context, it seems necessary to save any species and any ecosystem we can. Its disappearance might have consequences beyond anything we can imagine. We could possibly suggest that some ecosystems should remain off-limits for human beings until we figure out a way to co-exist within important ecosystems. In other words, we should not invade a wilderness area as part of an ecopolitical experiment. We should instead restore disrupted ecosystems around us, but with an eye to a better collective, so that we have a place in it. This does not mean that we re-create a forest by including an entertainment park, or plastic trees (see Krieger 2000), but people should be able to live in the forest, even in large numbers.

As already mentioned, ecosystems are often very hospitable and often fail to recognize a threat. When new species arrive, the new *oikos* can be quite welcoming. While the ecologist labels this act of welcoming as "invasive" on the side of the new species, we could also reconsider the ecosystem itself as nomadic, ready to change in order to find new opportunities.[7]

Here we return to Leopold, who forces us to ask how a mountain thinks. Does it think in terms of invaders and native as opposed to non-native? Or does it think in terms of hospitality, or fluidity? Do ecosystems perhaps prepare for climate changes, adjusting to dryer, wetter, hotter, colder, or more extreme conditions? Does nature perhaps already adjust to changes, while we are still debating the cause of such changes and whether the changes really happen? Life has survived extreme climate changes before. The novel ecosystems approach discussed above addresses global climate change and has in a few instances welcomed non-native species. This change in approach is a major paradigm shift in restoration ecology, since it moves the discipline from a retrogressive thinking – going back to a historical ecosystem – to a forward way of thinking – to a time that may or may not ever be there.

Some ecosystems might become stronger (in the sense of being better prepared to deal with climate change) with the introduction of new species. Esposito points out that protection and security in an extreme sense can actually limit one's freedom. Immunity as the solidifying of one's thinking can be very dangerous, as I have argued. To stop nomadic or homeless thinking would prevent us from crossing boundaries and creates rigid, fact-minded people. Ecosystems likewise might be limited by too much immunity in their freedom to grow, to adapt, and to find new opportunities in an ever-changing world. Moreover, too much protection and security for plants and animals might lead to a limitation of freedom.

We encountered the opposite of immunity, in the ideas of "infection" (Krell 1996) and "transmission" in Chapter 3. Nietzsche places the philosophy of the *Übermensch* over and against our morality, arguably including the morality of immunity. Is it possible that an organism or even a whole ecosystem can overcome itself, become stronger, and live according to a life-affirming principle? Are we perhaps making a mistake when we try to save the weak plant out of pity? Immunity, Esposito suggests, can become life-denying. Do we not need to expose ecosystems to the other so that it can affirm and embrace life? Does the future earth not need strong trees and forests that do well, instead of forests and lakes that need to be protected against any otherness? While organisms do change their environment, evolution is still partly adaption. This is nomadism in the form of plants and animals that move. Even mountains are walking, as we learned from Dōgen. Thus, I suggest that an ecopolitics moves toward *Überbaume, Übertrees,* and *Überwalde* or *Über-forests,* i.e., trees and forests that are life-affirming and wills to power that can redeem themselves, wherever they need to go.

The homelessness discussed throughout the book also provides an important hint for our discussion of species. We could paraphrase Dōgen by saying that mountains are non-native; they are practicing everywhere. The oikos of ecology suggests a neat categorization of what belongs and what does not belong where, or what is nature and what is culture. Dōgen suggests that we can only seriously engage with the mountain and with ourselves if we first let it wander and practice without a home. Study "is the work of the mountains. Such mountains and waters of themselves become wise persons and sages" (Dōgen 1985, 107). It is exactly this insight that we miss today: the mountains and waters, the landscapes themselves, have an understanding. Thus, we create wilderness areas so that we leave the mountains and rivers "undisturbed" even while its *logos* has included humans for thousands of years. We rip out or poison invading foreigners, and we plant species that *we* think are native, wild, and thus good. We may even look ahead and plant for a future climate. In doing so, mountains and waters are reduced to sets of formulas and measurable qualities. We follow the logos of the data, not that of the landscape.

Both Leopold and Dōgen question our human understanding of nature: we, or the instruments with which we measure, create categories and distinctions, boundaries and homes, or households. Snyder writes, "'Mountains and Waters' is a way to refer to the totality of the process of nature. As such it goes well beyond dichotomies of purity and pollution, natural and artificial" (Snyder 1990, 103). And so, we can add, it goes beyond the household of native and non-native.[8]

What does this concretely mean for ecopolitics? The Greek word for homeless is *aoikos,* so perhaps we should change ecology to "aecology" or "anecology," the logos of being homeless. A new ecopolitics is then an "anecology," the *logos* and *politikos* of homeless beings. It is, then, first of all, letting go of its categories. It listens to the howl of Leopold's wolf and the secrets it might hold. It first studies the practices of the mountain without its instruments, language, and ideas. More concretely, it lets go of notions of household, of belonging and invasion, of native and stranger. In this way, we no longer see ourselves as a stranger, but find ourselves in the wild and the wild in ourselves. The mountains are walking and thinking. We find the mountain in ourselves and become something else – a mountain, an ape, perhaps a bear, even a tree, or (more likely) something else altogether. Let us not forget Nietzsche's insight that man is a bridge and not an end.

Notes

1 For example, Dobson and Lucardie (1993) and Mathews (1996) fall into this category. A few works in the field of political science use the concept of ecopolitics, all within the framework of a strictly human political system. One example is Bluhdorn and Welsh (2008).

2 Why Haeckel exactly chose the word "ecology" might be explained by the fact that he also speaks of an economy of existence, as discussed by Tauber (2008, 229).

3 It could be tempting to distinguish between the interests of the masses as we find it in Heidegger's *they* and the work of the scientist. Starting with philosophy, we can immediately debunk the claim that academic philosophers are not falling prey to the temptations of the they and are their own being, by constantly reflecting on the very meaning of existence and taking up the very possibilities that we are. In a busy semester academics should be happy to find a few hours every week to do some research-related reading and writing. Original thinking is rare, especially since anxiety over tenure processes or job security forces researchers to play it safe and stay within the established discourses. Originality consists of a clever commentary on some secondary literature, strategically chosen to point out some subtle problem, important exercises that involve little risk. Publishing is as such not a result of a creative process, but a means to another end. Other obligations involve teaching, service, applying for grants and travel funds, traveling to conferences, processing receipts for said conferences, and endless meetings to discuss all of the above. The extremely unjust separation between adjunct and full-time faculty takes advantage of those who, for whatever reason, have been unable to secure a permanent job – a situation that creates a lot of anxiety and is detrimental to thinking. Many conferences are driven by ego, vanity, and gossip. Paper sessions are often centered on classifications and distinctions that no one outside of the field could find in any way relevant. Heidegger discusses this as a problem of the institutionalizing and naming of thinking. "The Greeks thought without such headings [logic, ethics, and physics]. They did not even call thinking 'philosophy'" (Heidegger 1977a, 220). When we name and categorize our activities of thinking, and claim to engage in this activity it becomes something else at best. More likely, we destroy it. We are extremely suspicious of intruders who do not have the proper training, but write about philosophy. Instead of engaging in a conversation, we keep it to ourselves (having forgotten how Socrates engaged everyone, whether they liked it or not). By protecting our discipline in that way, we in fact make it only less relevant. In other words, by making a discipline "our home," we appropriate what should not be appropriated. In claiming it to be our own, we, in fact, destroy it.

4 In order to grasp the relationship between ecologist and ecosystem we could also suggest here some other political system such as a Hobbesian body politics, a

mechanism that tries to control the subjects as members of one body (a country, or in ecology, an ecosystem). The leader (or leadership) is the head, which has absolute sovereignty over its subjects. Body politics is also not entirely applicable to restoration ecology: the ultimate goal of ecology is to restore the autonomy of an ecosystem, so that it can govern itself again. The intervention is always understood as temporary. Hobbes did view human subjects as beings driven by a natural instinct: egoism. His negative view of human nature resulted in a political system that sought to control those egoistic subjects through a leadership that had absolute sovereignty. Human self-interest constituted both the problem and the solution for Hobbes: human beings need to be in a political environment that controls them and has absolute authority over them; otherwise they will wreak havoc. Controlling them, however, is relatively easy, since one already knows what they want: The best for themselves. If society is set up in such a way that it is of an individual's best interest to, for example, pay taxes without facing penalties, subjects will comply. Again, we find that humans seem to be fairly easy to control. Animals and plants are presumably also driven by self-interest, but do not comply with any rules or laws.

5 To provide a current example: in the USA many ash trees are dying because of emerald ash borers, an invasive Asian beetle that destroys ash trees as it lays its eggs. It is now pretty much accepted that the beetles will kill many ash trees. How many ash trees will be killed is under debate, ranging from 60 percent to 99 percent of the eight billion ash trees that live in the USA. While the scale of the loss is under debate, ecologists agree that the effects of the loss will be huge. It will change the amount of sunlight, temperature, and humidity in a forest, and consequently will dramatically alter the ecosystems in which ash trees live. Although these unpreventable changes might seem bleak, ecologist Koerth-Baker points out that a similar issue in the past led to hemlocks largely replacing the American chestnut: "Few people living today remember when the Northeast was covered in forests of American chestnut. That species all but died out more than half a century ago from a series of fungal infections. Today, the forests and the life they harbor are very different; in many cases, hemlocks replaced the chestnuts. And now something else will replace the hemlocks" (Koerth-Baker 2014). The future will again bring a different tree; we will not have empty forests, but different forests. See also Gandhi and Herms (2010).

6 One could draw a parallel here with interracial relationships. When different races of human beings lived separately in different parts of the world, a certain norm was established that was called into question as people became more mobile and moved either voluntarily or involuntarily to different regions of the world, encountering people that looked very different. Although Freud claimed that, in particular, men were attracted to someone who looks like their mother (if not their mother), the number of interracial marriages tells a different story. Similar to the idea that interbreeding between different species is not "natural" or "normal," interracial marriages faced the same struggles. In fact, this is not a too distant history: Only in 1967 were the anti-miscegenation laws repealed in all of the USA. Arguably, gay marriage faces similar struggles, and slow recognition as a new norm today.

7 Another example are the infamous coqui frogs on the Big Island of Hawaii, considered by many to be a plague, an infestation of paradise. They are loud. At night they produce high-pitched shrieks and since there are thousands of them you will hear nothing but coqui frogs. Eradication as well as control efforts, both by the government and community groups, have been under way for some time. The Big Island has a coqui whisperer, as well as a group of Coquistadores. PETA has published guidelines on how to humanely kill a coqui (in case you wonder:

one of the methods is *deep freezing* after the frog has been rendered unconscious by a topical anesthetic). Coquis are loud, for sure, reproduce quickly (and loudly), and eat insects, leaving less for birds, and probably, most importantly, they are a non-native invasive species. They somehow made it to the Big Island from Puerto Rico and are – for many – an unwelcome guest, an intruder, an invader. It is relatively easy to draw a parallel with racist discourses. First of all, the coqui frog's home is Puerto Rico. Ecology, the logos of the house, indicates that the frog should have stayed there, and not disturb us Americans and threaten and harm our native birds. We did not invite them and now that they are here they quickly and loudly reproduce and we are the victims of this colonization. Housing prices might drop with these strangers in the neighborhood, and so forth and so forth. Yet, it was, most certainly, humans who, knowingly or unknowingly, brought them to Hawaii.

8   In the *Rambunctious Garden*, Emma Marris critically discusses several restoration projects and suggests that we should move away from the idea of wild nature, to a rambunctious garden (Marris 2011). I am drawn to the idea of rambunctiousness, since it implies that we are unable to control what is wild. Yet, the notion of the garden suggests that we are managing it nonetheless. For sure, we humans have touched all nature either directly or indirectly and, thus, we perhaps have no nature anymore. As has been argued many times before, nature has ended. This claim in itself, including Marris's claim of the garden, is, I believe, extremely anthropocentric and affirming that we are in control, an idea that I question throughout this book.

References

Appleyard, Bruce. 2015. "Can creating livable and complete streets improve children's spatial knowledge? A cognitive mapping study of the influence of traffic and Safe Routes to School (SR2S) projects on schoolchildren in a US suburban context." *Journal of Transport & Health*, 2 (2), Supplement.

Bluhdorn, Ingolfur, and Welsh, Ian. 2008. *The Politics of Unsustainability: Eco-Politics in the Post-Ecologist Era*. London: Routledge.

Dobson, Andrew, and Lucardie, Paul. 1993. *The Politics of Nature: Explorations in Green Political Theory*. London and New York: Routledge.

Dōgen. 1985. *Moon in a Dewdrop*. San Francisco: North Point Press.

Esposito, Roberto. 2011. *Immunitas: The Protection and Negation of Life*. Cambridge: Polity.

——— . 2013. "Community, immunity, biopolitics." *Angelaki: Journal of the Theoretical Humanities*, 18 (3), 83–90.

Gandhi, Kamal J.K. and Herms, Daniel A. 2010. "North American arthropods at risk due to widespread *Fraxinus* mortality caused by the alien emerald ash borer." *Biological Invasions*, 12, 1839–46.

Glazebrook, Trish. 2000. *Heidegger's Philosophy of Science*. New York: Fordham University Press.

Heidegger, Martin. 1977a. *Basic Writings*. San Francisco: Harper.

——— . 1977b. *The Question Concerning Technology, and Other Essays*. New York: Harper & Row.

Klinkenborg, Verlyn. 2013. "Hey, you calling me an invasive species?" *New York Times*, September 7.

Koerth-Baker, Maggie. 2014. "After the trees disappear: ash forests after emerald ash borers destroy them." *New York Times*, June 30.

Krell, David Farrell. 1996. *Infectious Nietzsche*. Bloomington: Indiana University Press.

Krieger, Martin H. 2000. *What's Wrong with Plastic Trees? Artifice and Authenticity in Design*. Westport: Praeger.

Lyotard, Jean-Francois. 1988. *The Differend: Phrases in Dispute*. Minneapolis: University of Minnesota Press.

Marris, Emma. 2011. *Rambunctious Garden: Saving Nature in a Post-Wild World*. New York: Bloomsbury.

Mathews, Freya. 1996. *Ecology and Democracy*. Portland, OR: Frank Cass.

Mugerauer, Robert. 2010. "Toward a theory of integrated urban ecology: complementing Pickett et al." *Ecology and Society*, 15 (4), 31.

———. 2011. "The city: a legacy of organism–environment interaction at every scale." In Ingrid Leman Stefanovic and Stephen Bede Scharper (eds.) *The Natural City: Revisioning the Built Environment*. Toronto: University of Toronto Press.

Nietzsche, Friedrich Wilhelm. 1995. *Thus Spoke Zarathustra: A Book for All and None*. New York: Modern Library.

———. 2006. *The Nietzsche Reader*. Hoboken: Wiley-Blackwell.

Orr, David W. 1994. *Earth in Mind: On Education, Environment, and the Human Prospect*. Washington: Island Press.

Snyder, Gary. 1990. *The Practice of the Wild*. San Francisco: North Point Press.

Stauffer, Robert C. and De Beer, Gavin. 1957. *Haeckel, Darwin, and Ecology*. New York: Stony Brook Foundation.

Tauber, Alfred I. 1994. *The Immune Self: Theory or Metaphor?* Cambridge and New York: Cambridge University Press.

———. 2008. "The immune system and its ecology." *Philosophy of Science* 75 (2): 224–45.

Wells, H.G, Huxley, J., and Wells, G.P. 1931. *The Science of Life*. Garden City: Doubleday, Doran & Co.

Index

Please note that page numbers relating to Notes will contain the letter 'n' followed by note number.

For Product Safety Concerns and Information please contact our EU
representative GPSR@taylorandfrancis.com Taylor & Francis Verlag GmbH,
Kaufingerstraße 24, 80331 München, Germany

Printed and bound by CPI Group (UK) Ltd, Croydon, CR0 4YY
08/05/2025
01864329-0004